NAPOLEON'S LOVE CHILD
A Biography of Count Leon

NAPOLEON'S LOVE CHILD

A Biography of Count Leon

DENNIS WALTON DODDS

Foreword by
Count Gaston Leon of Le Raincy

WILLIAM KIMBER · LONDON

First published in 1974 by
WILLIAM KIMBER & CO. LIMITED,
Godolphin House, 22a Queen Anne's Gate,
London, SW1H 9AE

© Dennis Walton Dodds, 1974
ISBN 07183 0333 4

Typeset by Eyre & Spottiswoode Ltd, Portsmouth
and printed in Great Britain by
W. & J. Mackay & Co. Ltd., Chatham

Contents

List of Illustrations

LIST OF ILLUSTRATIONS

Foreword

REFLECTIONS ON MY GRANDFATHER

by Count Gaston Leon

The destinies of the two little boys brought to the Emperor on the eve of his exile — Count Leon and Count Walewski — were very different.

A comparison of the life of Count Leon with that of Count Walewski reveals a deep injustice. It might well have been thought that at the outset the chances for each of them were equal; it was not the case. Alexandre Walewski had an attentive mother, and a legitimate and powerful father, who protected this son. The path of the young Walewski was made plain from his infancy. He had but to follow it, supported and guided by the enlightened circle of his Polish family and to profit from their distinguished influence. Neither his family nor his country at any time contemplated repudiating him. When the hour arrived for him to settle in France she welcomed him with kindness; and recollecting the birth of so noble a person, Napoleon III lavished his favours upon him. He was helped greatly by a sense of diplomacy and opportunism, in which Count Leon, it must be acknowledged, was sadly lacking.

Having regard to all the advantages that were Count Walewski's portion at birth, what were those of Count Leon? Quite simply — none at all.

Napoleon, overwhelmed with joy at the possession of a son, had him removed immediately from his mother in order to keep the child close to himself, alone, at the Tuileries. And so Count Leon grew up knowing neither the tenderness nor the protection of a mother; and what is more, he was obliged to apply to the courts to have himself officially recognised as her son!

Napoleon was a good and affectionate father; had he lived his son's destiny would have turned out vastly different . . . Unhappily, he was only fifteen when his father died, and he remained alone, abominably orphaned during one of the most troubled periods that France has ever experienced.

Nevertheless, the Emperor considered he had done everything necessary to assure to his son the material security and independence worthy of his rank. Little did he anticipate that the Bourbons with the stroke of a pen would make a nullity of his will. He did not believe that his son would be exposed to the hostility of the Royalists — abandoned by the Bonapartists, who had difficulties enough in extricating themselves from the debacle.

For Count Leon the price of being tolerated was the necessity of effacing himself, of consigning himself to oblivion. Who has ever seen an eagle transform himself into a mole though his talons were drawn and his pinions sheared!

But even if Count Leon's worldly goods had all been misappropriated, he would still have retained the courage and love of action he had inherited from his father.

Throughout his life he suffered from a compulsive need to act; to achieve something useful and great. Unhappily he was insufficiently aware of the limits of his resources and abilities. It is perhaps also true that the modicum of luck which is indispensable to success eluded him.

He disliked the press which he found malicious, indiscreet and unfair. They avenged themselves in spiteful and slanderous articles the echoes of which reverberate to this day.

Up to the end of his life he was robbed. When Napoleon III restored the investment of 100,000 francs that the Emperor had bequeathed to his son, Leon received only the annual interest; the capital was assigned to Count Walewski.

Even into old age he was hounded by the newspapers, who vied with each other in describing his last wretched moments — the ultimate lie upon his grave! For up to his death in 1881 he received an inalienable pension of 10,000 francs which allowed him a modest but decent existence.

His children, also, spoke of him with respect, remembering him as a distinguished and handsome old gentleman; and when they read the stories of which he had been the object they trembled with anger.

COUNT LEON
Le Raincy
Seine-et-St Denis

Acknowledgements

To Count Gaston Leon, who together with his hospitable wife gave me freely of his time at Le Raincy, showing me his souvenirs and discussing his celebrated grandfather. I am grateful to Count Leon, also, for permission to reproduce his letter written in 1904 to M. Georges Montorgueil, the editor of the *Intermédiare des Chercheurs et Curieux,* and his article *Reflections on my Grandfather,* which originally appeared in the journal of the Société Historique du Raincy et du Pays d'Aulnoye to whom I am also indebted.

To Mme. Colette Tillie, who graciously lent me the few existing personal letters of her great grandfather Count Leon; and her father Monsieur Repiquet who has listed and preserved the rare documents and pictures in the family collection.

To Lady Pauline Chapman, archivist of Mme. Tussaud's, who has given much personal help, and the Directors of Mme. Tussaud's for permission to reproduce the wax portraits of Count Leon and Napoleon's Lying-in-State and extracts from the writings of Joseph Randolph Tussaud and John Theodore Tussaud.

Mr Ernest Weal of the Société Britannique Napolèonienne, and Dr. Fernand Beaucour, President of the Société de Sauvegarde du Château Impérial de Pont-de-Briques, for sources of information which have proved invaluable.

M. Jules Lambert of the Hôtel de Ville, Pontoise, who gave directions for tracing the homes of Count Leon; and M. Claude van Peteghem who searched the dusty greniers of the Town Hall for old registers, not to mention the charming lady receptionist who introduced me to these gentlemen.

M. F. Brosseur, of the Société Historique et Archéologique de Pontoise, du Val-d'Oise et du Vexin, and the staff of the Syndicat d'Initiative of Pontoise.

M. Gaspard Lemoyne, Rédacteur en Chef of the *Intermédiatre des Chercheurs et Curieux,* Paris.

The Librarian of the National Book League.

Mr. John F. C. Phillips of the Director-General's Department, Greater London Council.

Mr. Wm. R. Maidment, Director of Libraries and Arts, London Borough of Camden.

Mr. Philip Ward-Jackson, Conway Library, University of London, Courtauld Institute of Art.

The staffs of the Archives Nationales, the Bibliothèque Nationale, and the Archives du Département de la Seine et de la Ville de Paris.

The staffs of the British Library at Bloomsbury and Colindale, Camden Central Library, and the Public Record Office, Chancery Lane.

Librairie Plon, and Robert Hale for permission to use copyright material.

PRELUDE

'J'ai un fils!'

'I have a son!' shouted Napoleon.

New Year's Eve, 1806, and snow was falling heavily outside the Emperor's Polish quarters, as Marshal Lefebvre — husband of the irrepressible 'Madame Sans Gêne' — told Napoleon that he was a father. His sister, Princess Caroline Murat, had sent off a courier through Mainz and Bamberg as soon as she received the news at her town house in the Rue de Provence, the street next to that in which the Emperor's son was born.

The mother of Bonaparte's first child was Caroline's own lady-in-waiting — Eleonore Denuelle de la Plaigne.

'The weather was appalling,' recalled Rustam, Napoleon's Mameluke servant. 'All the soldiers were complaining of the cold. It was there that I received a letter from my mother-in-law telling me that my wife had given birth to a son.' Napoleon congratulated Rustam; but it was apparent that his own good news had not yet arrived. The Emperor had just met the Russians in battle for the first time and the Grande Armée had emerged badly mauled from the encounter at Pulstuck.

Rustam was not exaggerating when he described the atrocious winter conditions in Poland. Napoleon raged against his grumbling troops. Hardened veterans who only a couple of months earlier had trounced the Prussians at Jena and Auerstädt gave up the fight and committed suicide. With 35,000 French locked in combat with 60,000 Russians the result was a stalemate, except for the losses claimed by each side. According to the Russians, 8,000 French soldiers had died in the encounter, while their own killed and wounded numbered 3,000. Marshal Lannes had attempted to break through the left wing of the Czar's army under the command of General Bennigsen and his 120 guns. The French had maintained their own positions with difficulty; and after the battle, which took place on December 26, 1806, the Grande Armée, decimated, hampered by bad supplies, and its spirit shattered, split up and went into winter quarters.

So it was that the news of the birth of Leon Denuelle de la

Plaigne arrived at precisely the moment when Napoleon's morale, like that of his army, needed a bolster. The Empire was scarcely two years in being, and the legend of the invincible little corporal was in danger of foundering in the winter mud of Poland.

Napoleon had been declared sterile by his doctor; and Josephine — now forty-three and with ten childless years of marriage behind her — had built all her hopes of preserving her marriage on Corvisart's opinion. But now — 'This is my child,' shouted the Emperor. 'There's no doubt about it! Tell them to give Eleonore anything she wants.'

Dr. Corvisart had been proved wrong![1]

'Now I can start a family,' said Napoleon, his mind already teeming with schemes. 'Nature has answered my call: at this moment the future belongs to me!'[2]

So long as Napoleon was not sure of his ability to sire children, Josephine was able to contemplate the future with equanimity, wrote the French historian Frédéric Masson:

> In order for him to be certain of his fertility a peculiar circumstance was necessary. This was it. It came from a passing flirtation which seemed at the time to be without consequence and to which the Emperor attached not the slightest importance.
>
> Henceforth the spell was broken and the Emperor could be certain of having an heir of his blood. More than any other fact, perhaps, this secret birth of a child without a name influenced the remainder of his life and determined the great resolutions he took from the time of Tilsit and which he only fulfilled two years later.

This was also the opinion of Baron Fain, who was at one time the Emperor's secretary:

> Napoleon left two natural sons. Their birth had refuted the vain allegations of Josephine, and contributed not a little to the divorce, by giving Napoleon the knowledge that he could obtain an heir from a second wife — younger than the first.

The birth of Leon was the event which was to end Josephine's idyll of the Villa Bonaparte and set Napoleon on the journey which would culminate in the ravagement of Europe and the occupation of France by foreign armies for the first time since the sixteenth century.

During his confinement on St. Helena, Napoleon spent much time re-writing history. Verbally, gossip said, he claimed Leon was not his son but Murat's, his sister's husband who was a notorious womaniser.

> I have talked a great deal about the Emperor with Monsieur
> de Las Cases,

wrote Viel Castel, the diarist of the Second Empire.

> He told me that at St. Helena Napoleon sometimes spoke of
> his weakness in the 'amorous diversion'; it was a most trivial
> matter; he attributed the child's paternity to Murat.

But by his actions he betrayed the effect that Leon's birth had produced on his life; indeed his very last moments were occupied in making financial dispositions for his eldest son.[3] And, as the French biographer Charles Nauroy states: 'At his worst moment when France was already threatened, on the eve of Brienne and Champaubert, he did not forget Leon.'

Leon's mother's first husband, the dragoon officer Revel, observed:

> After Leon's birth Eleonore's standing could not have been
> higher. Bonaparte gave his mistress everything she wanted.
> Madame Campan's pupil demanded the arrest of her mother:
> Madame de la Plaigne was hauled off to prison. Next she
> asked for her banishment: the Minister of Police arranged it.
> Eleonore reigned, in short, and it would have taken little for
> Bonaparte to share his crown with her. What I am saying is
> not imagination; if Bonaparte had not met with strong
> resistance in his own family, Eleonore would have become
> empress.

Revel exaggerates, but the Emperor was undoubtedly overwhelmed.

Napoleon is even said to have proposed that his doctor should certify Josephine's pregnancy, in order subsequently to present to the French people a natural child who would be made to pass for the heir to the throne — as Louis XIV had legitimised the Duc de Maine and the Comte de Toulouse. Dr. Corvisart refused — and Bonaparte decided on a divorce. It is arguable that Napoleon would in any event have divorced Josephine. To a proud Corsican her constant philandering was an embarrassment; furthermore, she had served her purpose in civilising the young provincial and introducing him to her influential set. Sooner or later he would have sought an alliance with one of Europe's old royal houses; and the encounter with the aristocratic Marya Walewska on New

Year's Day, 1807, following so soon on Leon's birth, was a spur to his later ambitions.

As Guy Breton succinctly wrote, Josephine, without knowing it, was now no more than a figurehead.

CHAPTER 1

Marie Antoinette's Chamber-Maid

At St. Germain-en-Laye, patronised from its inception by Josephine and later blessed with the presence of Napoleon's sisters, was the Institution Nationale de St. Germain, run by a woman who was royalist to the eyebrows. Jeanne Genet-Campan had been lady-in-waiting to Marie Antoinette; had taught that unhappy Viennese princess to speak English, and accompanied her singing of Grétry's airs on the harpsichord and harp. She liked to recall the custom of the ladies of the Court to drop a curtsey whenever Louis XVI or his queen sneezed; and described the field-day they all enjoyed when the royal couple both had heavy colds.

Towards the end of the Revolution Mme. Campan opened an establishment for young ladies at the former Rohan mansion in the Rue de l'Unité on the outskirts of St. Germain-en-Laye; and one day in the year 1799 she received a visit from the young General Bonaparte.

'I must entrust you with my little sister Caroline, Mme. Campan,' announced Napoleon when he visited the school. 'I warn you she knows absolutely nothing.' Caroline was fifteen years old and unable to read. Pauline Bonaparte later joined her sister at Mme. Campan's *pensionnat*. Napoleon placed his young brother Jerome in the Irish College for Boys at the house next door. The principal, Mr. Patrick McDermott, who numbered among his pupils Eugène de Beauharnais, Josephine's son, charged 5,000 francs for the first year and 4,000 francs per annum thereafter.

Mme. Campan reserved four places for girls whose parents were unable to pay the fees. Their names were kept secret and only their parents knew they were being educated free. The school consisted of four classes, each distinguished by the colour of the girls' hat-ribbons: the youngest wore green ribbons, and progressed through *aurore* (golden yellow), and blue, to *nacarat* (orange-red) for the seniors. Mme. Campan's method of education was to 'instruct by amusing' and she particularly excelled in the art of conversation. 'Today,' she would begin gravely, 'we shall discuss an outbreak of fire, a shipwreck, a ruined picnic, and the break-up of a marriage.' At Mardi Gras and certain other festivals throughout the year Mme. Campan entertained her girls to dances with Mr. McDermott's boys next door.

During the night following *18 Brumaire* (November 9, 1799) the girls were aroused by the noisy arrival of a party of horsemen outside Mme. Campan's front-door. They had come to announce Napoleon's seizure of power at St. Cloud, and turned out to be a troop of General Murat's cavalry. Caroline Bonaparte was eighteen years old, and her brother's flamboyant *chasseur* married her while she was still learning to read at the *pensionnat* in the shadow of François Premier's red sandstone château.

Josephine had bestowed her *cachet* on the school shortly before by sending to Mme. Campan her daughter Hortense and a whole brood of nieces including Stephanie de Beauharnais — who inspired in the Emperor the most heated desires before he married her off to a German prince. The number of aristocratic pupils, and even of daughters of the new bourgeois regime dwindled; and the woman who had taken under her wing Elisa Monroe, the daughter of the American Ambassador who later became his country's fifth President, had to lower her sights.

It was thus that she accepted as a pupil Louise Catherine Eleonore Denuelle de la Plaigne.

Eleonore was the daughter of Dominique Denuelle de la Plaigne, *rentier,* and Caroline Sophie Couprie. The French word *rentier* covers a multitude of sins, but may be loosely rendered as 'of independent means': Eleonore's father lived by his wits from day to day. With the help of his wife, who contributed to the family budget by equally undefined means, he kept a comfortable apartment at 340 Boulevard des Italiens, where they held court to a mixed bag of guests. Caroline Sophie was still young and attractive and something of a flirt — her daughter was after all only sixteen.

High society being denied to her, Mme. Denuelle de la Plaigne displayed Eleonore at the evening entertainments. It was at the Gaieté Théâtre on the raffish Boulevard du Temple that she came to the notice of Jean Honoré Francois Revel, a captain-quartermaster in the 15th Regiment of Dragoons living at 20 Rue du Faubourg Saint Honoré. Eleonore was probably still at school at this time for, of their first meeting, Revel records she was only at Paris during the holidays.

The Denuelles and Revel — who stressed his captaincy and

soft-pedalled on the quartermaster — seem to have suffered a mutual deception, and the dragoon and Louise Catherine Eleonore were married at St. Germain-en-Laye on 25 Nivose an XIII. January 15, 1805. Two months after the wedding Revel was arrested for forging a bill of exchange and Eleonore was discreetly hidden at an educational establishment for unfortunate girls directed by a Mme. Pingre in Chantilly. She took part in religious processions, reported the inquisitive captive Revel, carrying the 'banner of salvation which her hands profaned'. But Eleonore's religious interlude was not of long duration, for it was from Chantilly that she was rescued by her old school friend Caroline Murat, who engaged her as a reader.[1]

Caroline Bonaparte had on January 20, 1800, married her own cavalryman against Napoleon's wishes, and was now beginning to spread her wings. She had bought, with her husband Joachim Murat, the magnificent Thelusson mansion in the Rue de Provence on the lower slopes of the hill of Montmartre. The hôtel du Gouvernement as it became known, stood on the site of the Rue Lafitte. It was built for Director Barras, who was Josephine's lover and the young Bonaparte's patron, and had been occupied by the unfortunate bather Marat. Guiseppe Fesch, Caroline's half-uncle, a cardinal and an art-collector on a massive scale, furnished the house with pictures and objects of vertu.

Writing about a visit to Paris he made with Charles James Fox, John Trotter — the Whig statesman's private secretary — described the Murat mansion:

> On the day previous to the great levée, we went to see the house of General Murat, since King of Naples. Nothing could be more superb. The apartments were beautifully and sump-tuously fitted up. The grand staircase was very noble — the bed-chamber was extremely elegant and rich — and one circular room, in particular, was deserving of attention. It was lighted from the top — a great number of beautiful white marble statues were placed in niches, holding branches for lights, and the intervening recesses furnished with silk and containing small couches had an excellent effect. There was so much symmetry and beauty in this room that I was much struck with it.

It was probably at the hôtel du Gouvernement that Napoleon first saw Eleonore. 'In 1804,' the Emperor's valet Constant recalled.

> Her Royal Highness Princess Murat had in her house a young

companion, Mlle. E. She was tall, slim, well-formed, a brunette with beautiful dark eyes, vivacious, very playful and aged possibly seventeen or eighteen.

Certain persons who took it upon themselves to separate His Majesty from the Empress his wife, noted with pleasure the inclination of the lady-in-waiting to prove the power of her glances on the Emperor, and that of the latter to be trapped. Astutely they fanned the flames, and one of them it was who assumed charge of all the diplomatic moves in the affair.[2]

Propositions made by a third party were immediately taken up.

The lovely E. came secretly to the palace, but rarely, and remained there only two or three hours.

She became large. The Emperor rented a mansion for her in the Rue Chantereine (later the Rue de la Victoire) where she was delivered of a fine boy, endowed from his birth with 30,000 francs in stocks and shares,

concluded Constant in his tantalisingly brief reminiscence.

Revel's account of the first meeting is typically extravagant; though it may well be true. On Eleonore's return from Chantilly Caroline organises a party to which Napoleon is invited. Catching sight of Eleonore the Emperor maladroitly spills a cup of coffee down her dress; and 'the focus of laughter and sarcasm, she weeps with an enchanting grace and modesty.' Touched, troubled and transported, the Emperor whispers his passion, as a lover, in Eleonore's ear. Napoleon usually made known his seignorial choice of a favourite by a mere glance.

Whatever the true history of Eleonore's first encounter with Napoleon may be, it is a fact that his sister, as Mme. de Remusat wrote, 'flattered his tastes and lent her home, if some sudden whim made it necessary to him' and, with her husband, Caroline 'strived to assure their credit in encouraging the Consul's passing fancies, and reaping benefits from the secret intrigue.'

Napoleon had returned in triumph from the Austerlitz campaign on January 26, 1806, and entered Paris at ten o'clock that night. The day after his arrival he chaired a meeting of the Council of State, and on January 28 held an audience for senior officials. He inspected the new building works at the Louvre on January 29, and the same evening attended a performance at the Théâtre Feydeau.

Eleonore was installed in the house next to the Elysée-Bourbon

palace in the Rue du Faubourg St. Honoré on January 30, 1806.
Access to the Elysée was achieved by the celebrated garden gate
through which down the years the mistresses of French emperors
and presidents have furtively tripped. One of these, Miss Howard,
occupied the hôtel Sebastiani in the adjacent Rue du Cirque. She
was the English mistress and benefactor of Louis Napoleon, and he
relinquished her when, as Emperor Napoleon III, he married
Eugenie de Montijo Y Kirkpatrick, the granddaughter of a Scots
wine merchant.

In view of the numerous Paris mansions of the Murats, it is
understandable that Revel, writing poems in his lonely prison cell,
found it difficult to keep track of his wife's movements. 'After the
Neuilly entertainment,' said the captain:

Eleonore was inaugurated into the temple of pleasure at the
Rue des Victoires under the custodianship of Regnault de
Saint Jean d'Angely, a eunuch of a new species who, more
than the sultan, enjoyed the favours of the odalisque.

With Napoleon's gift to Eleonore of 29 Rue de la Victoire, the
eternal triangle was enshrined in stone. At the eastern end of the
street, Number 60, stood Josephine's honeymoon villa, the hôtel
Bonaparte, while a few doors away Number 48 was to become the
home of Marya, Countess Walewska.

Napoleon spent the whole of March 1806 in or near Paris,
moving between the capital, Malmaison and St. Cloud. On March
23 he visited Versailles to inspect the works he had ordered done
on the Trianons, and returned to Malmaison. However, on March
1, 3, 8, 10, 11, 12, 17, 18, 23 and 24, Napoleon did not leave the
capital.

Eleonore became pregnant during the first fortnight of March
1806; and, as the old saw has it, 'a tired man begets a son'.

'Love is a folly committed by two people,' once observed
Napoleon, and there is no doubt that it expressed his sentiments
on the man-woman syndrome. 'We will hear nothing in derogation
of women — we peoples of the West,' said Bonaparte. 'We hold
them — which is a great mistake — as being almost our own equals.
The peoples of the East are wiser and juster than we. They have
declared them the natural property of man. And in effect, Nature
has made them our slaves. It is only because of our foolishness
that they have dared to pretend to be our equals. They abuse their
privileges in order to corrupt and rule us.'

Mme. de Remusat, who with her husband was a member of the

Imperial household and therefore an eye-witness of Napoleon's intimate behaviour, observed: 'Bonaparte was lacking in education and good manners . . . The Emperor mistrusted women. That is not the way to learn to love them.'

Mademoiselle George, who shared a light-hearted romance with Napoleon before power became his mistress, declared: 'The Emperor's love was gentle. There was never anything shameless in the most intimate moments, nor any obscene words.' But Georgina did not omit mention of the 'dreadful cab' containing Napoleon's police spies which drew out and followed her whenever she left the house.

The omniscient Constant tells how one day Napoleon summoned another actress, Mme. Duschenois, to the famous alcove in the Tuileries palace. He kept her cooling her heels for a couple of hours and then sent an order that she was to undress. Without putting in an appearance he kept her waiting a further hour — and then ordered his valet to send her home. Napoleon would take a woman between periods of work much as another man would break-off for a drink or a smoke. Women were his *merienda* and his *quatre-heures*; and the Emperor may well have been the innovator of that hallowed Paris institution — the *cinq à sept*.

'Napoleon was not always of an exquisite gallantry with the ladies,' noted the Marquis de Bonneval in an elegant piece of understatement.

Le Hodey de Saultchevreuil was more to the point. Napoleon, he maintained, 'had the ways of an Arab . . . a tiger in his affairs . . . He had the manners and the brutal instinct of that wild ferocious beast.' Medical evidence on the Emperor, however, does not take the analogy further. Chateaubriand described Napoleon's way with the ladies at greater length and with more subtlety.

In the age when French gallantry sweetened manners and gave urbanity to the most ferocious characters, Bonaparte escaped that empire which intelligent women acquire over all beings endowed with a little sensibility. Time has shown that that wise age was not concerned with the purity of his manners; but rather with the peculiar disposition of his pride which did not allow him to render homage to beauty.

Brutal in his manners, Napoleon never knew the considerations which can soften the thorns of dependence; and even into his pleasures he carried that cynicism which humiliates others and that hardness which is the proof of egoism.

The celebrated alcove in the Tuileries to which Napoleon retired —

in the words of Balzac — to 'ride the horse of St. Benedict' was situated above the suite of rooms occupied by Josephine. Here the Emperor practised his doctrine: 'Love,' he claimed, 'is the occupation of the idle, the distraction of the soldier — and the danger of the monarch.'

In her memoirs, Mademoiselle George, the actress from the Théâtre Française who preceded Eleonore, described the Emperor's love nest:

I can still see the little windows above the state apartments: the salon, and the bedroom in which there was a kind of boudoir. I liked them so much that I used to bathe at the bains Vigier because I could see my dear little windows from my bath. To reach the pretty little apartment there was a horrid climb, and I had to go down long dark corridors.

'Oh! Constant, how high it is! I can't go any further — ' — 'Hush! No noise!'

Here we are. I entered through a little study which led into the bedroom . . . Constant, daft as a post, ordered the carriage to wait by the small door on the side facing the water. I told the Emperor that this annoyed me; so in future the coachman waited at the end of the lawn.

Napoleon summoned Georgina to the Tuileries two or three times a week. He undressed and dressed her himself; and he made her replace her buckled garters with round ones. The impatient lover found the buckles took too long to unfasten, while the round garters slipped quickly over Georgina's feet![3]

From the Emperor's suite, formerly the apartments of the three Louis, XIV, XV and XVI, a narrow lamp-lit stairway led down to Josephine's rooms immediately below.[4] Napoleon's playmates entered the palace of the Tuileries by the Pavillon de Flore; they were smuggled up a wide draughty staircase, by the guardroom, across the great audience chamber, through the Emperor's state bedroom with its ornate four-poster — rarely used — and finally into the study and boudoir. The tiny room where Napoleon dallied between acts of state was formerly the private chapel of Marie de Medici — who built the Tuileries. Duroc, Grand Marshal of the Palace, occupied a modest office close by; and the only opening to this sealed little world was a small hatch through which the Emperor's papers were received and despatched at all hours of the day and night. The door to the Grand Salon always remained locked. But as the alcove was adjacent to Josephine's private staircase her ears must have burned many times at midnight.

Captain Revel described a typical visit made by Leon's mother
to the Tuileries:

Eleonore lived obscurely under the name of Madame de St.
Laurent. She has said herself, that in the depths of the alcove
in Napoleon's room, where he received her, hung a clock, and
that while the Emperor was busy she found a means of
moving the large pointer and advancing it thirty minutes. The
time which Napoleon gave to his diversions was strictly
limited; so when he looked up and saw the clock he said:
'Already!' — and the lover was free.

This anecdote, together with the account of Mademoiselle George
suggests that the Emperor worked and made love in the same
room. Genius that he was, Napoleon had found a way of
combining business and pleasure.

CHAPTER 2

An Absent Father

Leon was born at two o'clock in the morning of December 13, 1806, with the aid of the distinguished *accoucheur* Pierre Marchais, of 29 Rue des Fosses Saint Germain l'Auxerrois, and the Medical Director of the Invalides, Guillaume Andral, Member of the Academy. Together with the Military Treasurer of the Legion of Honour, Jacques René Marie Aymé, who lived round the corner at 24 Rue St. George, they attested the child's birth at the Town Hall of the 2nd Arrondissement in the Rue d'Antin. The entry read: 'Léon, son of Eléonore Denuel, of independent means, aged 20, and of an absent father.'

There has been much speculation on Napoleon's doubts about Leon's parentage. Sharing as he did Murat's view of the proper rôle of a woman, the Emperor would naturally expect his flamboyant marshal to seize any opportunity offered by the proximity of his master's mistress. However, there exists no hard evidence that Eleonore was promiscuous. It is indeed likely that her brief childhood marriage to the rascally Revel turned her against men as a source of physical delight forever. Eleonore invariably exacted a consideration for her favours — usually a wedding ring. And she had nothing to hope or fear from the Gascon tavern-keeper's son: Caroline Bonaparte was Eleonore's *protectrice* and benefactor as she was that of Joachim Murat, her husband.

While it is not *known* that Murat and Eleonore shared the same bed, there is ample independent evidence that between January and September, 1806 she visited the Emperor not once but several times and that they did not discuss affairs of state. Indeed it was because of her tendency to display her intellect that Bonaparte tired of Eleonore. She preferred to talk politics.

Significantly, the two principal sources of the allegations against Murat are both virulent anti-Bonapartist: ex-Queen Hortense, Josephine's daughter and a woman of fine character; and Eleonore's ex-husband Revel, a convicted forger.[1] Neither Hortense nor the ex-quartermaster was a first-hand witness.

In his pamphlet, *Nouvelles Preuves du Rapt de Mme. Revel,* Eleonore's first husband can cite no witnesses to his allegation that she consorted with Murat in 1806, even though he freely names

names; and he is writing in the year 1816 when there was no risk of Bonapartist reprisals during the first year of the Bourbon Restoration. Surely Revel could have found some compliant *femme de chambre* to support his allegations?

Using that vague preamble beloved of the *carnadiste*, 'it is common knowledge', Revel says — on page 61 of his pamphlet — *'Il est notoire à Paris qu'Eléonore a vécu en concubinage, depuis mon arrestation, avec Murat, puis avec Buonaparte, en qualité de maîtresse en titre; puis avec des subalternes . . .'* As for the quartermaster's artful use of the phrase, 'since my arrest' it should be remembered that while Revel was arrested for fraud two months after he married the seventeen year old Eleonore — on January 15, 1805 — she was not taken into Caroline Murat's household until January, 1806. During the intervening year Eleonore was at a particularly strict boarding school in Chantilly!

'We are all bastards,' exclaims Posthumus in Shakespeare's *Cymbeline.*[2] But certainly it is *possible* that Murat was Leon's father; just as it is possible that Napoleon did not sire Alexandre Walewski and the King of Rome; and that Joachim Murat was not the father of his wife Caroline's children . . .

The inept handling of Leon at the most impressionable stage of his life was to prove disastrous.

Constant, the Emperor's all-seeing valet, recalled, 'He was first of all confided to Mme. Loire, the nurse of Achille Murat, who kept him for three years.'

Napoleon pontificated: 'I am of the opinion that the good or bad conduct of a child depends upon its mother.' But before Leon was two years old he was taken out of the hands of Eleonore, and mother and child were not to be re-united until he was sixteen. Eleonore had aroused the wrath of the Emperor by taking Leon to see his father on a surprise visit. Constant as always was there.

> The liaison did not last long. One day we saw her arrive at Fontainebleau where the court was gathered. She came up to the apartments of His Majesty and asked me to announce her. The Emperor was beside himself with rage at this request, and ordered me to tell her from him that he forbade her ever to visit him without his permission and to remain not a moment longer at Fontainebleau.

A crushed young Eleonore was turned away and re-traced the forty mile journey to Paris. After that late autumn day in 1807 she and Napoleon would not meet again.

During his formative years Leon was given into the charge of three nurses and was deposited in three different boarding establishments. Revel, to whom Leon was bound in no way whatsoever although the ex-dragoon continued to receive a substantial pension from him until his death in 1835, said: 'In the second month of his birth he was taken from his mother and confided successively to three nurses. The first, a lady named Martin, preserved his threatened days.'

Whether Revel is referring to the high infantile mortality of the early 19th century, or whether to some more sinister menace is not known, for he merely goes on; 'A lady named Loire was the last of his nurses . . . He was brought up secretly under the name of Macon.'

General Pierre Macon had died on October 18, 1806, at Leipzig, of which he was the District Commandant. He was eulogised in the 26th Bulletin of the Grande Armée, published in Berlin on November 3, 1806, thus: 'He was a worthy soldier and a perfect honest man. The Emperor was concerned with his death and much afflicated by it.' Napoleon chose a singularly bizarre method of perpetuating the memory of a gallant friend. Leon was to be saddled with the name of Macon until 1826, when he immediately abandoned it at his majority.

Napoleon dallied with the idea of adopting Leon. As Frédéric Masson wrote:

To avoid a break with Josephine to whom he was sincerely attached and whom with all her faults he loved, and at the same time to meet the provisions of the law of heredity, he undoubtedly conceived the idea of adopting his natural child, that he talked it over with Josephine; and that he went over the ground with those in his confidence. He searched for examples, invoked precedents, invented justifications.

If he withdrew it is because it would have been going too far to resort to a measure that was appropriate in the time of Louis XIV, when that monarch called to the succession the Duke de Maine and the Count de Toulouse.

Furthermore, less than two years previously Napoleon had imposed upon the commission met to draft the new Code Civil his views on illegitimacy. He wished to deny to bastards the proof of their paternity on the grounds that this would confer no benefit on the state. 'Society is not interested in knowing who their parents are . . . To give to illegitimate children the capacity to inherit would be an offence against public morals,' said Napoleon. He pondered the adoption of Leon until 1811 when, on March 20, his new wife, the Empress Marie Louise, gave birth to the King of Rome.

During the intervals of wrestling with the Imperial conscience, Napoleon had Leon brought to Caroline's home and to the Tuileries, while he was dressing or eating. 'He caressed him,' said Constant, 'gave him hundreds of sweets, and was amused at his liveliness and repartee.' When Joachim Murat was created Grand Duke de Berg in 1806, the Municipality of Paris made him a gift of the Elysée-Bourbon palace; and it was here that Napoleon came to play secretly with his little son.

In 1810 Mme. Loire, Leon's nurse, received a summons to the Elysée palace. Ironically enough it was from Michel, the husband of the woman who had supplanted Eleonore as lady-in-waiting to Caroline Murat:

> The Queen of Naples, Madame, instructs me to ask you to come tomorrow at one o'clock in the afternoon with the child, and to enter by the garden gate. You will kindly wait in the silver boudoir.
> Friday morning.
>
> M. Michel.

Maître Crémieux, the celebrated advocate, speaking for Leon in 1846, declared: 'The *boudoir d'argent* was in the Elysée-Bourbon: it is still there, but it is no longer used as a boudoir.'

President de Gaulle had the wing of the Elysée palace of which the boudoir forms a part restored to its Imperial elegance, after it had been used for many years as offices. The little dressing-room has been the scene of several dramatic events in French history. It was here that on June 22, 1815, Napoleon signed his final abdication; here that on December 2, 1851, Louis Napoleon took from a bureau drawer a folder bearing the legend 'Rubicon'; and it was in the silver boudoir that on February 16, 1899, the President of the French Republic, Felix Fauré, collapsed and died in the arms of his mistress.

'I have also had mistresses who loved me,' Napoleon told Lord Ebrington on Elba, 'but I have never had a *maîtresse en titre,* and I have never allowed myself to be ruled by a woman.'

Marya Louchenska came as near to the title of acknowledged mistress as any of the women who graced Bonaparte's bed. And her son was to be heaped with honours by two Emperors, while his half-brother Leon — Napoleon's first-born — was a mere spectator.

The romantic story of Napoleon's first glimpse of the eighteen year old Polish countess has been given a wide distribution. While his coachman was changing horses before the gates of the little town of Bronie, the Emperor espied for only a few tantalising moments the lovely young Marie, before he continued on his way to Warsaw. It was January 1, 1807, and the news of Leon's birth had reached him only the previous day. Later, in the Polish capital, Countess Marya Walewska was introduced to Napoleon, and the two lovers spent their nights in the old boudoir of Warsaw Castle. Marie at first refused him her favours; but the Polish nobles appealed to her patriotism. What was one woman's virtue compared with the liberation of her country from the despotism of the Czar?

Napoleon's love-life was regulated with military precision, and he did not leave his sexual rendezvous to the caprice of chance encounters, as Mme. de Remusat recalled.

Whenever the Emperor made a journey, or even went on campaign, he never omitted a certain distraction which he arranged in his short respites from affairs of state or his battles. Murat, his brother-in-law, or his Grand Marshal, Duroc, were given the task of seeking out the means to satisfy his passing fancies.

During the first invasion of Poland, Murat, who had preceded him to Warsaw, received the order to find for the Emperor an attractive young woman — preferably of noble birth. He accomplished this mission adroitly, and fixed on a young and aristocratic Polish girl married to an elderly husband. We do not know what means he employed and what promises he gave; but finally she consented to all the arrangements, and even to a nocturnal meeting at Warsaw Castle where the Emperor was in residence.

Here then was this beautiful creature delivered up at the place of her fateful rendezvous. She has recounted this adventure herself, confessing that she arrived in fear and trembling. The Emperor was shut up in his study. The stranger's arrival was made known to him. Without interrupting his business he gave orders that she be taken to the suite allotted her, told to take a bath and to eat. She would then be free to get into bed.

Nevertheless, Napoleon continued to work until late in the night. 'Having at length finished his tasks,' continued Mme. de Remusat, 'he went along to the room where Marie Walewska had been waiting a considerable time, and suddenly appeared in all the aspect of a lord who considered preliminaries a waste of time . . .'

During an expansive moment on St. Helena Napoleon told Gourgaud: 'I owed to Talleyrand my connection with Mme. Walewska,' and he proceeded to demolish the legend of the reluctant heroine by confiding, 'She did not put up much of a struggle!'

On Monday, April 2, 1810, less than four months after his divorce from Josephine, Napoleon married the Austrian princess Marie Louise; and the following month his second illegitimate son — Alexandre Walewski — was born. Countess Walewska received a pension of 10,000 francs a year; and after living for a while at No. 2 Rue du Houssaie, Chaussée d'Antin moved into 48 Rue de la Victoire. Alexandre Florian Joseph Colonna Walewski was born at Walewice Castle, Poland, on May 4, 1810. His mother had arrived pregnant in Paris; but Napoleon sent her away so that the child would be born in his native country.

In contrast to his treatment of the three year old Leon, Napoleon immediately gave Alexandre Walewski a title, and made him the beneficiary of a settlement subsequently funded from a grant of lands in the kingdom of Naples. This public act of recognition had no relevance except in the context of the Emperor's affair with Marie Walewska; and it made a nonsense of his assertion: 'Immorality is without possibility of contradiction the worst thing that can be found in a sovereign, for the reason that it at once makes immorality fashionable.'

It is true also that the young republican Bonaparte had mellowed into an Emperor with a great respect for the old titled families of Europe. If Napoleon had been born to the purple he could, like Charles II, have founded a ducal line from the offspring of an orange-girl. In fact the etiquette of the Tuileries was more strict and elaborate than that of the Bourbons. The English visitor Bertie Greatheed noted that a certain 'R^d G' 'had been refused introduction to Bonaparte on account of not having been presented in England.'

Marya Walewska had vainly sacrificed her honour. In lieu of granting her country, Poland, its independence, Napoleon had created her son a count of the French Empire. Meanwhile the three year old Leon, brought up by strangers, still bore the second-hand name of a dead general.

While the court was at Fontainebleau, Napoleon elevated to the barony another person whose life would be bound with that of

Leon until the end of the tragedy on St. Helena.

On November 2, 1810, Joseph Ignace Mathieu, a member of the Electoral College of the Oise, and father-in-law of Napoleon's private secretary, Meneval, was created a baron of the Empire with a state pension. It is not surprising, therefore, that when Leon was five years old, as Baron Fain noted, 'M. Mauvières, notary, and father-in-law of my comrade Meneval wished very much to be his guardian.' Baron de Mauvières (Mayor of St. Forget), who lived at 331 Rue Saint Honoré, appeared on Wednesday morning, March 25, 1812, before the Juge de Paix, Jean Thomas Defresne and his court bailiff, Joseph Prague, at that same Town Hall of the 2nd Arrondissement where Leon's birth had been registered. Leon was now at boarding school and the object of the meeting was to make him financially independent of his mother, who had received a dowry of 20,000 francs in 1808. The memory of Eleonore's visit to Fontainebleau haunted Napoleon like a spectre.

Mauvières bore no authority from Leon's mother and he had not the slightest legal grounds for assuming guardianship over the child. Therefore, to answer the routine objections of a knowing judge the fiction was advanced that the boy's mother and father could not be found! (Eleonore was in Paris; and Napoleon was staying at the Elysée palace a couple of hundred yards from the home of Mauvières — in the same street!)

Nevertheless the legal farce was solemnly played out.

Whereas M. Joseph Ignace Mathieu, Baron de Mauvières . . . has explained to us that a child of masculine sex, born in this city and in our district, at 29 Rue de la Victoire, December 13, 1806, of Mlle. Eleonore Denuelle and of an absent and unknown father, was registered under the name of Leon . . .

That this minor is now at boarding school, and that a person equally unknown, after having placed him there, has until now paid all his expenses;

That the applicant has been called by diverse circumstances to look after the interests of this child; that he is aware that funds — sufficient at least for his education — must be permanently granted. It therefore follows that the necessity arises, in the absence of the mother and because of the very doubt of her existence, as also the ignorance in which we are left by the birth certificate concerning the father, to appoint to this child a guardian receive such funds as may be forthcoming, and a deputy guardian to protect his interests should they conflict with those of the guardian.

Judge Defresne had already given his verbal permission for the setting up of a family council and the following members now appeared before him:

Denis Charles Francois Bonnomet, of 43 Rue du Mont Blanc, member of the General Council of the Department of the Seine, tontine administrator, honorary notary, and advocate of the Imperial Court; Jean Baptiste Louis Anne Adrien Leroy de Camilly, 14 Rue de la Madeleine, former counsellor at the Court des Aides; Antoine Louis Gillet, of 340 Rue Saint Honoré, Paris notary and member of the Electoral College of the Department of the Yonne; Charles Auguste Bernard Fauquet, 346 Rue Saint Honoré, former advocate, 'all friends of the minor in default of his parents, who with Baron de Mauvières, and ourself as President,' intoned Judge Dufresne, 'constitute the family council, promising to deliberate and to give their opinion on their soul and conscience under the oath that they have sworn before us.'

The deed of guardianship then rehearsed the glowing benefits which Leon might anticipate from the arrangement.

Considering that nothing but good can result to the minor Leon to have a supervisor; that his fortune can reap only benefit from it, and that it is proper to give him as guardian the person who is already watching over his needs and interests, it is our unanimous opinion to appoint the said M. Joseph Ignace Mathieu, Baron de Mauvières, to administer the assets of the infant . . . authorising him at the same time to receive gifts and to effect all dispositions for the inscription of bank shares and entries in the Grand Book of the National Debt.

As a guarantee of his good faith, Mauvières was obliged to mortgage his estate of Mardilly, at Evry-les-Chateaux, in the arrondissement of Melun, Départment of Seine et Marne, near Fontainebleau.

A week later Napoleon left Paris for Châlons to inspect the Grande Armée: the first step on his journey to Moscow; and Leon joined the children of Baron de Mauvières in the Hix school at 3 Rue Matignon, conveniently situated near the Elysée palace. Jacques Antoine Hix was well connected, having been in 1807 Master of Ceremonies of the Saint Napoleon masonic lodge of Paris.

The distinguished drama critic of the *Journal des Débats,* Geoffroy, who had been a pupil and later director of studies at the

Eleonore Denuelle de la Plaigne
From a portrait by Philiberte Ledoux

The Emperor Napoleon
From a picture by Delaroche

The Palace of the Tuileries showing the Pavilion de Flore and Napoleon's apartments

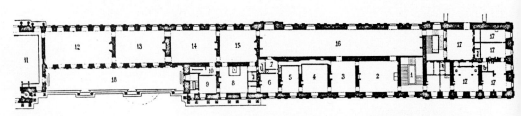

1. Escalier de l'appartement d'habitation.
2. Antichambre.
3. Salon de service.
4. Salon de l'Empereur.
5. Cabinet de l'Empereur.
6. Cabinet topographique.
7. Garde du Portefeuille.

8. Chambre à coucher de l'Empereur.
9. Cabinet de toilette de l'Empereur.
10. Huissier de l'appartement.
11. Salon des Maréchaux.
12. Salon des Officiers.
13. Salon de la Paix.
14. Salon du Trône.

15. Grand Cabinet du Conseil.
16. Galerie de Diane.
17. Appartement du Pape.
18. Terrasse sur le jardin.
19. Petit appartement de l'Empereur.
20. Escalier de service.

Plan of Napoleon's apartments in the Palace of the Tuileries, showing the famous alcove and spiral stairway, between the map room (No. 6) and the office of the *Garde du Portefeuille* (No. 7) school, recalled in tranquillity the dreadful year of the Terror.

I entered the college of M. Hix, in the Rue Meslay, one of
those Parisian institutions from which a number of brilliant
students emerged. The terrible year of 1793 slipped by as
peacefully as if I had been studying with the Benedictine
refugees abroad. Two more years passed during which I
carried off prizes which augured for me a shining future; but
due to the political situation my grandmother no longer had
sufficient funds to keep me there and I was obliged to leave.
Goodbye then Rageneau de Sainte Colombe, Lesbros,
Feroussat, Bergerot, Sainte Marie . . . Goodbye! I was twelve
years old . . .

Leon, by all accounts, was a worthy pupil of M. Hix and received
what has been described as a brilliant education. A syllabus of a
typical Paris boarding school will indicate the amount of knowledge that students were expected to absorb:

Subjects	Teachers	
PHILOSOPHY		
Morale	BERTRAND	former tutor, Member of several learned societies he is assisted by several private tutors
*Logic		
BELLES-LETTRES		
*Grammar, general and particular		
*Poetry and Rhetoric		
*Latin, *Geography and *History		
English (100 francs a Year	CORBIN	They speak these languages with an incomparable purity
German (100 francs a year)	BERGER	
Italian (100 francs a year)	BLANVILLIAN	translator of *Paul et Virginie*

ADVANCED SCIENCES

*Pure mathematics and physico mathematics sciences	CALLET	the author of tables of logarithms, former professor of the Schools of Engineering and Marine. Assisted by two tutors he prepares pupils for the Polytechnique
*Mineralogy		an officer of mines, who also teaches mathematics
*Handwriting	BERNARD	of the Lycée des Arts with the original examples of Rossignol
Bookkeeping and Foreign Exchange (50 francs a year)	BONNET	former professor

FINE ARTS

Drawing and Wash Architecture, Painting (100 francs a year)	CHARBONNIERES	of the Department of Roads and Bridges
Tonic Sol-fa and Violin (100 francs a year)	GRIOT	of the Opera Comique
Piano (2 francs a lesson)	DOIX	
Clarinet (2 frs a lesson)	PERRET	of the Opera Comique
Dancing (100 francs a year)	DESCHAMPS	of the Theatre des Arts

PHYSICAL TRAINING

Boxing and Gymnastics (100 francs a year)	BLOT	a pupil of Ray
Riding (30 francs a year)	VIEILLARD	at his Establishment, Rue de Varennes
Swimming (30 francs for five Months)		

A dentist, Citizen Carlier, and a doctor, Citizen Gastaldy, visit the college at frequent intervals.

The pupils are taken for walks; and, from time to time, to museums and state factories.

The fee, including subjects marked with an asterisk, is 600 francs for pupils up to the age of twelve, and 800 francs for older students. Private tutors are provided at a saving of two thirds on their fees in town. Whatever be their number, Citizen Bertrand makes himself responsible for everything for 1,200 francs; the only extra being for clothes.

Note: Pupils are never allowed to go out without a teacher or a servant. When enrolling they should bring with them a bed, three pairs of sheets, a dozen napkins, cutlery and a mug. Fees are payable in advance at the beginning of each term. Hire of a bed costs 36 francs; and laundry, including care of linen, 50 francs a year. Pupils paying 1,200 francs are relieved of these charges.

(It is interesting to note that the riding master was Captain Vieillard — most probably the ex-Artillery officer who later became private tutor to the two sons of Hortense and Louis Bonaparte, and afterwards of Leon.)

Leon did not remain with Monsieur Hix, but was removed to the pension Bourdon, and thence to a third institution — the College Muron. A Mlle. Natalie Bourdon at one time directed a school in the hotel Mailly, 279, Rue d l'Université, Faubourg St. Germain; and her syllabus has a curiously modern ring: 'My time is completely my own and all my moments will belong to my young friends.' Her young friends were obliged to enter details of their twelve francs pocket money in a little account book. 'This will indicate their leaning towards charity, thrift, miserliness or coquetterie,' she wrote in her leaflet, which advised that the school was 'particularly destined for foreigners' *with distant parents.*

Like many absent fathers, Napoleon salved his conscience by keeping his child liberally supplied with cash. During the period from Leon's birth in 1806 until June, 1815, Napoleon — on a generous reckoning — spent less than four and a half years in Paris.[3]

In January 1814, before leaving Paris to join his army at Chalons, the Emperor instructed the Duke de Bassano to add to Leon's assets 12,000 francs represented by ten shares in the canals.

CHAPTER 3

The Angel of Malmaison

Each time that his father returned from the wars Leon was brought from school, dusted off, and dandled for a few short moments on the Emperor's lap; until one summer day he was taken by his guardian to say good-bye to his father — 'Père Violette' — in the rose gardens of Malmaison.

Napoleon once observed that it was imagination which lost battles; certainly on the day of June 18, 1815, he preferred his own fantasies to the sober reports of his generals. 'I tell you Wellington is a bad general, the English are bad soldiers; we will settle the matter by lunchtime,' said the Emperor. The time: 8.30 a.m., the place: Waterloo. The immovable Irishman and the irresistible Corsican had at last come face to face across a few fields of Belgian corn. The matter was not settled by lunchtime; and at 3 p.m. the Emperor revised the odds. 'This morning we had ninety chances in our favour,' he announced. 'We still have sixty.'

On June 22, 1815, he signed his final abdication, and a few days later, accompanied by Bertrand, he slipped out of the Elysée palace by a garden gate into the tree-lined avenue which had been named by the Revolution the Route de la Montagne du Bon Air, but which the Empire had known as the Elysian Fields. Napoleon saw the Champs Elysées for the last time as he drove to Malmaison to receive the hospitality of his step-daughter, Hortense.

While the ex-Emperor was strolling in what had been his private garden, and perhaps thinking of the idyllic hours he had spent with Josephine at her country home, Baron de Mauvières brought to him the eight year old Leon from the Hix school.

Hortense, the ex-Queen of Holland, describes the scene.

One day at noon, the Emperor sent for me. He was in his little garden with a man whom I did not know and a young child who appeared to be nine or ten years of age. Taking me aside, the Emperor said: 'Hortense, look at this child. Whom does he resemble?'

'It is your son, Sire, he is the image of the King of Rome'.

— 'You think him so? Then it must be true. I, who never believed myself soft-hearted — but the sight of him moves me. You seem to be aware of the circumstances of his birth. How do you know about him?'

'Sire, the people have discussed him a great deal; and this similarity proves to me they were not mistaken.' — 'I admit, I had doubts that he was my son. Nevertheless I had him brought up in a boarding-school in Paris. The headmaster wrote to me to ask what my plans were for his future. I wanted to see him and — like yourself — his resemblance to my son has shaken me.'

'What are you going to do with him? I would look after him with pleasure, Sire, but do you not think it would give them an opportunity to stir up ill-feeling against me?' — 'Yes, you are right. It would make me very happy to know he was with you. But people would lose no time in saying that he was your son. When I am settled in America I shall send for him.'

Then he rejoined the gentleman who waited some distance away; and I went up to this child — who was as beautiful as an angel. I asked him if he were happy at school, and how he amused himself. He replied that for some time he and his companions had been playing at fighting with each other and that they had formed two teams: one called the Bonapartists and the other the Bourbons.

I wished to know on whose side he was. — 'The King's side,' he told me. And when I asked him why, he answered, 'Because I like the King and I don't like the Emperor'.

I guessed how little he suspected his parenthood, and the identity of the person he had just seen; and I found his situation so bizarre that I questioned him on the reason for his dislike of the Emperor. — 'I have no reason,' he repeated, 'save that of being on the side of the King'.

The Emperor rejoined us, sent away the person in charge of Leon, and went in to lunch. I followed him, and over and over again he remarked, 'This sight has moved me. He resembles my son. I would not have believed myself so susceptible of the feelings he has created in me. His resemblance to me and my son has struck you very much?' And his conversation continued in this strain throughout the whole of lunch.

The ex-Emperor was no longer in a position to give orders; and

when he sailed from Rochefort his destination was not America
but a tiny island in the South Atlantic.

With Napoleon safely borne away to the Southern Oceans —
Revel prepared the publication of his pamphlet: *Buonaparte and
Murat, Abductors of a Young Wife, written by the outraged hand
of J. H. F. Revel, Captain, retired,* in which he recounted the story
of his nine-week marriage with Eleonore. Some three months
before his release from Dourdan jail,[1] Captain Revel had entertained his fellow-prisoners with a poem he had composed entitled
La Matrimonimanie. A released prisoner hurried to Mme. Campan
to regale her with a few stanzas; and in January 1807, the work
was seized, together with many other documents and nineteen
dossiers, by one Quartermaster-Sergeant Guérin in a raid on
Revel's two furnished cells.

Two months after his marriage to Eleonore, Revel had been
arrested for forging a bill of exchange. The Murats interceded on
behalf of the husband of Caroline's school-friend; and, although
Revel was sentenced to two years imprisonment by the Criminal
Court of Seine-et-Oise at Versailles, he was spared the ignominy of
the branding with a hot iron — an integral part of the penalty.

From his prison cell the ex-dragoon (and now ex-army con-
tractor) had contested his wife's action for divorce in April 1806,
taken under the awesome protection of the Emperor, whereupon
Eleonore wrote chillingly to her husband: 'You have no other
choice: it is either the convict-hulks, or a few short months in jail.'
Menaced with transportation to the French penal colony of
Cayenne if he did not give his written consent to the divorce,
Revel decided to foreswear the heat of Devil's Island, in order — as
he said — to avert hardship to the children of his first marriage.
The final decree significantly described Eleonore as being
'attached to the household of Her Royal Highness the Princess
Caroline.'

In January 1808, a year almost to the very day after the
romantic encounter in Warsaw Castle, Napoleon sent for the
nineteen year old Marie Walewska. The countess arrived in Paris at
the end of the month and took up residence in a house on the
Quai de Voltaire — conveniently near to the Tuileries across the
Pont du Carrousel, but discreetly separated from the palace by a
narrow stretch of the Seine. Eleonore was now more than ever *de
trop* and it was high time she was re-married and out of the
capital. On February 3, she sold No 29 Rue de la Victoire, where

Leon was born, and re-conveyed the house to Jean Claude Henry, a lawyer of the Rue Feydeau and Murat's confidential agent, who acted as a man of straw in delicate negotiations touching the Emperor.

The following day Eleonore received from Henry a dowry of 20,000 francs and married Pierre Philippe Augier, an infantry lieutenant. Her parents were not consulted about the proposed marriage and as a result of their protests were promptly committed to prison at the instance of Eleonore herself for indulging in 'unguarded talk'! They had merely demanded a formal request for the hand of their minor daughter. (Eleonore was still only twenty years old.)

This was denied us, [said Mme. de la Plaigne] and on January 17 we were conducted into the presence of Desmarets at police headquarters where we were told we must sign the marriage contract.

In vain did we invoke the sacred rights of parenthood. We were told that my husband would be taken to the Temple prison and myself to the Madelonettes.

I wish to state that I would never have believed possible such encroachments on my liberty for refusing to sign my daughter's marriage contract; but M. Desmarets replied that he was perfectly able to involve me in a conspiracy which would lead to my utter ruin. I was at once forced into a cab by a certain Pasques, who called himself a police inspector, and was driven to the Madelonettes where I was placed in a cell.[2]

My husband was detained all night at the police station, and having been given a promise that I should be set free as soon as he had signed, he complied without reading the document.

In spite of this proof of submission, I remained shut away for three weeks, and during this long torture my daughter was married and the ceremony dishonoured by the imprisonment of a wretched mother in a cell, where — they assured my husband — my legs were being eaten away by rats.

A week later M. and Mme. de la Plaigne were ordered to remain at a distance of three hundred miles from Paris. They sold their furniture, of which the greater portion was bought at a knockdown price by the policeman charged with their custody!

However, at the moment of their departure the Denuelles petitioned the Senate for redress:

Your Excellencies,
Come to our aid. Please address yourselves to the Prefecture
of Police and learn the circumstances of the case. They are so
abominable that they will strain your powers of credibility.
When you are made aware of the facts we are confident we
shall receive justice from you, as you must be persuaded of
our gratitude and deep respect.

Madame de la Plaigne

Paris, February 26, 1808.
Eleonore's former husband Revel was named lieutenant in the
64th Regiment of the line at Besancon in March 1808; but on
April 4, he was refused permission to see his children at Paris
before rejoining his regiment. The Bonapartist authorities had
effectively cleared the capital of all remnants of the Emperor's
passade save one — he was too young to speak. Revel tells how at
the end of March he found himself seated next to the Denuelles,
including Eleonore's aunt Zulma, in the dining room of the Hôtel
National at Besancon. His in-laws had been exiled to the eastern
frontier post when Ravel was banished to Tours. The dragoon had
with difficulty effected his re-entry into the army; but this chance
meeting so alarmed Eleonore's mother that she wrote to the
Ministry of War and the unfortunate Revel was transferred to the
Rhine army at Worms. Eleonore and her new husband were
packed off to the French army in Spain where Murat was
providing Goya with material for his painting of the massacre of
Spanish patriots — *Tres de Mayo*. Although Augier was a man of
blameless character his presence in Paris was inimical to the
Emperor, and in order to keep him out of the French capital he
was obliged to leave his preferred infantry. To Augier's protests
that he was not a cavalryman the War Ministry ordered: 'Make use
of him in the cavalry . . . Motives already known to this Ministry
demand that he should not any longer remain in Paris.' As a
solatium he received a gratuitous ribbon of the Legion of Honour.
     Eleonore's second marriage had lasted little more than three
years when Augier, now serving with the 7th Cuirassiers, disappeared in the retreat of the Grande Armée from Moscow. In the
crossing of the icy Beresina at the end of November 1812, he
received a musket ball in the shoulder and was left for dead by his
groom, who took back to the regiment Augier's horse and
breastplate. The servant had been mistaken, however, for the
squadron-leader reappeared at Wilna. He was last reported in a
Polish hospital, dying as the cossacks were entering Marienbourg.

Eleonore's third husband was a German diplomat. Charles Auguste Emile Louis, Count de Luxbourg, was born at Zweibrücken. The title stemmed from his grandfather who had named his new barony after the family château on the shores of Lake Constance. His law studies completed at Göttingen and Heidelberg, de Luxbourg entered the Diplomatic Service as an attache at the Bavarian Legation in Switzerland. During Jerome Bonaparte's short but expensive reign in Westphalia, de Luxbourg was *en poste* at Kassel. He was a member of the Bavarian mission in Paris from 1811 to 1813, and it was at this time that he met Eleonore. She followed the count to Bavaria and they were married on March 23, 1814, at his home in Seckenheim.

Some ten months after their return to Paris the de Luxbourgs were assailed by Revel with pamphlets and law suits; Eleonore's Imperial protector was now on the distant Mediterranean kingdom of Elba busily decreeing that his island subjects should not sleep more than five to a bed. On December 3, 1814, Revel — who had received a legal education — instituted an action for nullity of the divorce of 1806. 'The law has been polluted,' he complained, 'public decency diminished, and the security of the family compromised.'

Revel was a Vicar of Bray with a disastrous sense of timing. As soon as he received news of Napoleon's return to France — near Cannes at four o'clock in the afternoon of Wednesday, March 1, 1815 — the ex-dragoon enlisted with his son in the volunteer forces of King Louis XVIII. After placing his daughter in a convent under the reluctant patronage of the Archbishop of Rheims, he hurried back to Paris: but on arrival at the Tuileries he learned that Louis had fled to Ghent.

However, Revel remained in Paris and coolly applied to Napoleon's newly-appointed Minister of the Interior for a job. Carnot — the architect of the Grande Armée — sent him to Chartres as Secretary-General of the Eure-et-Loir; but a few weeks later the ex-quartermaster was back in Paris. Napoleon had been defeated at Waterloo and a royal decree of July 24, 1815, cancelled all official appointments made by the Imperial government during the Hundred Days.

In his pamphlet Revel made a comprehensive round of attacks upon anyone who had been remotely connected with his marriage, including not only the Emperor's lawyer, Masson, but his own advocate, Lebon, to whom he had once addressed fulsome verses. Mme. Campan was charged with enjoying a large and handsome slice 'of the cake for the immoral banquet of the rape of my wife.'

Jeanne Genet-Campan also lost, on July 19, 1814, her Imperial perquisite as director of the Maison de la Legion d'Honneur under the royal decree which dissolved that institution. She withdrew to Ecouen with 60,000 francs of debts, a tric-trac table, a game of bagatelle from Josephine, and a whirligig from Hortense. More fortunate than Revel, Mme. Campan received from Louis XVIII a pension of 6,000 francs and a similar amount from Hortense. She had, on June 21, 1814, written a letter on paper bearing in watermark the image of Napoleon and the Imperial eagle assuring King Louis that she had never solicited the Bonapartes. This was probably true: as in so many other matters, Napoleon was indebted to Josephine for his introduction to the female pedagogue of St. Germain-en-Laye.

Five months after the Emperor's arrival on St. Helena Revel resumed his suit for the annulment of his shot-gun divorce from Eleonore, and the hearing took place on December 15, 1815, before the Court of First Instance of the Seine. The substitute *Procureur du Roi,* de Marchangy, gave his answer on January 5, 1816, when he demanded the dismissal of Revel's claim and the suppression of his pamphlet as a defamatory and injurious libel. The court, accepting the advocate-general's submission, threw out the claim, banned Revel's book, and condemned him to costs!

The ex-dragoon returned to the charge two years later with an accusation of bigamy and trigamy against Eleonore. He wrote to the Ministry of War for evidence supporting his contention that Augier had survived the Russian campaign, and received a reply, dated January 1, 1818, which confirmed that the death of the squadron-leader of the 7th Cuirassiers could not be established — only that he had disappeared at the river Beresina and had not been heard of since. Revel wrote also to Augier's aged father who, in the absence of proof positive, not unnaturally believed his son might still be alive.

Eleonore, too, had been importuning the War Minister for a certificate - stating that her husband was *dead*; but in reply to a letter of April 21, 1819, she was told that the Ministry was unable to furnish her with the necessary document.

In the middle of all this paper work, Revel opened a second front. He was still awaiting the result of an appeal against his action for annulment of divorce; but on April 9, 1819, the quartermaster brought against the twelve year old Leon a suit for disavowal of paternity, advancing as his motive the fear that the child would claim legitimacy under Articles 312 and 315 of the Civil Code. As French law would not entertain an action against a minor, Revel called a family council to nominate a guardian against whom a case could be brought. It is hardly credible that the adolescent Leon was not aware of the controversies of which he had been the object since his birth.

On April 21, 1819, Eleonore's father, now living at No.6 Rue de la Michodiere, and two other of the Denuelle clan, Jean Simon a retired naval officer, and Francois Claude, Eleonore's cousin, appeared before the Juge de Paix of the 3rd Arrondissement, together with a member of Revel's family and two of his acquaintances. The judge confessed bewilderment at the reason for this spectacle and adjourned the case for four months, in order, as he said, to make some inquiries *into Leon's religion*! Every *persona* drawn into the drama of Leon seems to have been impelled to add his own bizarre contribution to the story. When the court re-convened at 7 a.m. on Saturday, August 12, 1819, the judge appointed as guardian *ad litem* Leon's grandfather, Dominique Denuelle, and again adjourned the hearing.

The matter dragged on for two more years, until Revel proposed to Baron de Mauvières that the claim should be settled with the ex-dragoon receiving a pension of 3,600 francs — as recognition of the services he, Revel, had rendered the child 'in protecting him from the avarice of Eleonore and her father'! In return he would postpone his action for disavowal of paternity until Leon had reached his majority.

Mauvières bought off Revel with a pension of 1,200 francs (out of Leon's assets); but when his request for an advance of 300 francs was not immediately satisfied, Revel again took up the suit. The baron, now living quietly in the valley of the Chevreuse, wearied of the charge committed to him by the Emperor, who had these six months past rendered up his own stewardship, and transferred the burden of Leon to his son-in-law, Meneval.

Claude François de Meneval had entered the service of the Bonapartes as Joseph's secretary, and at the age of 24 replaced the sharp Bouriennes, as *chef de cabinet* to the First Consul. On February 3, 1806, Napoleon appointed him his private secretary, and the next year paid for his wedding and honeymoon, adding 50,000 francs for good measure.

'A real treasure . . . ' was Napoleon's description of his secretary, 'amiable, reserved, zealous and absolutely discreet.' Not surprisingly, he confessed, 'I was unable to keep — nor in fact did I keep — any secrets from Meneval.' Leon's birth was therefore not concealed from the man who always possessed the Emperor's 'secret of the day'. On April 13, 1810, — still in the aura of his fortnight old marriage to Marie Louise — a grateful Napoleon created Meneval a Baron of the Empire.

At first the Emperor considered entrusting the guardianship of Leon to his young secretary; but decided instead to confide his son to de Mauvières (who had received his barony six months after Meneval's).

The Bonapartes had a conspiratorial obsession for doing things at two steps removed; and Napoleon retained effective control over Leon through Meneval and his father-in-law. It was well that Meneval did not immediately receive the tutelage of Leon, for after the first fall of Paris he was given the duty of escorting the ex-Empress Marie Louise to Vienna.

In order to transfer the guardianship of Leon from Mauvières to Meneval a new family council was summoned before the Juge de Paix of the 2nd Arrondissement, on October 22, 1821, consisting of Leroy de Camilly, Count Lavalette, Las Cases and Baron Denon. A student of numerology would find significance in the triumvirates of Leon's early life: three arrondissements, three nurses, three schools, three guardians, three family councils . . .

As well as giving him a new guardian, the family council allotted Leon an income of 12,000 francs which he proceeded to spend like a Bonaparte. Philibert Audebrand believed that Leon most physically resembled Napoleon's youngest brother (whose voice vividly recalled that of the Emperor). At sixteen Jerome went out and spent 10,000 francs on a silver mounted toilet case containing razors for which he had no use whatsoever. Like Leon, Jerome Bonaparte was to suffer throughout his life because of the lack of control exercised over his youthful spending.

The fifteen year old Leon started the New Year of 1822 in style by laying out 34 francs on theatres and hackney cabs; and on February 8, treated himself to 15 francs worth of perfumery. He purchased a miniature portrait of the Emperor at 300 francs and an accompanying pocket case for 25. A further six francs he spent on a box to hold a portrait of Eleonore. For the pre-Lenten festivities he hired a horse at the Mardi Gras rste of 20 francs. Bechu and Lafitte, tailors, reaped 391 francs for clothing the young dandy, and Leon's footwear cost another 91 francs.

The new tutor received the customary *douceurs* paid by a young debutant to his mentor. Narcisse Vieillard had been brought from Rome where he had been coaching the future Napoleon III. On April 2, 1822, Leon and the ex-Imperial artillery captain set up home in an apartment strategically situated near the Odeon theatre and the Luxembourg on the borders of the Latin Quarter and the aristocratic Faubourg St. Germain.

At No.3 Rue de Crebillon, Leon and his tutor slept on beds of bird's eye mahogany, behind muslin curtains at 18 francs 45, cunningly sewn by a Mme. Roux for 72 francs 35. The new ménage was lavishly appointed with the products of the Restoration *faïenciers* and *orfèvres* and the *maître menuisier* ébénistes of the Faubourg St. Antoine. Lemoine the goldsmith supplied a canteen of cutlery for 395 francs, while a mere 50 francs bought a china service from Laplé. The linen presses were stocked at a cost of 359 francs 95, and knives for the table accounted for 12 francs. Below stairs, Josephine the cook made do with a humbler set of instruments for which she paid a trivial 4 francs 10.

Leon and Vieillard took coffee in armchairs costing 340 francs — a fraction of the total furniture bill of over 3,000 francs mostly spent on *gros meubles,* but with a representative assortment of the Louis XVIII chairs — *causeuses, dormeuses, veilleuses;* and tables — *vide-poches tables à secret,* and *guéridons.*

The walls were papered and tapestried at a cost of 76 francs 55, and below them the bookcases began to fill with an embryo library. Leon spent 12 francs on his father's favourite romance, *Paul et Virginie* (which, Napoleon confessed, he could never read without weeping), and the *Memorial de Sainte Hélène* (56 francs plus 12 francs for binding). A pair of alabaster vases stood on the chimney-shelf, and Leon counted the hours by a pendulum clock — like the one Eleonore had regulated with her feet in the Tuileries alcove seventeen years before.

One day Baron Fain turned up at Meneval's where he experienced what was to be the inevitable reaction of all who met Napoleon's first son:

I saw Leon Maçon at Meneval's in 1822; he would be fourteen or fifteen years old, and I cannot say how moved I was to see come to life in the face of this child the young General Bonaparte himself, more or less as I saw him the first time in 1796 when he presented himself at the headquarters in the Rue des Capucines to take command of the Army of the Interior.

Six weeks after Leon moved into his own flat, Revel's case was again thrown out by the Court of First Instance. On May 21 and

August 16, 1822, the First Chamber delivered two more decisions
unfavourable to the quartermaster; and Leon's funds were dunned
for a further 3,273 francs in costs to buy Revel off.

Eleonore, Countess de Luxbourg, was living in Mannheim where
her husband was director of the court theatre; but her *homme de
confiance* — one Miel — waited in the wings at Paris, describing in
honeyed tones to Meneval's ward the delights of life in Baden.
Miel would soon give the cue for Leon to leave a performance of
the adventures of Aladdin to play the *jeune-premier* in a real-life
pantomime.

Leon arrived in Germany early in 1823. On the evening of
January 11 he had been taken by his tutor, Monsieur Vieillard, to
the Gymnase Theatre in Paris, at the corner of the Boulevard
Bonne Nouvelle and the Rue Hauteville, to see '*La Petite Lampe
Merveilleuse*', a fairy operetta in three acts by Scribe and
Mélesville with music by Alexandre Piccini. Aladdin was played by
Léontine Fay.

In his history of Paris theatres, Chalons d'Argé notes with
approval, 'the good taste which almost always presides'.

The Gymnase is the most agreeable of the minor Paris
theatres and the best society of the capital is always found
there. Like everywhere else it has its flops; but unlike
everywhere else it has never witnessed the outrage of decency
and taste . . .

The Gymnase Dramatique was a branch of the Théâtre Francais,
where young actors were put through their paces; and it was there
that Rachel made her début. In 1821 a young actress named
Virginie Déjazet began her career at the Gymnase. Later, at the
height of her fame, she was to make a fleeting but agitated
appearance in Leon's life; and on the night when Vieillard's
impatient young pupil sat among the audience she was a member
of the troupe.

During the interval of *The Wonderful Lamp* Leon asked permission to go out for refreshments. Placing his hat on his seat he
left the auditorium and slipped quickly downstairs to the theatre
exit, where Eleonore's agent Miel was waiting for him with a
carriage. Leon jumped into the cab and the coachman, whipping
up his horses, drove eastwards along the boulevards, out of Paris
and on to Strasbourg. From there Leon was taken across the
Rhine to Mannheim where his mother was waiting. Eleonore had
last seen him when he was a year old. For fifteen years they had

been kept apart at the Emperor's command; yet Napoleon had been dead almost two years before Eleonore dared to defy his wishes.

At the Gymnase Leon's tutor spent some anxious moments. When the curtain fell at the end of the performance and Leon had not reclaimed his hat, Narcisse Vieillard searched the theatre. As there was still no sign of his pupil he became thoroughly alarmed and questioned the attendants. Reluctantly Vieillard decided that there was nothing for it but to report Leon's disappearance to his guardian. A furious Meneval called in the police. Although they were happy enough to see Paris with one Bonaparte the less, the Sûreté scoured the city with their usual thoroughness and mounted an investigation. But the Quai des Orfèvres was baffled. Leon had left no trace whatsoever; and it was not until after a week had elapsed that Meneval learned of the manner in which his ward had been abducted.

In high dudgeon he wrote to Eleonore's husband, Count de Luxbourg:

Paris, January 19, 1823

M. le Comte,

After a week passed in painful anxiety I have been informed, as a result of inquiries following statements I was obliged to make at police headquarters, that Leon — who had organised and carried out his plan of flight with consummate dissimulation — had made for Strasbourg, there to be met and conveyed to Mannheim.

I refrain from all personal reflection on the ingratitude and insensitivity shown by the young man in this escapade, and on the reprehensible behaviour of M. Miel, whose counsel and assistance have once again proved harmful to him.

I address myself to you with confidence, monsieur, for I am persuaded that it was without your knowledge that this scheme was planned and executed.

It is not for me to tell you what you must do. My own task is clear. I know what duties my office of guardian imposes on me. I shall fulfil them completely; for heavy as is the burden that has been laid upon me, I have neither the right nor the power to evade it.

Count de Luxbourg, it appears, did not reply. However, on the day after Meneval had committed his frustrations to paper, Eleonore was writing to him a long and sentimental letter which concluded with a request for 10,000 francs a year for Leon's education! Meneval ignored it.

In the summer Leon went for a trip down the Rhine and recorded his impressions in a slim pocket-book bound in red Morocco leather. He entitled it *Voyage du 1823*.

'The weather was pretty good when we left Mannheim at six o'clock in the morning,' he wrote on Thursday, July 3, 1823. At Worms the private coach stopped at the Black Eagle; and while the horses were being attended to Leon went to visit a relative. The journey by road from Mannheim to Mainz took twelve hours, and it was here that the party with which he was travelling embarked the following day.

On his arrival in Cologne Leon dismissed the city with the observation that it was 'dirty and ill-built'; but after a night's sleep he modified his verdict.

At seven in the morning we visited Cologne cathedral, which is superb and very high. We were shown some rare objects; among others the veritable heads — it is said — of the three kings: Gaspar, Melchior and Balthazar. Their shrine is of silver-gilt, four and a half feet high and three feet wide, encrusted with rows of precious stones, and it stands in the centre of another tomb of marble, closed by an iron door, with a lamp at each corner which is perpetually aflame.

Although it was high summer, Cologne enjoyed its usual heavy downpour of rain; and after crossing the Dutch border Leon found the roads covered in two feet of mud. Worse still — while the coachman was paying the toll the horses wandered off and overturned the coach in a ditch three feet deep. Leon and his companions were obliged to scramble out and right the vehicle in the mud and the rain. 'When we arrived at Cleves at two o'clock in the morning our first thought was to get between the sheets.'

The party wisely decided to continue their journey by diligence as far as Utrecht where they again took ship. Leon found Utrecht 'large, most attractive, very clean together with its inns, and its inhabitants very honest.' At Amsterdam the apartments of the king and queen were 'magnificent and furnished in the style of Versailles.' The clock in the tower played a tune; and from it could be seen the ships arriving from the high seas to the accompaniment of roaring cannon. Leon visited the shipyards where each vessel, sixty feet long, occupied twenty-five workmen four years in its building.

He is continually astonished by the cleanliness and honesty of the Dutch, and devotes eight pages to a description of Broek:

Eleonore, Countess of Luxbourg, by a pupil of David. The portrait was damaged when the ship bringing it back from the United States sank in the port of Havre.

Eleonore, by an unknown artist

This village, at a quarter of a league distant, offers the traveller something for his curiosity, and the nearer he approaches the more he discovers its splendour and its people's good taste. We went into an inn where the cleanliness of the rooms and of the refreshments, and the honesty with which these Dutch folk explained to us what we did not know, astonished us. As soon as we were replete they lent us their daughter to show us the noteworthy features of their village.

On the edge of the water we were astonished to see very pretty Turkish kiosks whose doors of sandalwood inlaid with ivory and ebony were painted with great artistry. All the streets and courtyards were laid out in mosaics made from marble and other remarkable stones of an astounding cleanliness. The fronts of the houses were shaded by rows of trees bordering flower beds and lawns. These trees, were shaped and neatly trimmed after a manner which it is impossible to describe. Sea-shells were used to decorate many of the streets in this village — which carriages are forbidden to enter. The facades and forecourts of the houses are so clean that their owners enter their homes only by the rear courtyards for fear of dirtying or damaging something.

Leon was completely captivated by the ways of the people of the Netherlands:

We observed also the scintillating good taste of the Dutch in their gardens: arranged with an inconceivable order and symmetry, they have in them rivers, bridges and little boats. The church that we saw was very pretty, but quite small and narrow. Its chandeliers are of silver-gilt, and the pews, as also the pulpit, are constructed out of mahogany in a uniform style with the names of their occupants on the back.

According to hearsay this village is the most tiresome, but also the prettiest and the richest of all the villages in the world.

At Rotterdam Leon's party booked passages, surprisingly, on a steamship; and paid for their temerity in adventures which might well have ended fatally, as the hardy Dutch mariners had apparently not yet mastered the new invention: 'On Tuesday, 15 July, 1823, after visiting a sugar refinery — which was large and clean', they went aboard the steamer.

Hardly had we gone three miles when an extraordinary event occurred — it began to ship water and was about to sink below the waves when by a most fortunate chance we found ourselves close to a village where we immediately drew in and disembarked. The ladies did not wish to linger; so the boat was drawn up, the hole repaired, and our voyage resumed. After resting ourselves for two hours we dined aboard; and at eleven o'clock the pilot came to tell us that the weather being sombre it was too dangerous to go on and he intended to drop anchor. After a quarter of an hour the anchor was lowered and we were obliged to sleep on board.

Leon did not find the Dutch sailors as admirable as their landsmen, for on the next day he recorded further misadventures:

Finally at seven o'clock the anchor was raised; but the pilot having discovered that he had lost his way was obliged to steam three miles astern, so that instead of making Antwerp at nine o'clock — as we were informed at Rotterdam — we arrived the following morning at noon for lunch.

During a visit to Brussels Leon drank beer in a café named Rendez-vous de la Promenade des Champs-Elysées; and here again he was kept indoors by the pouring rain.

On his Dutch holiday Leon never got out of bed later than seven o'clock; and on his arrival in Aix-en-Chapelle he says;

Saturday, 19 July, 1823: At five in the morning, after an immersion in mineral water had refreshed our bodies, we visited the baths which are very remarkable. And then — accompanied by the maître d'hôtel who was very friendly, and by the family we met on the boat going from Mainz to Cologne — we visited the gambling casino, went for a stroll and saw the source of the mineral springs. In a large cavity we could see the water which gushed from the earth at boiling-point. Some distance further on we came to the fountains from which hot mineral water continually pours. Afterwards we went to the superb cathedral which contains several objects given to the church by Mary Queen of Scots. We saw too the head and arm of Charlemagne — who was said to be seven feet tall — together with his hunting horn, his crown of solid gold, and his marble throne which was locked away in his tomb for three hundred years and upon which ninety-six emperors were crowned. There was also a tooth of the apostle Peter, a piece of the cross, and the girdles worn by Jesus and Mary.

After this rigorous day Leon was still able to record:

On our return to the hotel we partook of a dinner which

equalled our fatigue, and at five in the evening we boarded a
private carriage in which we passed the night.
But on Sunday, July 20:

Not having been able to sleep a wink in the coach the whole
night and ready to drop from exhaustion, we entered
Cologne at 8 a.m. After resting an hour and breakfasting at
10 a.m. we left in a private carriage for Bonn. Here we
lunched with a former lycée professor who showed us some
very curious things in the anatomical collection.

Leon began the last leg of his journey in typical Rhineland
weather:

20th day — Tuesday, 22 July, 1823 — At five in the morning
we remounted our carriage which brought us to Mainz at
eight. There we had lunch, and — after the storm died down
— changed coaches, arriving at Dienheim for dinner. At
Worms we freshened up, and slept at Mannheim where we
regained our table, our room and our bed.

Leon's style is vivid and his writing copper-plate. Each page of his
journal contains marginal annotations but there are practically no
corrections. The thirty pages of manuscript are a model of clarity
and afford striking evidence of a fine, sharp intellect — even at the
age of sixteen. He concludes his account with a table summarising
his journey under four headings, giving at the side of each day the
place where the trip commenced, where he dined and where he
spent the night. Characteristically, he adds above his signature
'Léon' the warning: 'This work must not be amended'! The last
two pages used out of the sixty in the notebook contain two
intriguing poems, *Sur les vieillard qui fait l'amour*[3] and
Déclaration d'amour de Réné à Sarotte.

Leon's tutor in Paris, the ex-artillery captain Vieillard, had now
become superfluous, and he was sent back to Rome to educate
Leon's fourteen year old cousin — the future Napoleon III — who
had also received a German education, in Augsburg.

A harassed Meneval wound up the bachelor establishment at the
Rue Crebillon and sold the contents of the flat for some 4,000
francs. After the deduction of 333 francs 50 centimes for expenses
a balance of 2311 francs 10 centimes remained. Dissatisfied with
the poor prices offered, Meneval bought-in the furniture from the
salon for 410 francs; but on its re-sale he made a profit of only
two francs. A few of Leon's old clothes brought in a further 18.

Meanwhile the *dramatis personae* of the Empire continued
quietly to make their exits. While Leon was in Germany, Josephine's

son, the gentlemanly Eugène de Beauharnais, died, on February 21, 1824; and on September 16, 1824, Charles X, the former Comte d'Artois, ascended the throne of France with the passing of Louis XVIII.

In Mannheim Leon was ambitious to join the army of the Grand Duke of Baden and with this aim he bombarded his guardian with letters.

Finally Meneval responded:

> Paris, June 16, 1825
>
> I had decided not to reply to your letter until you had made good your fault.
>
> The way in which you took it upon yourself with the help of evil counsels to repay my care and solicitude, and the respect that I owe to myself, have imposed on me an obligation.
>
> I shall not speak of the annoyances and embarrassments of every sort which your imprudence has cost me; in that regard you have wounded only me.
>
> *Mon ami,* today, when you are about to take up a profession, my personal feelings are silenced in the light of your future interests. I have no objections whatsoever to the course you have in mind.
>
> You will find me ready to help you by all the means that my position of guardian puts at my disposal. I await the approaches you mention and particulars of the corps you will enter, as well as the name of the person in authority with whom I must deal.
>
> I heartily desire that in the career you are to follow you will obtain the successes which are achieved only by good conduct and praiseworthy sentiments.

Meneval received the anticipated approach from cavalry major Jean Henri David de Hennenhofer, diplomatic chief and aide-de-camp to Grand Duke Louis of Baden. The squadron-leader, an unamiable character, wished to know a good deal more about Leon before he was prepared to let him loose among the chocolate soldiers of the Grand Duchy.

To Hennenhofer's queries Meneval gave the following reply:

> Paris, July 29, 1825
>
> I received from Karlsruhe the letter of July 11, which you did me the honour of writing. Allow me to thank you personally for the interest and goodwill you have extended to my ward; for whatever displeasure he has caused me, this will

never in any way influence my actions in his regard. Higher considerations and motives arising from a sentiment that you will appreciate will be my compass.

In order to attain the object that I wish to see realised — an aim which you appear equally to desire — you are correct in thinking that Leon's situation must be clarified and the circumstances of his birth and the facts regarding his name and fortune legally established. To determine his personal status there exists only his birth certificate which I have the honour of enclosing.

As for his assets, these consist of (1) 10 non-negotiable shares in the Canal du Midi, and 10 similar shares in the Canal of Orleans and the Loing. The income from these 20 shares, purchased in March, 1812, for the sum of 240,000 francs, and entrusted at the time to his guardian (Baron de Mauvières) was in the region of 12,000 francs a year. Since the peace the income has risen steeply; (2) 13,000 francs at 5 per cent in the Great Book of the National Debt, acquired with the proceeds of savings out of income after the expenses of his education and maintenance had been met. Such, at the time I write, is the state of Leon's finances.

These in sum, are the documents which exist to clear up the points raised in your letter. I do not hesitate to give you them, sir, inspired as I am by confidence in your character and in the part you wish to play in this matter.

I trust they will inform your judgment and enlighten your concern for Leon.

Meneval must have known that this letter was the kiss of death to Leon's military hopes. But it is doubtful whether it worsened his case. At the court of a petty princedom where the *Almanach de Gotha* was prescribed reading, there was little hope of acceptance for the illegitimate son of an obscure girl and an 'absent father'.

Hardly more than a decade earlier Napoleon had forced Charles the hereditary prince of Baden to break-off his engagement to Princess Augusta of Bavaria and marry Josephine's niece — Stephanie de Beauharnais. To complete the square, Princess Augusta was then married off to Prince Eugène de Beauharnais. The hereditary prince of Baden had little choice; defiance of the Emperor would have meant annexation of the Grand Duchy — the fate of Brunswick.

With all this passing through the crafty Hennenhofer's mind there was little prospect of service for Leon in Baden.

If he did not know it before, Leon must now have realised that he was a nameless outcast. His great protector was dead on St. Helena. Henceforward Leon would be an outsider. In default of Hennenhofer's cavalry, Leon threw in his lot with the *Burschenschaft* of Heidelberg.

Academic freedom 'consists in allowing young people to live in debauchery, to attend courses of study at their whim, to get into debt, to dress like fools, and to assault philistines.' So wrote Kotzebue. The year was 1819 and the writer had in mind German university students — particularly the *Burschenschaft*. August Friedrich Ferdinand von Kotzebue, German playwright and paid agent of the Emperor Alexander of Russia, was stabbed to death on March 23, 1819, by Karl Ludwig Sand, a member of the *Burschenschaft*.

It was perhaps inevitable that when Leon came to study in Heidelberg he should, in preference to one of the aristocratic Corps, have joined a society which was strongly anti-French and credited with Napoleon's downfall at Leipzig; a student organisation which in 1817 celebrated the fourth anniversary of that battle, on the Wartburg mountain, by burning French flags, and books.

After Kotzebue's murder the *Burschenschaft* was proscribed; and when Leon joined the re-constituted society its activities were non-political and consisted chiefly of drinking and duelling. Members of the Corps and the *Burschenschaft* were differentiated by their mode of dress. In contemporary illustrations of the crude *Mensur* the duels are invariably between students belonging to the two groups. Judging by his flawless features Leon had never taken part in one of these hacking contests; accomplished swordsman as he was he probably found them lacking in finesse.

For the remainder of the summer of 1825 Leon remained in Heidelberg living comfortably on his 6,000 francs a year; while his cousin 'Bo-Bo' — the Camberwell-born son of Jerome Bonaparte and Elizabeth Patterson of Baltimore — had managed to get through 2,500 dollars in fifteen months at Harvard. Early in 1826 Leon's mother left Mannheim for the Unter den Linden where her husband had on February 1st been accepted as Minister to the Court of Prussia. The German writer K. A. Varnhagen von Ense records: '25 March, 1826 — The new Bavarian ambassador the Count de Luxbourg arrived here: he has had an audience of the King.'

Leon, too, was reaching the end of his Baden chapter and on March 27, 1826, Meneval wrote a letter of introduction for him, addressed to Napoleon's mother — 'Madame Mère' — who was living in Rome.

Madame,

I beg your Imperial Highness to welcome with kindness the bearer of this letter. He is the young Leon in whom the Emperor took a fatherly interest, and the wardship of whom he confided first to my father-in-law, and latterly to myself. He has completed his studies at the University of Heidelberg and at the moment is living in Germany.

As he is now already in his twentieth year he has been granted his independence and I have every reason to hope he will show himself worthy of his freedom by wise and sober conduct.

My duty as guardian and my trust in your Imperial Highness's kindness lead me to the fervent wish that he should make your acquaintance, and I am fulfilling the desire of his father in placing this young man under the exalted protection of your Imperial Highness and of your august family, in which I venture to beseech you to be his introduction and his support.

I deeply regret that I am unable personally to present my ward to your Imperial Highness and to render to you the homage of my feelings of reverence and boundless affection, with which I shall never cease to be, Madame, of your Imperial Highness the very humble and very obedient servant.

The letter to Letizia must have appeared to Meneval his final act as Leon's guardian. Only the previous day he had rendered an account of his four years' stewardship, consequent upon Leon's emancipation by a family council of February 2, 1826. In the chambers of the Paris notaries Outrebon and Grivel, on February 26, Meneval presented his final accounts. Against an income of 142,952 francs 75., Leon had received 137,478 francs 44. Meneval immediately paid over the balance of 4,474 francs 3 centimes; and Leon's affairs were put into the hands of a receiver — Alexandre Henry Fournel, senior, a valuer of 18, Rue des Fossés-Saint-Germain-l'Auxerrois.

Leon returned to Paris and took an apartment on the Rue de la Paix — the first street in the capital to be lit by the new hydrogen jets of the Compagnie du Gaz Portatif.

A frequent visitor to Paris during the Restoration was the

controversial Irish writer Lady Morgan. In 1829 she wrote:

> The peace of Europe would not be disturbed more than it at
> present is, by the personal appearance of Napoleon
> Bonaparte's eldest son, who is seen in every street and
> assembly of Paris, without one glance of conspiracy being
> turned on him, save those from the bright eyes of ultra
> duchesses, of which he is the cynosure. 'They monopolise
> him, as they monopolised his father,' said a gentleman to me,
> as we sat in a public assembly at the Institute, admiring the
> fine intelligent countenance of this interesting young man,
> who was hitched between two beauties of the Château — the
> victim, and not the agent, of a conspiracy which he was
> doubtless alike unable and unwilling to resist.

It has been suggested that this passage refers to the eighteen year
old Alexandre Walewski. But Sidney Morgan knew her Bonapartes.
Moreover, Lady Granville had sometime previously described
Walewski as 'dull, civil . . . a tall pale, inanimate boy . . .' a
description which could hardly be applied to Leon!

In Rome Leon's twenty-one year old cousin, Louis Napoleon,
was diverting local society in a different manner: Lord Malmesbury was describing the son of ex-King Louis of Holland as a 'wild
harum scarum youth, riding at full gallop down the streets to the
peril of the public, fencing and pistol shooting, and apparently
without serious thoughts of any kind,' the same Bonaparte who as
a child had been nicknamed 'Oui Oui' because of his compliant
disposition.

In the spring of 1831, Leon and his Bonaparte cousins con-
verged on London. Their arch-enemy — the last of Thackeray's
Four Georges — had died at Windsor on June 26, 1830, and was
succeeded by his brother, the Duke of Clarence.[4]

After a foul Channel-crossing in a travelling-carriage lashed to
the bridge of the *Royal George,* Hortense and Louis Napoleon
arrived at Fenton's Hotel, 63 St. James's Street. Josephine's
daughter reserved rooms on three floors and complained: 'The
rooms that we finally discovered were only passable — and for
them we had to pay four louis (about £4) a day when we had been
so comfortable in Paris for 30 francs.' Between May 10, and
August 7, 1831, Hortense and her son enriched the London
merchants to the tune of 20,000 francs; and while she may have
found Paris 'so comfortable' Hortense was not yet *persona grata* to
Louis Philippe, who had accepted the French throne after the July
Revolution of 1830.

On May 13, 1831 the Duchess of Glengall, who had met Hortense at Plombières in 1802 called at Fenton's with the news that Alexandre Walewski and Leon were in town; and a few days later she sent round an invitation to a family party with Leon. Hortense declined this opportunity of a Bonaparte re-union.

Leon returned to Paris. Lacking even the restraint of Maneval's slack rein he gambled away the francs that he did not lavishly bestow on Eleonore and her family; and his gaming brought him eventually into armed conflict with a man who had assisted at the eclipse of his father on the battlefield of Waterloo.

CHAPTER 4

Wellington's A.D.C.

Charles Hesse was the son of a Berlin banker ruined by Napoleon's Prussian campaigns, although it was rumoured that he was the natural son of the Duke of York. He had been brought up by Elizabeth, Margravine of Ansbach — the former Lady Craven — who lived at Brandenburg House in Hammersmith. Under the protection of the Duchess of York, Princess Frederica, he joined the 18th Hussars.

Caroline of Brunswick, the wife of the Prince Regent, encouraged a hot flirtation between Hesse and her daughter Princess Charlotte Augusta — the heir to the throne. In all probability she instigated the romance; certainly she acted as a post-box, and arranged for the young hussar to enter her private apartments through a gate in Kensington Gardens. The Princess of Wales went so far as to lock the two lovers in her own bedroom — *telling them to amuse themselves*! The attempt to encompass her daughter's seduction failed and Charlotte emerged with her honour intact. But Hesse was posted abroad, being severely wounded at Waterloo where he almost lost an arm.

As Princess Caroline's equerry he formed part of her travelling ménage. Even before Waterloo Caroline had fallen heavily for Murat's charms; and Charles Hesse in his turn joined the line of Caroline Murat's lovers. In the subsequent scandal he was hustled from the Kingdom of Naples under armed escort. Princess Caroline returned to England on the accession of her husband as George IV.

It was in Italy that Hesse met the Baron de Rosenberg. In the spring of 1831 the baron came to Paris — possibly because he had killed one Romanovich in a duel and judged it politic to move on. He opened a lavish establishment on the first floor of the hôtel Montmorency on the Boulevard Montmartre. This was no more than a crooked gambling club, where Captain Hesse seems to have been de Rosenberg's partner.

The baron kept a large stable and lived in great style at the hôtel Montmorency, where he installed a celebrated opera singer as his mistress. Outside the apartment a she-bear delighted the passers-by as it padded back and forth on the balcony. It was de Rosenberg's practice to separate young bloods from their inheritance, and to facilitate this he served them a vicious drink called 'cardinal', a mulled wine of which the ascertainable ingredients were a pineapple and several mixed vintages.

One of the baron's victims was the young D'Alton Shee de Lignères, later politician and writer and a founder of the French Jockey Club. In his memoirs the count describes how he began feeling odd after two or three glasses of the baron's infusion. Invited to guess the number of hazel nuts in a dessert bowl at five louis (25 francs) a go, he accepted the bet 'out of politeness'. Under the influence of the cardinal he lost 36,000 francs — and paid up. It was thus that he met Leon at the hôtel Montmorency.

Leon was four years older than Edouard D'Alton Shee — and far less docile. In the company of Felix, Marquis de Lavalette, he had lost 16,000 francs to Hesse, for which he gave the captain an I.O.U. After a sharp exchange of words a duel was proposed. (Years later Leon's son Gaston claimed that Hesse had spoken disparagingly of Eleonore.)

Count d'Esterno and a German officer acted as Hesse's seconds, and Leon was accompanied by Colonel Fournier and an officer named May. In the hope of avoiding a fatal result Colonel Fournier had drafted a set of rules. Each man would use his own arms; but they were to be checked by the seconds to make sure that there was no discrepancy between them. Two distant limits each ten paces apart were marked out. Leon and Hesse would walk ten paces from these points and stop at a distance of thirty paces one from the other. Having reached this spot each would then be free to advance as far as his limit and fire as soon as he wished.[1]

Leon faced Hesse in the shadow of the great fortress of Vincennes, where Henry V of Agincourt had died; and where the Duc d'Enghien was murdered. Was the quarrel merely over a gaming debt of 16,000 francs — or was it partly the spirit of a Corsican vendetta: the son of Napoleon against the Prussian who had served as aide-de-camp to his father's conqueror? Perhaps Leon — twenty four years old and with little prospect of glory in battle — felt he must face death to prove himself the son of the Emperor. He gave Captain Hesse choice of weapons.

Charles Hesse who had survived the Peninsular War and the campaign of 1815 was to lose his life over a game of écarté — which only two could play and in which there were no aces. In the woods of Vincennes a large party had gathered on that early spring day of 1832. Gaspard Gourgaud was there, who as a young general had gone into exile with Napoleon on St. Helena. Leon was carrying that day for the first time a talisman. In Rome the year before, his aunt, ex-Queen Hortense, had given to him a button telling him to wear it in time of danger.

The young Leon and the middle-aged hussar faced each other at thirty paces. Hesse shot first — and missed. It was a habit of English gentlemen to fire wide; but if Leon knew about the custom he had no intention of deloping. He had been cheated in Paris and Hesse would pay at Vincennes. Leon stepped forward five paces and fired. Captain Hesse received the shot full in the chest and fell to the ground.

Dominique Larrey, the Emperor's humane surgeon-in-chief, who had amputated 200 limbs at Borodino, using snow as an analgesic, and been wounded and made prisoner at Waterloo, now performed a last duty. He had drummed up the medical services of the 11th Regiment of Artillery in garrison at Vincennes. Their ministrations were in vain: Hesse's wounds were so grave that he could not be transported to Paris, and he died a few days later.

The debt was not wiped out by Hesse's blood; for Leon was obliged to sign a bill at twelve months in de Rosenberg's favour. After an inquiry by the prosecutor's office, Leon was summoned before the Assize Court on a charge of manslaughter — and acquitted. De Rosenberg continued to be troublesome and the young Leon complained to the police; whereupon the baron, who had decided that the climate of Paris had now become as warm as that of Florence, departed with the cardinal for fresher fields.

Leon, also, judged it politic to absent himself awhile from his beloved boulevards. After the death of the Duke of Reichstadt, he says, 'I went to Rome to make my condolences to Madame Mère, and while I was in the isolation hospital at Civitta Vecchia I received a letter from the Cardinal.'

Choosing his words with care, Cardinal Fesch wrote to Leon:
I hope that you will soon be allowed to leave the quarantine station at Civitta Vecchia, and I want you to know that it will give me as much pleasure to see you as it gave me on your last trip to Rome . . .
In a letter dated August 28, 1832, Leon promised his uncle that he would never again lose 45,000 francs in gambling; and expressed his sorrow at the death of *l'Aiglon*, 'to whom was transmitted the glorious name of the Emperor Napoleon, my father.' In the same letter Leon begged the cardinal's influence to effect his discharge

from the quarantine clinic, where he was being detained as a cholera suspect. During the summer the disease had carried off 18,000 Parisians in a single month.

Moved by the death of 'Napoleon II' in Vienna on July 23 — in the room in which Napoleon had dictated peace terms to the defeated Austrians — Leon's uncles Joseph (now head of the family) and Lucien were at work in Joseph's sumptuous new home at 23 Park Crescent near Regent's Park, drafting a constitution to return them to power. Joseph was not the first Bonaparte to take up residence in England, for after his capture in 1807 Lucien lived at Ludlow in Shropshire and afterwards spent several tranquil years as a country squire on the banks of the Severn at Grimley in Worcestershire, where he had paid 20,000 guineas for the 18th century stone mansion of Thorngrove.

In 1834 Leon left the house at 370 Rue Saint-Honoré, which he had occupied since 1832, and moved to 64 Rue de Paris in St. Denis, the better to launch out on his new attempt at a military career. Since the advent of Louis Philippe, 'the citizen king' for whom Leon was good propaganda, he habitually referred to himself as 'the natural son of the Emperor Napoleon' and with his father's illustrious example before him he joined the National Guard with the rank of major.

On April 20, 1834, he took the oath of fidelity before the Mayor of St. Denis, M. Boyé. The Colonel of the regiment was M. Benoist, with whom Leon was soon at cross-purposes — Colonel Benoist had had the temerity to invite Leon rather forcefully to shut up while the two were at dinner. On June 4, Leon wrote to the mayor requesting authority to take command of a detachment of 41 men for service at the royal palace of Neuilly. Mayor Boyé granted Leon's request without referring to Colonel Benoist, who quickly reacted pointing out that a regulation of October 4, 1832, required the mayor to correspond with him and not with Major Leon.

The bureaucratic snowball was gathering momentum nicely. At once Mayor Boyé replied that never having received the said. Ministerial decision he was not obliged to abide by it; and he referred the question to M. Mazères, the Deputy Prefect of St. Denis. This official found the regulation after a three-day search through the back numbers of the *Journal des Gardes Nationales* and told the mayor to comply.

After less than six weeks in uniform Leon had managed to set at loggerheads the Town Hall, the Prefecture and the National Guard.

The major engagement, however, commenced on June 23 when Colonel Benoist wrote to the mayor suggesting some changes in the regulations for guard duties. M. Boyé replied two days later that he could see no useful purpose in these modifications — and sent the letter to the deputy prefect.

The very next day Colonel Benoist told the mayor he had no right to show the letter to the deputy prefect, and added, 'Furthermore, I must inform you that in matters affecting duties I have ordered the major to correspond only with me, as his immediate superior, and I have told him that he is not to recognise any commands other than those emanating from myself, in accordance with Article 87 of the law of March 22, 1831.'

Mayor Boyé's response was to pass all the correspondence to the deputy prefect — who told Colonel Benoist for the future to keep the Town Hall in the picture. But on July 8, Leon, with a fine Imperial panache, advised the mayor to ignore any duty regulation which had not been submitted by him, in accordance with the terms of Article 78 of the law of 1831. Mayor Boyé welcomed this Bonaparte initiative 'written in the true spirit of the law' — and passed it on to the deputy prefect, at the same time observing sadly that it would only complicate the feud with the colonel.

Letters continued to pass between St. Denis and the prefecture, until July 16, when Leon told the deputy prefect that only he had the right to propose a regulation. M. Mazères and Colonel Benoist dubbed this letter 'unseemly' and decided to discipline Leon.

On July 26 Leon was relieved of his duties, and immediately he became a folk hero to the citizens of St. Denis. The bistros resounded with cries of 'Long live the count! Down with Benoist!' Children took up the chant, and the slogans echoed and fireworks were set off in the Place des Armes until well into the night.

Benoist distributed a leaflet on August 19 in which he made a violent attack on the mayor. And, as Leon records, 'M. Boyé, outraged by this libel and incensed by its misrepresentation of the facts, published a refutation which shamed M. le Colonel Benoist.'

Leon was out of St. Denis by July 29, and took the opportunity to visit his uncle Joseph in England. It was, therefore, with some astonishment that Meneval received a letter from his old master the ex-king:

    Denham, near Uxbridge, September 13, 1834. I have had
the pleasure of making the acquaintance of Count Leon.[2] He

found Lucien here whom he had seen at Madame Mère's house in Rome. I know he was particularly recommended to you by the Emperor and it was to you he confided his wardship; I was also surprised that you had not introduced him to me yourself by letter.

You know that my confidence in you, and my friendship are of longer standing even than those accorded you by the Emperor and of which he gave such eloquent witness when he confided to you the interests of a child whom he left too soon to make sure of his destiny in a more solid manner. I should like you to tell me all you know about this affair.

He has been with me two days; he resembles the features of the Emperor. He appears to me to be full of soul, of warmth, and envious to render himself worthy of the kindness shown to him by his fellow citizens. He wishes also to devote his time to persuading the Chambers to repeal the law of exile which burdens the Emperor's family.[3]

He possesses a natural eloquence and appeared to me as having the love of study which is evidenced by the informed nature of his conversation.

If he so desires it would be useful for you to introduce him to the handful of friends that events have left to me. You know that their number is not large — at least of those who have the courage to declare themselves.

Avail him constantly of your advice; I have counselled him to follow it as that of a friend for whom I cherish the most sincere feelings of esteem and tender friendship.

Do not doubt it: my thoughts are as unchanging as your own.

Yours affectionately,
Joseph, Count de Survilliers.

While engaged in his dispute with Colonel Benoist, Leon had taken on another opponent. Like Louis Napoleon, Leon was a brilliant horseman, and if in nothing else his estimate of a good horse may be accepted. His father, on the contrary, was no equestrian and what he looked for was a docile mount: Napoleon on one occasion fell off his horse three times in a single afternoon.

The first record of Leon's recourse to the Restoration pastime of litigation appeared in a Paris newspaper that was to log his passage through the *salle des pas perdus* during half a century.

On June 15, 1834, the *Gazette des Tribunaux* reported a suit against one Letulle junior, a horse dealer, from whom Leon had bought two bay horses for 6,000 francs. He had paid 2,500 francs in cash and had given in part-exchange a splendid animal which no longer suited him. When Leon had an opportunity of inspecting at leisure the two bays supplied to him by Letulle, he found that they were not the ones he had bought. Accordingly he returned the horses and claimed a refund of the purchase price. Letulle refused to disgorge and retained Leon's money and all three horses.

The Tribunal de Commerce ordered the appearance of both parties for June 24, the day after Colonel Benoist's famous letter to the Mayor of St. Denis. Leon did not appear at the hearing and a verdict in default was entered against 'the young count' — as the *Gazette* described the twenty-seven year old major.

Appealing against the decision on July 9, Leon spoke in person and was listened to 'with a lively interest' — no doubt engendered by the current events at St. Denis. The unfortunate Letulle, however, was received with scorn, and 'more than once incredulous smiles greeted his speech', as he affirmed that Leon had returned the two bay horses to be sold. At the postponed hearing on July 22, the court annulled the contract and ordered Letulle to refund to Leon the sum of 1,700 francs in cash and return the horse given in part exchange, or its value, fixed at 3,500 francs.

On September 29 Leon resumed his duties at St. Denis; and without any delay he published an order protesting against his 'illegal and unjust' suspension and cancelling the duty regulations promulgated during his absence by the colonel.

Benoist reacted swiftly and on October 11, 1834, Leon was again suspended for two months. A royal decree, of October 28, dismissed him finally from the service. No doubt Louis Philippe hoped thus to end Leon's tapping of the Orleans purse, as alleged by Philibert Audebrand, for the officers of the National Guard were regularly entertained to dinner by their commander-in-chief, the king. Leon had hoped that his sensational order of the day would result in his being tried before the Court of Assize. But — so he maintained — the French Government recoiled before the enormity of hauling before a criminal court 'a man bound by the closest ties to the family of Napoleon' and preferred to condemn him behind the closed doors of the Prefecture of the Seine!

Despite Leon's three-cornered fight with the authorities of St. Denis and the suit against Letulle, he demonstrated that — like his father — he could handle three matters at once by acting as election agent for General Gourgaud *at St. Denis*. Leon had moved back into Paris and was now living at 15 Rue Taitbout near the Boulevards.

In terms of great affection Gourgaud wrote:

Have the kindness, my dear Leon, to give me some news of our election.

With your powerful intervention I have excellent prospects . . . Remember that in working for me you are also working for yourself, for I should be quite happy to quit the Chamber to make room for you.

It sufficed but two years for the battle of St. Denis to recede into limbo, for in 1836 Leon again appeared in the town's National Guard, this time as a lieutenant in the 2nd Company of Chasseurs, a regimental title which immediately recalls the portraits of the Emperor in his favourite costume — the green and red undress uniform of the hussars.

At this time Leon was frequently to be seen in the company of his mother and her husband, Count de Luxbourg; and on July 22, 1836, he applied to the Intendant General de la Liste Civile for seats at the opening ceremony of the Arc de Triomphe, the building of which had begun as long ago as May 1806. Leon wrote: 'The inauguration of the Arc de Triomphe brings back to me such dear memories that I am impelled to ask you for seats for my mother and her friends in the private stands.'

For the nonce everything in Paris was sweetness and light; (at the British Embassy Church, on August 20, a Miss Parry was married to William Makepeace Thackeray). But elsewhere two other Bonapartes were keeping the family reputation alive. In Canino, where Lucien Bonaparte's Italian estates were situated, his son the twenty-one year old Prince Bonaparte, trapped by twenty-eight foresters, killed the head keeper with a hunting knife and wounded two others; while Prince Louis Napoleon was writing to his mother, Hortense, telling her he was going hunting. With the help of an opera-singer named Eleonore to attract a wavering lieutenant to his cause, Louis re-entered France by the route which Leon had taken in reverse twenty-three years earlier. His attempt to rally the Strasbourg garrison failed, however, and he was captured and tried in Paris. In spite of a stroke of Napoleonic luck (at a crucial moment fog blotted out semaphore communication with Paris) 'Oui, Oui' bungled the plan.

The future Napoleon III was given 14,000 francs and put on a ship bound for the United States. Louis Philippe had confiscated 200,00 francs found on his rival at Strasbourg, and thus made a profit of 186,000 francs on the deal. Fourteen years later Napoleon III was to remember the incident when he sequestrated the Orleanist lands. On his arrival in New York, Prince Louis put up at the Washington Hotel on Broadway and announced his intention of becoming an American farmer.

By the summer of 1837 Leon's extravagance was beginning to take effect and he began selling off some of his possessions. Accordingly he handed over a picture valued at 6,000 francs to one Dubois, a dealer, for him to sell. Leon received half the value of the picture in the form of a bill of exchange. The bill turned out to be worthless and when he tried to recover his painting he found out that it had disappeared — together with Dubois.

Leon had spent the proceeds of the bill of exchange at a jeweller's called Fade, who claimed the value of the dishonoured instrument at a court hearing on June 2. Leon in turn counter-claimed on a gold enamel seal ring and two diamond studs, which — he affirmed — had been overcharged by weight on the invoice.

Leon was now thirty and his fading youth no longer charmed the royal courts. It was another dishonoured bill of exchange that resulted in his becoming the involuntary guest of a M. Charrier an alleged creditor. While Joseph Bonaparte was enjoying the English countryside at Brettenham Park in Suffolk, and Las Cases was petitioning an indifferent Chamber of Deputies for a pension for the dying Caroline Murat, Leon was living on 45 francs a day in the debtors' prison overlooking the Parisians' pleasure gardens of Tivoli.

CHAPTER 5

Unquiet Days in Clichy

The *cor de chasse* is something like a valveless French horn — and twice as big. It will fit comfortably over a man's head and shoulders; and the volume of sound which it produces is fully commensurate with its size. During his detention in the debtors' prison at Clichy Leon received permission to play this huge brass hunting horn — an instrument which was later banned from the streets of Paris by the Prefect of Police.

The prison for debt was situated at 70 Rue de Clichy and contained 200 cells for men, but only 18 for women. The size of each cell was approximately 12 feet by 10 feet; nevertheless Clichy was held palatial compared with the old Revolutionary jail of St. Pélagie which it supplanted. To make life more comfortable, a prisoner could hire mattresses, pillows, blankets, etc., and the cost of an iron bed was one centime a day. For pastimes there were open-air bowls and skittles, and inside the prison quoits, chess, draughts and other games.

Some time after Leon's tenure the prisoners formed a society and elected a committee. For a subscription of 10 centimes (1d) a day they were privileged to use an oven, take baths at reduced rates; and by purchasing food in bulk they were able to eat for 5d a day. They even managed to build up surplus funds with which to help the poorer debtors. Much interest was taken in the inmates of Clichy by charitable organisations, and de Villemessant, the editor of *Le Figaro*, stocked a reading room with magazines, newspapers and books, for the use of which the prisoners paid a subscription of a sou (½d).

To commit his client to jail the creditor obtained a court order, the arrest of the debtor being carried out by a *garde du commerce* of which Paris had seven. This special bailiff conveyed the bankrupt by cab to Clichy and paid out 45 francs for his first month's board. As long as the creditor paid for his maintenance the unfortunate prisoner remained out of circulation until he had settled his debt. This self-defeating practice persisted until 1860, when arrest for civil and commercial causes was abolished and

Clichy was emptied. A debtor could not be taken on a Sunday or
between sunset and sunrise. Therefore at dawn there was a great
exodus to the Paris suburb of Batignolles which lay outside the
city boundary to the north-west, and a trek in the return direction
at nightfall.

Leon either refused to join this undignified rout or believed the
bailiffs' men would never lay hands on the son of the Emperor; for
he remained in his old haunts near the Grand Boulevards.

His first trip to Clichy, in 1837, seems to have been an error. A
person named Charrier had him attached because of a dishonoured
bill which had come into his hands. Leon and he had never met,
and Charrier had no personal interest in the transaction. The court
freed Leon on March 30, 1838; but he was soon back inside at the
instance of one Louis Delpech who had advanced him several sums
of money to a total of 40,000 francs.

Leon's relationship with Delpech had commenced — as always
— on a very cosy plane, as a letter to the moneylender shows:

I am much distressed, my good Delpech, to see no improvement in your health. For the love of God take the advice I
gave you: follow a course of treatment — and do it regularly.

You are still in the prime of life; and with precautions —
which you are not taking — we shall have you with us a long
time yet. Just think, my friend, how indispensable you have
become to me. When I do not see you I am no longer gay; I
feel an emptiness in my soul. I have grown used to your
frank, loyal, brusque, but so generous and devoted character
that I am in the happy process of making plans for the future
totally different from those I have for many a long day
entertained.

My good friend, come soon. Do not deprive me longer of
the pleasure of seeing you, of showing all my gratitude; and
of thanking you from the bottom of my heart for all you
have done for me. One day, my good Delpech, I shall be able
to pay my debt to you: that is my most sincere wish.

You are like a father to me; I love you as I love my own.
He watches you from on high, my friend. You love his son,
you render him important services; you must find a great joy
in your heart.

Farewell, my good Delpech, my friendship and all my
gratitude. Leon.

According to Delpech Leon had also seen the inside of the prison
of St. Pélagie which overlooked the *Jardin des Plantes* at 18 Rue

de la Clef. The Empress Josephine, when Josephine de Beau-
harnais, and Mme. du Barry were imprisoned during the
Revolution in this former convent, which the cynical prosecutor —
Fouquier-Tinville — called 'the ante-chamber to the guillotine'.
The author of *La Marseillaise*, Rouget de Lisle, spent some time in
the debtors' wing.

Delpech gives an extravagant account of Leon's exploits while
he was detained in the grim 17th century building from which the
tumbrils had rolled. The moneylender's recital exceeds the inven-
tiveness of even Leon's fertile imagination; and the accuracy of
Delpech's allegations may be gauged from the fact that in his
original manuscript he continually refers to Eleonore as Leon's
niece.

He [Leon] was born of the marriage of Mlle. Eleonore
Laplaigne, wife of Revel, infantry captain, who was given a
heavy jail sentence. The Emperor had granted him stock
worth more than 40,000 francs in the canals and other
securities, and 22,000 francs at 5 per cent on the National
Debt, of which his mother took a life interest and of which
he would take the capital on her death. M. de Meneval — who
will no longer see or receive him — was his guardian.

For a long time he has existed by false pretences and lives
on the first floor of 39, Rue Neuve St. Augustin. His
furniture having been attached, he was gallant enough to
suggest to Mme. Buelle, the wife of a magistrate from
Corbeil, who lived on the mezzanine floor that they should
exchange apartments; and they transferred their furniture
accordingly. When the bailiffs came to carry out the seizure
on the first floor they found instead Mme. Buelle's furniture
there. The other pieces had vanished most timely to the
mezzanine, together with a fine lamp belonging to Mme.
Buelle and a few other little things. In his gallantry the noble
count also attempted to make off with a watch and some
diamonds belonging to Mme. Buelle, but she shouted for
help.

The noble count urged his mother to poison her husband,
the Count de Luxbourg; and threatened to murder her unless
she gave him money. She placed herself under the protection
of the Prefect of Police, who charged Inspector Wolff with
her safety. He reported his mother and Count de Luxbourg
to the police, accusing her of bigamy and trigamy. At St.
Pélagie he was reputedly the worst character in the prison,

swindling caterers, stealing the governor's watch, and
generally creating uproar and scandal. They put him in a cell.
He also accused the governor of sleeping with his mother —
whom he had never set eyes on.

I do not have a complete list of this bandit Revel's[1] debts
to hand. They amount to a total of over 100,000 francs in
which I figure for some 47,000.

The most important creditors are

M. de Roycourt, upholsterer, of the Rue de Miromesnil,	about	12,000 francs
Touchard, coachbuilder, of the Champs Elysées		5,000
Captain Toufay		4,000
Guichard		5,000
A host of debts large and small, including one to a jew of the Rue de Port Mahon		18,000
Mme. Maille, Montreuil, for board and lodging		6,000
The husband of the chambermaid		500
Mme. Pierson for board and lodging		4,000
The state pawnshop at Rue Bourbon Villeneuve, by false pretences		1,200

A swarm of tailors, shoemakers, restaurateurs, lawyers and
court officials, to whom he has promised the earth but has
given not a sou; a vintner from whom he recently purchased
12,000 francs worth of wine, which he immediately disposed
of for 4,000 francs; several clockmakers, jewellers, etc.

Leon's response was to haul Delpech before the criminal court on
a charge of usury, false pretences, and breach of confidence. The
case was dismissed at a hearing of December 31, 1839. He then
brought a civil action demanding damages of 100,000 francs,
alleging that Delpech had forged his signature.

Leon first fell into the hands of the moneylender when he
borrowed 25,000 francs from Delpech to meet legal expenses
incurred by his mother, in a suit at Château Thierry in which the
heirs of Murat's lawyer and business agent, Henry, were claiming
Eleonore's dowry. In Leon's absence, Delpech not only removed
furniture, linen, pictures and family papers, but to add insult to
injury had him committed to St. Pélagie. To get out of prison

Leon gave Delpech a note for 40,000 francs on his assets in Mannheim; but Delpech did not release him, alleging that Leon's property in Baden was mortgaged up to the hilt. It was because of this breach of trust that Leon brought the action for 100,000 francs damages; but his claim failed.

Delpech's account of Leon's expenditure approximates closely with the 94,000 francs of the 'dandy's budget', which the periodical *L'Entr'Acte* printed on January 10, 1839 — an ironic echo of the palmy days when the sixteen year old Leon shared a flat in the Latin Quarter with his spendthrift tutor, the ex-Imperial artillery captain, Veillard:

Rent of a suitable house in the
vicinity of the Rue de Rivoli   14,000 francs
In his stable three bays, and a
cheval de coupé for the
evenings; including harness, hay,
straw and oats   20,000
Tailor: black suits, coloured suits,
jackets, hacking and hunting
habits, overcoats   5,000
Shoemaker: walking shoes,
travelling shoes, polished and
unpolished, fancy shoes; and
polishing same   5,000
Hatmaker: grey hats, black hats,
long pointed, and fancy hats;
according to season, caps, berets   3,000
Linen; because a good supply of
linen articles is indispensable to
fashion. It is the item which
attracts the closest inspection.
Love and the Church need fine white
cloths on their several altars   4,000
Gloves   1,500
Perfumery: essences, oils, creams,
pomades   800
Jewellery: watches, chains, cameos,
rings, cigar-cutters, toothpicks,
shirt buttons   18,000
Canes, batons, cravaches, whips, and
other tree- trunks; plus the cost of
depositing them in theatres, museums,

concert-halls, etc.	1,000
Servants: a little tiger for drives in town	2,000
A herculean old soldier: lackey and coachman in one	3,000
A valet who knows how to shave, curl and dress the hair	3,000
Food	4,000
The thousand and one trifles indispensable to Parisian life; pince-nez, telescopes	200
Theatre	3,000
Bouquets	1,200
Gambling: wagers and losses at table; gifts and tips	6,000
Stationery, for notes, love letters, challenges, etc.	500
A total of, say	94,500 francs

As nothing is allowed for doctor or dentist it is presumed the dandy was as sound as his purse. Certainly Leon seems to have had the constitution of an ox.

While Leon was occupying his seven and a half square metres of cell with its iron bed, two straw chairs, and little white wood table, another dandy was being lionised in London. Louis Napoleon's personal expenses were estimated at a modest 90,000 francs a year, of which the rent of his house at 17 Carlton House Terrace accounted for only 625 francs. Montholon, however, believed the prince's total budget to be in the region of 600,000 francs — largely underwritten by Baring Brothers.

During his last year in Clichy Leon petitioned the sixty year old Meneval, and in return received from his former guardian the usual platitudes:

Paris, January 8, 1839

I was absent when your letter arrived and found it on my return from the country. The sight of the letter and its contents brought back the pain I experienced when I learned of your sad plight; and the prospect of my own inability to offer a remedy. It is one of my poignant griefs.

I had no need of the recommendations left by the Emperor to his testamentary executors — and of course to myself — to protect you. But what protection can I offer? The cult of old memories may perhaps be honourable in these times; but it is nothing but fine talk, and more of a hindrance than a help. In what way therefore am I able to serve you?

Have you not approached your mother? . . .

Towards the end of his stay in Clichy, Leon maintained, the Emperor's family entertained the hope that he might be received into Holy Church. Rome at this time was teeming with Bonapartes, and indeed Lucien was a member of the Black Nobility, having been created Prince de Canino by Pius VII in 1814.

'During my detention,' says Leon in his *Reply to the Editor of the Capitole*,

the Archbishop of Paris, Monsignor de Quelen [the former secretary and friend of Cardinal Fesch], conceived the idea of effecting my entry into the priesthood, and, without my knowledge, wrote to His Holiness, and to His Eminence Cardinal Fesch, my great-uncle. In view of the favourable letters he had received from the monsignor, the Holy Father did me the kindness to speak to the cardinal on my behalf, and found the latter so well-disposed in my favour that His Holiness encouraged him to persevere in his attentions towards me.

In fact, while Leon was in Clichy the main preoccupation of Hyacinthe Louis, Count de Quelen, Member of the Academy and Archbishop of Paris, was the conversion of that prince of trimmers — Talleyrand. To accomplish the return to the fold of the erring abbot had been Quelen's ambition for twenty years; and on May 17, 1838, shortly before his death, Charles Maurice de Talleyrand-Perigord, ex-Bishop of Autun, and sometime Ambassador to the Court of St. James, signed his Retraction which was immediately rushed to the Pope. A beatific Quelen died on December 31, 1839, without having seen Leon swing a thurible.

Years later Leon recalled this non-starter in a letter of May 1858 to another archbishop of Paris, Cardinal Morlot, Grand Chaplain to the Emperor Napoleon III.

At St. Helena, on April 22, 1821 — a fortnight before his death — Napoleon had said: 'The family will probably have popes'. But apart from Madame Mère's half-brother Fesch, the only other member of the family to assume the *capa magna* was Lucien's grandson, Cardinal Lucien Louis Bonaparte, who was born in Rome on November 11, 1828.

Archbishop Quelen had taken a benevolent interest in prisoners generally; but to Leon the slightest nod in his direction was enough to encourage in him the highest flights of fancy. He said, 'The cardinal adopted the opinions of the archbishop, and to encourage my realisation of them, showed himself disposed to help me attain high ecclesiastical office, and even to make testamentary dispositions to my advantage.

'His Eminence,' added Leon, 'always held me in high affection.'

Cardinal Fesch demonstrated his affection in a singular fashion: he left a will making Joseph Bonaparte his universal legatee. This was probably not so much an act of cynicism as a reversion to the ancient Roman institution of *paterfamilias* by leaving everything to the eldest surviving male.

On July 31, 1839, the *Quotidienne* published the following: No one has been forgotten in this will, unless it be Prince Jerome and his children.

Each bequest is accompanied by a particular clause: to wit, that any beneficiary demanding his legacy shall forfeit the same; for the reason that the entire will would be a mockery if the generous dispositions of Joseph were not to be relied upon.

Doubtless Leon's creditors had read this sanctimonious observation with interest; and it may explain why they released him from the debtors' prison on October 23, 1839 without — as he says — receiving the least satisfaction; *for Joseph Bonaparte* — now the source of Leon's great expectations — *was in London.*

When he went to see his grandmother on his discharge from jail, Leon caught up with the family news. Visitors were freely admitted into Clichy; but if his mother's relations had left him to languish in prison Leon does not criticise those whom he had helped so unstintingly in the days of his affluence. And although he is usually punctilious in giving details of locations, he carefully preserves the anonymity of their dwelling-place.

At my first visit to widow Delaplaigne, my aunt Mlle. Zulma Delaplaigne — a pious soul — told me what the Archbishop of Paris had done for me during my detention, and her opinion that the cardinal had made dispositions in my favour which had been entrusted to the conscience of Joseph Bonaparte, ex-King of Spain.

At this time the thirty-three year old Leon was living in utter squalor and it is difficult to understand why his grandmother and his religious aunt did not offer him shelter. They certainly hoped for further demonstrations of his generosity following his visit to his uncles.

In fact it was the mystic Coëssin who took him in. Leon's landlord, Fournol, had given him an ultimatum on January 30, 1840: either he settled his bill, totalling 686 francs, that very day, or his room would be re-let in the evening. Coëssin offered him bed and board at 290 Rue St. Honoré, close to the church of St. Roch — where Leon's father had first brought himself to the notice of his superiors with his 'whiff of grape-shot' administered to the citizens of Paris.

A police report of January 22, 1840, shows to what depths of misery the dandy of the 1830s was reduced:

Count Leon lives at the Hôtel de Bruxelles, Rue du Mail. His mistress is a woman of disreputable behaviour who lives with Lesieur, a married man employed at the Ministry of War. He left his wife for this concubine who treats him in the most indecent fashion.

This 'Madame Lesieur' practises magnetism, the proceeds of which — as well as Lesieur's salary — are devoured by Count Leon.[2]

They are living on the second floor of 21 Rue du Petit Carreau, with a rent of 200 francs; and they own not 50 francs worth of furniture and clothes. They have all been sold for Leon's upkeep in prison. With nothing left to sell, this woman has borrowed money to defray the costs of a legal action in which Leon is currently engaged. His mistress is quite sure he will win it, after which he will take her with him to visit Louis Bonaparte in London. At present she is selling some very fine napkins bearing the Count's cypher. We are assured that the furniture and clothes belonging to her are not worth 50 francs. The other tenants are indignant at the scandalous behaviour of Count Leon and the woman.

Leon confided to Coëssin his plans for visiting London to receive his share of Cardinal Fesch's estate from his uncle Joseph Bonaparte, who was staying at Marshall Thompson's Hotel, 28 Cavendish Square. Coëssin gave the expedition his blessing.

'I conceived the happy notion,' says Leon, 'of presenting to Prince Louis seventeen letters which Louis Bonaparte, ex-King of Holland, had written to Mme. Couprie my grandmother, in which he expressed the most noble sentiments.'

By means of this naive gambit Leon hoped to ingratiate himself with the thirty-one year old Louis Napoleon by handing to him a collection of letters written by the prince's father which probably contained some conventional phrases in praise of Leon himself.

Grandmother Denuelle had tried to bolster his financial adventure with her treasured souvenirs; but Leon was not allowed past the hall porter at 1 Carlton Gardens, and it is doubtful whether the pathetic bundle was ever delivered.

Leon still needed his cross-Channel fare. 'But how was I to make this journey?' he says. 'I was absolutely penniless; and when my landlord, Fournol, repossessed my rooms he took away all my belongings and papers.'

The problem was solved by the proverbial 'rich uncle from Australia' in the person of M. Alexander Contzen, who lived next door to Leon at 41 Rue Neuve Saint Augustin, near the Place Vendôme. He provided a loan of 300 francs for the tickets.

'I set off at once,' says Leon, 'with nothing but the clothes on my back.'

Together with a friend of Coëssin — Martial Kien — and some samples of the philosopher's patent oil-lamps with revolving base 'superior to those named Carcel', Leon sailed for England. With his many faults Leon, who always believed that something would turn up, had a touching belief in the goodness of human nature.

Baron Meneval, the former secretary of the Emperor, whom His Majesty on St. Helena had appointed as my guardian, gave me for the Count de Survilliers, Joseph Bonaparte, a letter in which he informed him of the kind plans that the Archbishop of Paris had envisaged for me.

On February 5, 1840, in his characteristic style, Meneval had written:

Leon is going to London and has asked me to give him a letter for you. I do it the more willingly because it affords me the opportunity of recalling myself to your memory, and of receiving news of you from an eye-witness. He has experienced reverses of fortune that I know of only imperfectly. If you are prepared to listen he will tell you himself. They are the result of his inexperience, and his independence of mind towards the advice of those who wish him well.

He seems to have many projects, and to exaggerate his resources; for instance the value of the presumed influence of the late Archbishop of Paris with Cardinal Fesch. He has an adventurous nature which is not always governed by prudence and a sense of what is right and proper. He talks of going to Petersburg to claim from the Duke of Leuchtenberg the payment of the legacy left to him by the Emperor from money in the hands of Prince Eugène. He is also in dispute with his mother who wishes to deal with the proceeds of 20,000 francs invested in the National Debt, which she owes to the generosity of the Emperor and of which Leon naturally has the reversion. The Emperor had himself left assignments of 300,000 francs on the sale of timber which were expropriated by a decree of Louis XVIII and on which there is no hope of recovering anything.

This, in a few words, is his situation. I will not permit myself to recommend him to your goodness because it were better that he should show himself rather more worthy of earning it in person. At all events, the interest attaching to his origins, acknowledged in some sort by the Emperor, and the good he desired for him, cannot be forgotten.

Meneval's epistolary style had changed little in fifteen years. His letter of recommendation assured for Leon a closed door wherever he knocked in London.

CHAPTER 6

Igniferous Balls and Incendiary Bullets

Leon arrived in London on February 13, 1840. The capital was slowly returning to normal after the festivities following the wedding of Queen Victoria three days earlier to Prince Albert of Saxe-Coburg. As Leon expected to stay at an hotel for only a few days until he should be received by his uncle, Joseph Bonaparte, ex-King of Spain, he put up at Fenton's, 'where,' he says, 'I had stayed in happier days.' In spite of Queen Hortense's instant dislike of the hotel when she arrived with her son Louis Napoleon on their first visit in the spring of 1831, Fenton's had become what can only be described as the London headquarters of the Bonapartes.[1]

On the morning following his arrival Leon sent his card to Colonel Bouffet de Montauban, 'whom I knew to be in almost continual contact with the Bonaparte family.[2]

Colonel Montauban lunched at Fenton's and Leon explained the purpose of his visit.

'I told him that I had come to London to find out from Joseph Bonaparte the bequest made to me by Cardinal Fesch, after which I would travel to Russia to claim from Prince Leuchtenberg, the son of Prince Eugène Beauharnais and son-in-law of the Emperor Nicholas, 300,000 francs due to me by the succession of Prince Eugene, his father, by virtue of the seventh codicil to the will of the Emperor Napoleon.'[3]

Colonel Montaubon advised Leon not to go personally to the Count de Survilliers — Joseph Bonaparte, — but simply to send his card, together with the letter of introduction addressed to Joseph from Baron de Meneval, Leon's former guardian. Leon lost no time in doing this.

After lunch at Fenton's, Montauban asked Leon to visit him that same day. In fact he returned the colonel's call in the evening. 'Hardly had I entered the colonel's room,' says Leon, 'when a German named Doctor Warbourg was introduced to me.'

The doctor told Leon of a new invention by means of which inflammable material could be made to burn even when plunged into water. This so aroused Leon's curiosity that he went with Colonel Montauban to Doctor Warbourg's home, in order that they might continue the discussion 'more at their ease'.

Dr. Warbourg ushered them into the underground chambers of his chemical laboratory where they met another German, Herr Wetter, the doctor's collaborator in the new process. Wetter handed to Leon a manuscript, written in German and bearing the title *New invention: Igniferous and Incendiary Balls and Bullets, by S.   , a senior officer in the service of   .*

'Although,' says Leon, 'I was quite familiar with the German language, I nevertheless asked him to send me a French translation of the manuscript.' It was after all some fourteen years since Leon had been a student in Heidelberg.

Meanwhile on February 15 Leon's plan to call on Joseph Bonaparte suffered a rude set back when he received from his uncle an *unsealed* letter addressed to Baron de Meneval. It is a comment on Joseph's character that he had already sent a copy of the letter to Meneval in Paris *direct*:

> . . . I am very sorry to refuse you anything, my dear Meneval, whom I have loved as a son ever since I knew you. But the conversations which your ward had with Doctor O'Meara — who was obliged to report them to me — are of such a nature that they have broken-off all relations between us. I desire his happiness; but I shall never again concern myself with him. It is my wish that he should forget me, precisely as I shall seek my own happiness in forgetting him. Because you know, my dear Meneval, bitterness gives no pleasure to my heart. . . .[4]

Leon had inherited his father's gift for the mellifluous phrase and he immediately sent off the following reply to Joseph:

London, 15 February, 1840

Dear Uncle,

This morning I had the honour to send you the letter handed to me by my guardian, Baron de Meneval.

Full of confidence and hope, I was waiting for you to appoint the hour of our meeting. This evening you sent your reply to my guardian's letter. You had not sealed it and I was therefore obliged to take note of the contents. It is with a feeling of deep sorrow and astonishment that I learn of the wounding remarks contained in the untruthful reports of Doctor O'Meara.

The Archbishop of Paris, Monsignor Quelen, who was kind enough to have my letters conveyed to His Eminence

Cardinal Fesch, had charged me with this journey to London. Baron de Meneval approved the mission.

Your kindness ever towards me; those affectionate feelings that constrained you to write to me as your son, and which have always been my joy, had led me to hope for a warm welcome from you. Must it be otherwise? Will you permit me to depart without having explained the motive that decided me to seek your presence? Must I bear the pain of giving to my guardian in person the letter you delivered to me for him? Or shall I be fortunate enough to obtain of you a moment's conversation?

I have the honour to be with the deepest respect your very humble and very obedient nephew,   Count Leon.

In spite of this carefully worded example of the old Napoleonic charm, Leon received yet another rebuff.

The following morning Maillard, the private secretary of Joseph Bonaparte, called at St. James's Street to tell Leon that his master had not changed the resolve expressed in his letter of February 15. In view of Joseph's determination not to see him, Leon asked Maillard to give a message to his uncle which was something in the nature of an ultimatum. Either Joseph should hand over the bequest made to Leon by his great-uncle, Cardinal Fesch; or state in writing that the cardinal's will contained no legacy in his favour, either officially or by way of conscience.

Maillard undertook to deliver this message; but as he was leaving Fenton's Hotel he counselled the employment of an intermediary in the person of the Count de Montfort. The count was none other than Jerome Bonaparte, Napoleon's youngest brother and a veteran of Waterloo. Charged with the duty of creating a small diversion at Hougomont, he had turned it into a private battle and diverted a substantial portion of the Grande Armée. A year later Jerome's father-in-law, King William I of Württemberg, created him Count de Montfort.

When Leon called at the home of Jerome his uncle sent out his secretary to say that he would not receive him until Leon had seen the Count de Survilliers (Joseph Bonaparte) who, of course, refused to see Leon! This series of affronts would have raised the hackles of a milder individual, let alone a Bonaparte.

However, Leon seems to have laid the pursuit of his legacy temporarily to one side; for as soon as he returned to his rooms he examined the German manuscript which had been given to him by Dr. Warbourg:

Eleonore Denuelle in 1838 when Countess of Luxbourg. *From a miniature*

The Emperor Napoleon

The Silver Boudoir in the Elysée Palace, where Leon played as a child with Napoleon; here Louis Napoleon directed his coup d'état, and here Felix Fauré, President of the French Republic, died in the arms of his mistress.

The igniferous incendiary balls cannot be analysed by any chemical process; any such attempt will destroy the building and the persons inside.

Should any article containing combustible material be struck by an igniferous ball, it will instantly catch fire, and the combustion cannot be extinguished by any means whatsoever, even if it is plunged into water, and indeed for such length of time as there remains the slightest particle of inflammable matter.

An incendiary ball shot into the water will create a great boiling turbulence; all combustible objects, such as a ship, which approach the seething disturbance will burst into flames and be destroyed.

The government which possesses the secret of the igniferous balls will own the means to master the world.

On February 17, 1840, Wetter sent the following letter to Leon:

Monsieur le Comte,

I have the honour to send you the enclosed translation of the details of the invention of Baron — as we agreed at Doctor Warbourg's. Since it would be most ill-advised to place such a destructive weapon into the hands of the English you would do well to offer it to the Emperor of Russia during your stay in St. Petersburg. Doctor Warbourg will give you all the necessary details and will himself familiarise you with the invention.

Leon now had further cause for indignation. It seemed hardly a coincidence that while he could not get within hailing distance of a Bonaparte, Louis Napoleon's close friend Colonel Bouffet de Montauban had lost no time in putting Leon in touch with two crackpot German inventors.

'The following morning,' says Leon,

I went in search of Montauban to reproach him with having introduced me to individuals who had the temerity to suggest appointing me the agent for an invention, the object of which was to serve the interests of Russia to the detriment of other nations.

The colonel tried as far as possible to reassure me of their intentions; but when I returned to my rooms I found a second letter from Wetter, in which he proposed to me an interest in the financial benefits which would follow the sale of the secret to the Emperor of Russia. He ended by saying, 'I have not seen Warbourg since I left you; but I have no doubt that I can persuade him to fall in with my suggestion, if you promise in writing that you will supervise the business in such a way that he will receive his share of the profit. Please let me have your reply as soon as possible.'

Wetter's insistence on a written reply from Leon made him fear that in order to compromise him Montauban had, in all innocence perhaps, been used to introduce him to Warbourg and his partner.

Leon then pondered on the fact that Montauban was almost always in the company of 'a Monsieur Persigny, the friend of Prince Louis Bonaparte'. The two were in constant attendance on Louis Napoleon whenever he visited Her Majesty's Theatre in the Haymarket, where the prince maintained an impressive box directly opposite that of the Queen.

Vicomte Fialin de Persigny was the same age as Louis Napoleon. Fialin, besides re-christening himself de Persigny, endowed himself with several styles including *loyal serviteur* and 'Loyola of the Second Empire'. A fervent Bonapartist, he first espied the young Louis in a coach in Augsburg — after the driver had shouted *'Vive Napoleon!'* — and attached himself to the prince for life. Fialin had enrolled in the army of Louis XVIII in 1825 and in his early twenties he became adjutant of the 4th Hussars. After a dispute with his superiors he left the Restoration army and became a journalist.

Leon's attention now turned to other members of Louis Napoleon's suite. At his home in Carlton House Terrace the prince had a 'court' of some seventeen persons.

Doctor Warbourg's wife, Leon discovered, was continually receiving visits from Dr. Conneau, Prince Louis Bonaparte's physician. Henri Conneau, the son of a French civil servant, was born in Milan in 1803 during its occupation by Napoleon's army. After studying medicine in Italy he acted as secretary to Louis Napoleon's father and later to the prince himself. He became doctor to Queen Hortense, who made him promise never to leave her son. Conneau was, in fact, with Louis until the end. In London Conneau aided Louis's projected invasion of Boulogne by sewing buttons on uniforms and producing stirring proclamations on a small hand press in the basement of 1 Carlton Gardens.

Having regard to Louis's well-known scientific interests, and the fact that he had actually published papers on ballistics which was his special subject, it is difficult to understand why he had not himself taken up the invention of the igniferous balls. He must certainly have been aware of the process, and might well have had a hand in it. The existence of Warbourg and Wetter was no secret to him; and the prince's concern for the two inventors was shortly to be made known in Louis Napoleon's own Paris newspaper.

Leon, certainly, was not deceived for he says, 'Prince Louis, or his favourites, wishing to destroy any chance of a rapprochement between the Bonaparte family and myself would have found it capital to give me the opportunity to go to Russia and offer to the Emperor an imaginary invention, or — if the invention were real — it would have suited them to land me in a perilous position by placing me in contact with individuals who by their intrigues were exposing themselves to grave measures on the part of the English Government. 'Under the influence of these thoughts,' he says, 'I called on Colonel Montauban to tell him that I perceived quite clearly that I was being led into a trap.'

Leon then went to Doctor Warbourg and said to him, 'Wetter is asking me for a reply in writing. He is not going to get it. I am the object of sinister designs. If a trap is being laid for me I will have satisfaction for it: I shall have you both sent to the Tower!'

When Wetter got wind of Leon's *démarches*, and of his dissatisfaction over the matter of the igniferous balls, he must have realised that the ploy had failed. Storming up to Fenton's Hotel while Leon was away, Wetter declared that he had some papers belonging to him and that if they were not returned he would wait outside the hotel and take them back by force.

Montauban's next step was, to put it in its most favourable light, disingenuous; for he told Leon, quite erroneously, that under English law he was permitted to kill a person who had insulted him on the public street. The Colonel followed up this extraordinary piece of legal advice by giving him a sword-stick 'to defend himself'. The mock Tuileries of Carlton House Terrace had now given Leon the means of embroiling himself with the London police. If Bouffet de Montauban's actions are to be taken seriously, it meant that he had incited Leon to attack a fellow-member of Louis Napoleon's entourage. Wetter's little charade outside Fenton's was then no more than bad play-acting.

Leon was now told that the threats he had made against her husband had made Frau Warbourg ill. 'Doctor Conneau, who attended her, invented all sorts of means to persuade Prince Louis Bonaparte to rid himself of me,' says Leon, 'and told him that I had threatened to have two of his friends sent to the Tower.'

On February 20, 1840, Colonel Montauban sent the following letter to Leon:

My dear Count,

Madame Warbourg is still in mortal fear of the threat you laughingly made to have those two gentlemen sent to the Tower. Since fear is an incurable complaint to those it afflicts, please be as generous as the Great Man, your father, and restore tranquillity to those who have lost it. I should be grateful if you would have the kindness to return to me, as you told me yesterday, the letters and documents that Wetter sent to you. I shall return them at once and explain how little importance you attach to this affair. Kind regards, Colonel Bouffet de Montauban.

P.S. I shall call at your hotel at about one o'clock or half past when I return from the king.

There was more disturbing news in the post however for on February 23 Leon received another letter from Maillard, the secretary of Joseph Bonaparte:

Monsieur le Comte,

I passed on the message you asked me to deliver but I was unable to change the Count's decision respecting yourself.

It must now have become obvious to Leon that if his uncle Joseph had received a bequest on his behalf from Cardinal Fesch, he had no intention of disgorging it. In making Joseph his universal legatee, Leon's great-uncle, the cardinal, had put all beneficiaries at the mercy of Joseph's conscience.

When Leon acquainted Montauban with this latest refusal, the colonel advised him to ignore the conduct of his two uncles and go to see his cousin, Prince Louis Napoleon.

Leon wryly observes, 'This was the state of things when Monsieur Guizot arrived in London to take up his appointment as French ambassador.'

Like Talleyrand before him, Francois-Pierre Guizot took up residence at Hertford House in Manchester Square, which the duke of that name had built in 1776. Guizot described the embassy as 'a large building between a little gravelled court and a small damp garden, with a handsome ground floor, well arranged for official and ceremonial purposes, but bare and inconvenient in the first storey for domestic life. . . '[5]

It would be interesting to know what took place at that interview at Hertford House between the son of the Emperor Napoleon and Louis Philippe's ambassador, whom Acton and Morley believed to be the greatest all round statesman of the 19th century.

Guizot makes no mention of the visit in his book *London, 1840, an Embassy*; while Leon merely observes:

Under the auspices of Monsieur Coëssin I was very well received by Monsieur Guizot, which led me to raise the matter of the igniferous balls in which an attempt had been made to embroil me.

Prince Louis had taken a lease of Lord Ripon's house at 1 Carlton Gardens, and on February 27,[6] the very day of Guizot's arrival in London, he moved from 17 Carlton House Terrace, just round the corner.

On four consecutive days Leon made the journey down Pall Mall to leave his card on Louis Napoleon. The first three visits produced no response; but at the fourth time of asking Leon was told that his cousin would not see him. The message was delivered to him by the *hall porter*.[7]

Leon canvassed the opinion of his acquaintances — notably that of Bouffet de Montauban — on Louis Bonaparte's refusal to see him. He was told that he had been complaining (with some justification!) about the scurvy treatment he had received at the hands of his uncle Joseph Bonaparte; that Louis found fault with him for threatening to have two of his doctor's friends sent to the Tower; and, furthermore, that the Bonaparte family had received letters from Paris branding Leon as a police agent sent to spy on Louis Bonaparte.

This latter and most serious allegation has been repeated — without any supporting evidence — by such authorities as Lord Malmesbury. Leon's own version of the episode was freely available in his *Réponse au gérant du journal le Capitole*. The doctrine of natural justice — *audi alterem partem* — at least, ought to have operated in Leon's behalf.

'The *Argus* and the *Capitole*, newspapers of the Bonaparte family,' he writes, 'have repeated this odious allegation.' The fact that Louis Bonaparte had taken upon himself the justification of Wetter and Warbourg confirmed Leon in his conviction that a trap was being laid for him. 'I resolved to deal with all three,' he concluded ominously.

Leon consulted an English lawyer — Mr. Buckley — who warned him that he would lay himself open to grave charges if the plans of Wetter and Warbourg came to light before he had himself alerted the British Government. But, before taking any action against the two inventors, Buckley asked them to call at his chambers.[8]

Wetter and Warbourg, however, judged it politic not to face

Buckley's questioning; so the lawyer drafted a letter for Leon to send to the Foreign Secretary.

Leon sent off the warning note on February 29, 1840. Did he know that Lord Palmerston was entertaining the French ambassador to dinner at Carlton House Terrace that very night? Bearing in mind Leon's astuteness it seems more than a coincidence.[9]

'In order to deal with all three at once,' says Leon, 'I sent the following letter to Prince Louis Bonaparte:

My little cousin,

It must be admitted that if I have shown much patience in trying to see you; you, on the contrary, have been guilty of a gross discourtesy is not receiving me. You have felt yourself able to interpret in the worst light, and without having heard me, my uncle Joseph's refusal to see me.

I have left my card on you several times and you have believed yourself able not to respond with your own. Do you not think, monsieur mon cousin, that you have behaved offensively towards me?

I was able to regard the bad actions and letters of my uncle Joseph and my uncle Jerome as malicious. At their age they believe that anything is permissible. But do you believe you can do likewise at your age, my little cousin?[10]

As you call yourself a Frenchman you must feel that my honour is offended by such disloyalty and that I must have just reparation.

I shall wait as long as you wish, or as long as shall be necessary. But I swear on the ashes of the Emperor Napoleon my father that your evil behaviour towards me will bring its punishment one day.

If I am mistaken, if you have not a drop of French blood in your veins, out of human respect, you are obliged to give me a reply to this letter, or abuse it at your fancy. I am resigned to anything.

With which, monsieur mon petit cousin, I have the great honour of paying my respects, Count Leon.

P.S. I am keeping a copy of this letter, and together with many others I shall have it printed at the appropriate time.

This letter, like the one to Lord Palmerston, was dated February 29, 1840. Leon had indeed dealt with all three at once.

On March 2, 1840, while Leon and some friends, together with a Colonel Ratcliffe, were gathered in the coffee room at Fenton's

Hotel, a tall, heavily-built man of soldierly bearing, Colonel Parquin, entered the room. He told Leon that Louis Napoleon had not believed it necessary to reply to his cousin's letter, and that for the future he wished to have nothing to do with him.

Then, somewhat embarrassed, and in a voice shaking with emotion, Parquin said, 'Monsieur le Comte, if you have something with which to reproach Prince Louis Bonaparte, it is with me you will have to reckon.'

'Is that all?' Leon replied. 'This confirms me in the opinion that the prince is a coward. Since I do not wish to have an affair of honour with you any more than with the other friends of Prince Louis Bonaparte, if another such scene occurs I shall lay a complaint before a magistrate. You may withdraw.'

According to Leon, the colonel retired without saying another word; but in such an extraordinary manner that he drew gusts of laughter until he had quite disappeared from sight.

Colonel Parquin, who was fifty three at the time of this incident, had been given the Cross of the Legion of Honour by Napoleon after serving in eleven campaigns. In Portugal he saved the life of the Duke de Raguse, and at Leipsig that of Marshal de Reggio. He married Mademoiselle Cochelet, the companion to Queen Hortense, the mother of Louis Napoleon, whom he first met in 1822 when the prince was fourteen.

After Colonel Parquin's departure from the hotel Leon took up his pen and sent off a further letter which Colonel Ratcliffe eagerly volunteered to deliver to Prince Louis.

Monsieur mon cousin,

A tall fat gentleman by the name of Parquin is leaving my hotel after having told me on your behalf that the letter which I wrote you the day before yesterday was the real reason why you refused to see me.

You will understand that I was quite unable to reply to the type of language which was capable of exciting such hilarity in the members of my entourage and others standing by. You abuse my letter in an extraordinary fashion.

I had foreseen this; and I am therefore obliged to repeat that the natural consequence of this comical visit is that you have not a drop of French blood in your veins.

If another such messenger appears I shall request Monsieur Guizot, the French ambassador, to accompany me to a magistrate.

With respect, Count Leon, London, 2 March, 1840.

Colonel Ratcliffe delivered this letter to Louis and gave him the following message: 'Count Leon says that if you persist in maintaining that he is a police agent sent to spy on you, he will challenge you to a duel with pistols. This ignoble thought is not in your heart, but in your mind. It is a stain that he sees on your brow, and one that can only be effaced by a bullet . . .'

CHAPTER 7

The Duel on Wimbledon Common

The hollow below the windmill on Wimbledon Common had for centuries been a notorious duelling-ground. It was well-known to the police of the metropolis as the spot where the noblest in the land settled their disputes, often by firing into the air like the Duke of York, son of George III, when he met Colonel Lennox after a Guards parade-ground tiff. The Windmill dropped suddenly out of favour after a haberdasher had settled an account there.

It therefore came as no surprise to Inspector Nicholas Pierce of A Division when he discovered that an extraordinary cavalcade was assembling in St. James's and heading west. He had received information at two o'clock that morning, March 3, from Superintendent Baker, 'that certain parties had an intention of meeting in a hostile manner at Wimbledon Common.'

At about seven in the morning a post-chaise left Fenton's Hotel and set-off slowly up St. James's Street, passed Crockford's Club House at No.50, and turned left into Piccadilly. Colonel Ratcliffe on horseback brought up the rear followed by Inspector Pierce. By the south-east corner of St. George's Hospital stood Tattersall's celebrated auction-mart, 'so renowned through all the breadth and length of horse-loving, horse-breeding, horse-racing Europe.'

Inspector Pierce had tried to make himself inconspicuous by hanging back, and when he arrived on the common the parties had left their carriages and were making their way to the hollow. Throwing the reins of his horse to a peasant, the inspector hurried down to the group of Frenchmen, who were arguing over the choice of weapons.

As the party challenged, Prince Louis Napoleon declared for swords; but Leon, as the party insulted, opted for pistols. Meanwhile, Colonel Parquin stood by holding in one hand a pair of duelling-swords and in the other hand *two* letters. By this time Inspector Pierce had reached the party and he immediately took charge of all four articles.

The discussion on choice of weapons continued, although with the confiscation of the swords the question had now become academic, so the prince and Count d'Orsay proposed that the matter should be decided by the drawing of lots. Leon maintained that as an expert swordsman it was all the same to him; but that as the offended party he had choice of weapons.[1] Prince Louis Napoleon finally agreed to the use of pistols, two brace of which were lying on the grass unnoticed by the policeman. Count d'Orsay then turned to Inspector Pierce and asked him what was his authority for interfering, and who had given notice of the duel.

No shot was fired. And the inhabitants of Wimbledon slept on, unaware that the son of Bonaparte had come so close to altering the course of history by shooting the future Emperor Napoleon III of France.

An awkward situation was avoided by the appearance of Inspector Partridge and Sergeant Otway, accompanied by a number of police constables. Unaccountably, Colonel Ratcliffe chose this very moment to take a brace of pistols from its case. He was immediately arrested.

This incident gave Inspector Pierce the opportunity to go up to the colonel, show his baton and tell him he was a police-officer, and duty-bound to take Ratcliffe into custody for attempting to commit a breach of the peace. Count d'Orsay again asked who it was that had told the police, after which the whole party was taken to the station-house.

As soon as Bow Street Court opened, Leon, Louis Napoleon and their seconds were brought before the police magistrate, Mr. David Jardine. This unhappy official was to be the object of a most extraordinary attack in the form of a book of verses by one Robert Ball:

> Hail! Bow-Street Court, where licences are paid
> For crimes once infamous, now venal made!
> Where scope to wealthy miscreants is given
> To doff the chain before the links are riven!
> Jardine, forgetful of thy sacred vow,
> To minister the laws alike to all
> Whose rights within thy jurisdiction fall . . .[2]

After listening to Inspector Pierce's description of the events of the early morning, Jardine asked, 'Have you since ascertained that the pistols contained powder and ball?'

'Yes, sir, there are balls in them and caps upon them.'

Colonel Ratcliffe then declared that there was no powder in the pistols which belonged to him, as could be seen, for it had been arranged that the duel was to be fought with swords. This was the second time within a few hours that Ratcliffe had put his foot in it.

Mr. Jardine then asked if any of the defendants who were foreigners and not sufficiently conversant in the English language would wish to have the evidence read over to them in French. Leon answered that he could not sufficiently understand the evidence that had been given but he was quite satisfied that all the proceedings were perfectly legal and correct. It was this flair for the disarming touch that had kept the disaster-prone Bonapartes afloat for so long.

Louis Napoleon said he was prepared, if required, to enter into an explanation of the circumstances which gave rise to the offence with which he was charged.

Mr. Jardine did not wish to hear any statement from either side; and said that his only duty was to prevent a breach of the peace. He hoped the defendants were prepared with the sureties he would require to prevent any further inconvenience.

Count d'Orsay said that he had come prepared with bail which he thought there could be no objection to. At this time the profligate dandy — 'Cupido unchained' — was in the last stages of insolvency. It had been his custom to drive Louis Napoleon around town in his hooded cabriolet with an immense horse between the shafts and a tiny groom on the box. Gillion Gaspard Alfred de Grimaud, Comte d'Orsay et du Saint Empire, born in Paris in 1801, was the son of one of Napoleon's generals and grandson of the man who negotiated the purchase of the British Embassy in the Rue du Faubourg St. Honoré from Pauline Bonaparte.

Louis Napoleon asked for the return to him of the two letters which Inspector Pierce had taken from Colonel Parquin. Mr. Jardine handed back the letters and bound over the parties to keep the peace with all Her Majesty's subjects, and particularly with each other, for the next twelve months.

Leon and Louis were required to find a total of £750 each, and the sum of £150 was received severally from Count d'Orsay and Colonels Parquin and Ratcliffe. The unfortunate Martial Kien who had travelled from Paris with Leon and the lamps was dunned for £100.

Count d'Orsay, still playing the moneyed dandy, although with empty coffers, suggested one surety might suffice for Prince Louis and Colonel Parquin. Mr. Jardine accepted the offer and Joshua Bates of Baring Brothers,[3] the bankers, who was financing Louis Napoleon in a big way, agreed to stand. The Honourable Francis Baring stood surety for Ratcliffe and d'Orsay; while Mr. Fenton, who owed so much to the Bonapartes, went bail for Leon.

The chief clerk at Bow Street, Mr Burnaby, then asked Mr. Jardine for directions as to the disposal of the swords and pistols. The magistrate said he could make no order about them; but he thought that as the defendants had furnished bail there could be very little apprehension of their committing a similar offence if the weapons were returned to their owners.

Then — in the words of Robert Ball — the relics of Napoleon's Empire were 'flattered, protected and finally let go.'

In the evening 'as a sign of family solidarity,' Louis appeared with his uncles Joseph and Jerome Bonaparte, sitting one on either side of him in his box at Her Majesty's Theatre.

On March 3, 1840, the Italian Opera gave its opening performance of the season, the first presentation in England of Donizetti's *Torquato Tasso.* While the singers were generally praised the work was given a sound drubbing by the critics. The *Morning Chronicle* called it 'monotonous, dreary, commonplace', while the *Atlas* likened it to the 'celebrated history of a piece of pack-thread — a vexatious enlargement on nothing.' The criticism might well have been applied to the events of that morning.

But the royal box at the Opera was in darkness. The Queen and Prince Albert were at Covent Garden playhouse. 'The excellent acting of Mr. Mathews as Motley in the farce *He would be an Actor,* elicited much laughter from Her Majesty and Prince Albert,' wrote the *Courier.* The twenty year old Victoria — already *enceinte* — was very much amused.

Meanwhile, back at Fenton's Hotel, Leon was packing Coëssin's lamps with the revolving base 'superior to those named Carcel'.[4] Until he was able to borrow the money for his journey home to Paris[4] he stayed with a family called Joy, who lived across from Bloomsbury Square in Hart Street (Bloomsbury Way).

On March 8, 1840, an article appeared in the *Argus,* a London weekly paper which Leon did not fail to notice.

The anonymous correspondent of the *Argus,* wrote:

Thanks to the vigilance of the A Division, one of those affairs *falsely* termed of honour, but which is dishonourable to

Christians, was put a stop to on Tuesday last. The public may take some interest in the subject from the position of the parties in fashionable life . . .

Count Leon, the challenger, is a natural son of Napoleon Bonaparte by a Mademoiselle de la Plagne [sic], a young French lady of family, who previous to the Emperor's marriage possessed his affections.

It is a moot point whether Louis Napoleon was the challenged or the challenger. A second inaccuracy by the *Argus* correspondent is shown by the fact that at the time of Napoleon's *passade* with Eleonore Denuelle de la Plaigne he was very much married — to Josephine.

The *Argus* report continues:

He is a gambler, and a *professional duellist,* a man of reckless character, who killed our countryman, Charles Hesse, in a duel at Paris, besides having been engaged in other rencontres that terminated equally fatally![5] Lt. Col. Ratcliffe was placed by chance in the Enniskillen Dragoons, he is not an Irishman, though he seems ambitious to become a blazer! His *renomé* chiefly consists in the possession of a sweet voice, and cultivated taste for singing, and the friendship of the late Earl of Essex, the Duchess of Canizzaro, and the Dowager Lady Farquhar . . .

Prince Louis received letters from the French capital informing him that a plot had been formed to deprive him of his life, and that it was intended to send this said Leon over to this country, who would attempt to engage him in mortal combat! Shortly after the debts of Leon were discharged, and, furnished with a passport, he proceeded to England.

[Count Leon] wrote an abusive letter to the Prince. When sent an aide-de-camp to explain, he refused to receive an explanation and sent Colonel Ratcliffe with a cartel!

It is proper to observe here that *no* previous intimacy existed between the colonel and the count, their acquaintance having been formed in the coffee-room at Fenton's; and yet a gallant officer, commanding one of Her Majesty's cavalry regiments, is found ready to carry a challenge to a gentleman because he has not returned the visit of an individual whom he was not desirous of knowing and whom he considered to be an undesirable acquaintance! We must candidly confess we think this *ground of offence* the most shameful we ever heard propounded, on which to pretend to

justify by *The Code of Honour* the shedding of blood, and
deep and awful is the responsibility of all who are implicated
in this disgusting business . . .

The *Argus* correspondent concludes:

. . . We beg to call Lord Palmerston's notice to this affair, and
if it be as we have heard that this Leon has been sent here on
this murderous crusade we sincerely hope that his Lordship
will employ the powers vested in him, and drive from our
shores this individual, in every way unworthy of hospitality
and protection.

In his *Reponse au gerant du journal le Capitole,* Leon refutes the
charge that he had been living extravagantly at Fenton's and giving
lavish parties. 'My position at that period,' he says, 'was so critical
that I was unable to accept the invitations I had received from
Lady Morgan and the Duke of Brunswick.'[6]

On 11 March, 1840, *The Times* reproduced a letter written to a
'friend' in Paris by Colonel Parquin, which had been dutifully
published by the editor of *le Capitole.* It purported to give details
of the 'circumstances which preceded the duel between Prince
Louis Napoleon Bonaparte and Count Leon.' Parquin writes as
follows:

On the 1st inst. Count Leon wrote a letter to Prince Napoleon
complaining of his refusal to receive him, but it was of so
offensive a character that he refused to reply to it. The Prince
however sent me on the following day to explain to Count
Leon the motive of the Emperor's family for not having any
intercourse with him.

On arriving at Fenton's Hotel, I found the Count at
breakfast with another person, and having given my name,
and requested a private interview with him, he replied that he
did not know me, and would have nothing to do with me.

Although hurt at this unexpected reception, and not being
able in a public room to make the intended communication, I
told him, that in consequence of his refusal to give me a
private interview, I would say in my own name, that his
insolent letter to Prince Napoleon fully justified the conduct
of the Imperial family towards him.

Some hours after this scene the Prince received another
letter from Count Leon, in terms as offensive as those of the
first, and in which he said, that if I should again present
myself at his hotel, he would place himself under the
protection of M. Guizot, the French Ambassador.

On the same day Colonel Ratcliffe brought a challenge to the Prince from the Count.

I was immediately placed in communication with the Colonel, who avowed to me in the first interview that he had known Count Leon only a few days, having met him at the hotel, but knowing that he had been received at the French Ambassador's and had dined there, he had not hesitated when asked to become his second in an affair of honour.

As I was not acquainted with the Colonel and was ignorant of the English laws, I requested that another person might be associated with me in the delicate mission with which I was charged and postponed any decision till another interview.

The Prince then sent for Count d'Orsay, who arrived immediately, and conferred with me on the subject, when he informed me that Col. Ratcliffe was a distinguished officer of the English army, and highly respected.

Informed of this, the Prince communicated to us his determination, and in the evening, in an interview with Colonel Ratcliffe, we informed him that the Prince, from personal considerations, would have paid no attention to the insolent letters of Count Leon, but that the intervention of an English officer in the affair entirely changed its character, and therefore the Prince accepted the challenge.

On the same day that Parquin's apologia for Louis Bonaparte appeared in *The Times,* Leon received a letter from a German baron — Herr von Hoofsteten:

The enclosed French newspaper, in which you are mentioned, has just come into my hands. It seems to me they could have better served your interests. As I know the editor well, and am persuaded that he would do something for me, I offer you my services as mediator.

Leon did not avail himself of the baron's kind offer, but preferred to wait until he had assembled all the documentary evidence before answering the libels.

In articles published on 6, 9, 10 and 12 March, 1840 [he says] the *Capitole* slandered me odiously.

According to these articles I am alleged to be a professional duellist and a man of deplorable morality. I, the son of the Emperor Napoleon, am said to have consented to become a police agent whom the French Government planned to send to London to provoke Prince Louis Bonaparte to mortal combat.

In order to have me play this infamous role, the doors of
the debtors prison at Clichy are alleged to have been opened
for me, all my debts paid, and large sums placed at my
disposal. On arrival in London I am supposed to have sent a
challenge to Prince Louis Bonaparte on the vain pretence that
he had refused to see me, and having arrived on the
duelling-ground, I did not have the courage to fight with the
agreed weapons.

Leon was being attacked on two fronts. 'On the 15th of the same
month,' he says, 'Louis Delpech, whom I have been pursuing for
three years in the civil and criminal courts, had a letter published
in the *Argus* in which he dares to describe me as a *convict* and a
horrible *brigand,* whom the Bonaparte family had good reason to
reject.'

While he was thus being, as he said, spurned and calumnied,
Leon received a letter from his friend the mystic, Coëssin.

Here is a large parcel. I believe you will have taken the
trouble to read the *Capitole* which is the paper of the
Bonaparte family. Nevertheless, to be on the safe side, I
enclose an article from this paper which concerns yourself.

At first I had the desire to reply to the odious and ignoble
insinuations that this article contains; but I reflected that this
might have spoiled your plans and lost you an opportunity. I
therefore limited myself to going to Fournol, the landlord, to
request of him the enclosed letter, which he has written quite
spontaneously and without the slightest prompting on my
part.

Leon has not reproduced the enclosure, and Coëssin does not hint
at the contents of Fournol's apparently favourable note, but he
says:

You know, Monsieur le Comte, that only I and the honourable friends who live within my circle, are in a position to
demonstrate mathematically all that is odious and infamous
in the cowardly insinuations of the *Capitole.* Neither I nor
mine will be found wanting in your need.

The founder of the *Children of God* now goes in for some heavy
sermonizing:

In so far as concerns your duel with Prince Louis, if you were
to ask my opinion I would myself advise you, always
supposing — and taken for granted — that the lofty and noble
sentiments which you manifested at the time of your
departure are rooted in you fundamentally and that you have

Count Leon, by David, probably painted when Leon was 17.

The Emperor Napoleon's Lying-in-State at Longwood. Compare Napoleon's profile (taken from the Antommarchi death mask) with that of Leon (*sketch facing page* 128)

conscientiously taken care to make them the rule for your most important as for your smallest actions . . .

Here Coëssin, having become lost in his moral discourse, forgets what advice he was about to give. He does, however, loose a shrewd parting shot against the Bonapartes:

I would very much like to know which of your uncles and great uncles, your aunts — and even your grandmother — would dare to declare themselves free from the youthful failings with which they reproach you.

Leon's first step on his return to Paris was to apply to the courts for the return of the papers which had been wrongfully removed from his apartment by Delpech and Fournol.

'I have received justice,' he writes, 'and on 20 June last I was put into possession of all the documents necessary to enable me to lay the slanders that have been spread against me.'

The next passage in his *Réponse* reveals poignantly Leon's yearning to belong.

It is clear from these documents, which will be produced at the trial, that until his last breath the Emperor never ceased to take the liveliest interest in me, and that his family have always considered me as his *son*! Furthermore, I possess a letter from Prince Lucien Bonaparte in which he calls me his *nephew*.[7]

All these facts sufficiently explain the good endeavours that Cardinal Fesch, my uncle, felt able to undertake on my behalf.

Among the papers that were returned to me may be found one in particular which proves conclusively, that at the time of his last journey to London the Count de Survilliers (Joseph Bonaparte) told a lie to justify his refusal to explain himself regarding the dispositions which Cardinal Fesch had been able to make in my favour.

From his newly-recovered papers Leon unearthed a letter which, he maintained, gave the lie to Joseph's excuse for refusing to meet him. To counter his uncle's charge that his conversations with Dr. O'Meara had been of such a nature as to rupture all relations between them, Leon says: 'Nevertheless, *after the death of Dr. O'Meara,* (in 1836) Joseph Bonaparte had written me a most affectionate letter, in reply to the condolences I had sent to him on the death of *Madame Mère* (on 2 February, 1836, in Rome). This letter which seems to have slipped his memory is dated 12 August, 1836, and runs as follows:

Monsieur le Comte

The sad news reached me in the New World. On my return to England I find myself in the same disposition and situated as you found me at Dr. O'Meara's the last time we saw each other. Fate is constant in its hardships; I never again found that excellent O'Meara, so good for me. Please accept, my dear sir, my regrets, and the reciprocity of the sentiments that you have expressed.

Your affectionate servant, Joseph Count de Survilliers.

Leon is stretching a point when he calls this formal note from his uncle a 'most affectionate letter'; but at least he has the candour to publish it.

Without haste — like Dumas's Monte Cristo — Leon continues to plan his revenge on the scornful Bonapartes.

I shall produce before the court in which this case is heard the proof of all the foregoing facts. I give to the *Capitole* in advance my consent to produce any evidence to the contrary, and I renounce any rule of law which might shackle that newspaper's defence by denying to it any species of proof whatsoever.

But since the odious libels of which I have been the victim, and which have had such repercussions in Europe shall become as clear as the day, I shall claim heavy damages.

In a century where only riches are held in esteem, it is good and just to punish the guilty by depriving them of that wealth which forms the object of their uncouth religion. Because they really do not believe that justice has touched them until it has succeeded in relieving them of a portion of their idol.

Leon published his *Réponse au gérant du journal le Capitole* on July 19, 1840 — almost five months after his encounter with Louis Napoleon on Wimbledon Common. On the same day the one Bonaparte of whom Leon could speak with affection died.

'Only Lucien received me with kindness.'

Bellemois the editor of the Parisian daily the *Capitole* was a young man of twenty five. He believed he had found a means of circumventing the French laws on defamation by reproducing inspired gossip which had appeared in the London press.

According to Leon, the London weekly, the *Argus,* was a Bonapartist paper. It is quite certain that Louis Napoleon was the absentee proprietor of the *Capitole.* He had originally owned two

Paris newspapers; but the other one, the *Commerce,* had ceased publication. Prince Louis had founded the *Capitole* in 1839 at a cost of 140,000 francs through the intermediary of a bizarre character named Crouy-Chanel.[8]

The *Argus* followed up its highly-coloured account of the duel at Wimbledon by printing on March 15, 1840, in its original French, a letter from Louis Delpech. 'a French gentleman ... well-known on the Bourse, and indeed by all the *bon vivants* of Paris, as a clever, spirited and gentlemanly companion ...'

He was also Leon's creditor. Delpech had written to an unknown correspondent in London on 6 March, 1840:

My dear friend,

I have hardly been able to leave my bed for a month and I write only with much pain, suffering terribly with my right arm. However when I read the newspapers my indignation brings back all my strength at the instance of the infamous bandit, the self-styled Count Leon, whom I have publicly accused of giving himself a title of count which he has never possessed. He is called Leon, the son of the infantry captain — the destitute and convicted thief — Revel.

This bandit was introduced to me ... by M. Bouffet de Montauban. In 1837 I was weak enough to lend him more than 40,000 francs of which he has defrauded me in the most unworthy manner.

In open court, before the whole of Paris, I described him as a thief, convict, etc. I said to him, 'You dare to call yourself the son of the Emperor. If that great man came back to life, his most painful torture would be to see his image displayed on the body of a felon such as yourself.'

There is no provocation I have not employed to make him fight with me; and give me satisfaction for his outrages and his ingratitude. I reminded him that he fought with the English colonel Hesse, after having paid a bank note for 25,000 francs that he owed him; that I would offer to make him a gift of the 42,000 francs that he owed me, if he would fight with me. If the air of England restores a morsel of his courage, I shall leave my bed to go to London.

In spite of his bravado it is remarkable how Delpech hangs on the fact that he has been confined to bed for a month and that his duelling arm is causing him considerable pain — otherwise he would certainly fight Leon!

Delpech continues:

His affair with Prince Louis is a lure — a snare. He has been
paid to play this infamous role. After he lost his case against
me he was living at 21 rue des Petits Carreaux, in an obscure
and disgusting midden, with a miserable midwife called
Lesieur, who fed him by her labour and by selling her old
rags. Suddenly he had lots of money — he left for London. I
know the tainted source which he tapped.

I would like this infamous monster made known in
London through the widest publicity. He is a social disgrace.
I shall lay out as much money as possible to dismask him.

Delpech concludes:

I can hardly conceive how an honourable man, an English
colonel was able to ally himself with this horrible brigand.
The Bonaparte family has good reason to repudiate him . . .

The *Argus* prudently withheld the name of the London recipient
of this invective. Could it have been Bouffet de Montauban who
had introduced Delpech to Leon in Paris three years earlier?

Bellemois, the editor of the *Capitole*, appeared before the sixth
chamber of the *Tribunal Correctionel* of Paris on 3 September,
1840, in a courtroom packed to overflowing.

The *Gazette des Tribunaux* reported 'This affair, in which the
name of Prince Louis Napoleon must frequently be mentioned,
has borrowed much interest from recent circumstances.' The
circumstances recentes were of course the arrest and imprisonment
of Louis Napoleon after his landing in August near Wimereux.

On 23 July Bellemois had been approached by Leon and asked
to print a repudiation of the allegations made in the *Capitole*. The
editor refused. A writ was accordingly served on Bellemois on 12
August, 1840, at the offices of his newspaper, rue St.-Pierre--
Montmartre, 17.

Whereas in issues of 6, 10 and 12 March last, on the occasion
of a duel which was prevented by the English police and
which was to have taken place outside the walls of London,
on the third of the said month . . . *le Capitole* was guilty of
defamation . . .

In fact, the issue of the 6 March declared that Comte Leon
was going to solicit help from the Bonaparte family, whilst
on the contrary he was invoking, in the name of honour, the
last dispositions made in his favour by his great uncle, His
Eminence Cardinal Fesch.

. . . the issue of 9 March carried a letter which stated that
Count Leon had been received at the French Embassy, that

he had dined there, and that he would place himself under the protection of M. Guizot, if a captain in the service of Prince Louis presented himself at his hotel again.[9]

The next indictment against Bellemois concerns a grave assumption that has been accepted without qualification by the various chroniclers of Leon's encounter with his cousin Louis Napoleon on Wimbledon Common.

Whereas the *Capitole* let it be understood that Comte Léon must be attributed with the intervention by the authorities that rendered the duel impossible, nevertheless, it is admitted in this same paper that Prince Louis had let his family into the secret of the duel. Count Leon had only mentioned the matter to his seconds.

It therefore follows that Jerome and Joseph Bonaparte knew of the proposed duel and could have sent a quiet word to the police. Both of Leon's uncles had everything to lose and nothing to gain by Louis's premature death. He was the last hope of a Bonaparte restoration, and Jerome did profit conspicuously from the generosity of Napoleon III receiving the custodianship of the Invalides — a handsome sinecure; but by that time Joseph was dead.

Leon felt himself most offended, however, by the allegation in the issue of 12 March that he was 'a gambler, a professional duellist, of a deplorable morality; that a plot had been laid against the life of Prince Louis; that Count Leon had been chosen to go to England in order to provoke him to mortal combat; that the count's debts were paid and that he was furnished with a passport to go to London.'

The *Capitole* rounded off its account of Leon's adventures by saying that he had stayed at one of London's most sumptuous hotels; (Fenton's in St. James's Street, in spite of Queen Hortense's initial dislike of the place, had in fact been the Bonaparte family's habitual London lodging for at least nine years); that he gave dinners, lived in great state and that certain persons believed him to be attached to the French embassy; people commented on his new found affluence, or wondered at his life of ease, following an existence of extreme wretchedness. It also affirmed that one of Leon's seconds, Colonel Ratcliffe had gone mad when he learned of his involuntary complicity in 'infamous political speculations'; and yet the colonel's mental derangement had manifested itself a week before the slanders published against Leon.

The charge against Bellemois also claimed that Leon's debts had in fact not been paid; on the contrary he was in such a distressed state during his visit to London that he was unable to reply to invitations for lack of decent clothes.

Finally, the statement of claim asked for damages of half a million francs, the publication of a retraction, and costs.

Bellemois was defended by Maître Moulin. Maître Nibelie was counsel for the plaintiff, or — as the *Gazette des Tribunaux* has it — *'Maître Nibelie soutient les prétensions de M. le comte Léon'.* The *Avocat du Roi,* Maître Mahon, prosecuting, demanded *'Une réparation éclatante.'*

The Court, presided over by M. Pinondel, decided that the evidence given and the documents furnished proved that in several issues of the *Capitole* — notably in that of March 12 — statements damaging to the honour and interest of Leon had appeared; that Bellemois in his capacity as editor of the *Capitole* was legally responsible for the context of the articles, and that his plea of good faith could not be sustained, being based merely on the claim that he did no more than reproduce articles which had already appeared in the English press; because the act of reproduction possessed the same criminal character as the original publication.

So far as concerned the refusal of the editor of the *Capitole* to publish the denial requested on July 23, his offer to publish an expurgated retraction did not cure the original offence.

Bellemois was found guilty of all the charges and ordered to pay a fine of 1,000 francs.[10]

With regard to the claim for civil injuries, the Court held that Leon had suffered moral damage which called for compensation. He was awarded the sum of 5,000 francs. Bellemois was condemned to two years imprisonment in case of default in the payment of the penalties. The judgment was ordered to be published in its entirety — and within the week — in the *Capitole* and in other papers to be chosen by Leon.

CHAPTER 8

The Return of the Ashes

On his thirty-sixth birthday Leon received a letter from the private secretary of Louis Philippe:

> The Tuileries, December 13, 1840.

Monsieur le Comte,

   The letter which you wrote to the King has just been passed to him. His Majesty could do no more than send it on to the Minister of the Interior, who has charge of all the details of the cortège and of the ceremony; but he sent off the letter at once under a note in his own hand.

> Le secrétaire du cabinet,
> Camille Fain

At the very moment when this message reached Leon the barge *Dorade* bearing his father's remains was moving slowly up the river Seine.

In his will drafted a fortnight before his death Napoleon had written: 'I desire that my ashes may rest on the banks of the Seine, in the midst of that French people whom I have loved so much.'

It was almost two decades later that his wish was fulfilled; and the process began with an exchange of letters between Leon's erstwhile host at Hertford House, Francois Guizot, and Lord Palmerston.

On May 5, 1840, the anniversary of Napoleon's death, Louis Philippe's first minister, Adolphe Thiers, applied through his country's ambassador in London for the removal of the Emperor's ashes. The French Government's ungracious letter was meticulously drafted to obviate any impression that a favour was being solicited:

> The undersigned, Ambassador Extraordinary and Minister Plenipotentiary of His Majesty, the King of the French, has the honour, conformably to instructions received from his Government, to inform His Excellency the Minister of Foreign Affairs to Her Majesty the Queen of the United Kingdom of Great Britain, that the King ardently desires that

the mortal remains of Napoleon may be deposited in the tomb in France, in the country which he defended and rendered illustrious, and which proudly preserves the ashes of thousands of his companions-in-arms, officers and soldiers devoted with him to the service of their country. The undersigned is convinced that Her Majesty's Government will only see in this desire of His Majesty the King of the French a just and pious feeling, and will give the orders necessary to the removal of any obstacle to the transfer of Napoleon's remains from Saint Helena to France.

On May 9, Lord Palmerston returned a courteous answer, which placed the remains of Napoleon at the disposal of France, concluding with the words:

The Government of Her Britannic Majesty hopes that the promptness of its answer may be considered in France as a proof of its desire to blot out the last traces of those national animosities which, during the life of the Emperor, armed England and France against each other. Her Majesty's Government hopes that if such sentiments survive anywhere they may be buried in the tomb about to receive the remains of Napoleon.

The result of this démarche was communicated amid much applause to the Chamber of Deputies on May 12, 1840, by Charles de Remusat, whose mother had written the celebrated memoirs of her experiences as a member of Napoleon's household. The French Parliament voted a sum of one million francs for restoring the Emperor's ashes to France, and the third son of Louis Philippe — the Prince de Joinville — was charged with the mission of bringing home Napoleon's remains.

On July 9, 1840, the frigate *La Belle Poule* and the sloop-of-war *La Favorite* sailed from Toulon for the far-distant island of Saint Helena.

The Special Commission entrusted with the transfer of Napoleon's body comprised the Count de Rohan-Chabot — Commissary of the King — the Abbe Coquereau, Generals Bertrand and Gourgaud, Emmanuel de las Cases — son of the author of the *Memorial to Saint Helena* — Arthur Bertrand, Marchand, St. Denis and Novarrez — valets of the Emperor — Pierron, his domestic officer, and Archambeau, his huntsman. All the members of the Commission, with the exception of the first named, had shared Napoleon's exile on St. Helena.

The ships arrived at Jamestown on October 8, 1840; but the

exhumation was deferred to October 15, the twenty-fifth anniversary of Napoleon's arrival on the island.

Napoleon's physician, Dr. Antommarchi, has described his last sight of the Emperor, who after lying in state on his campaign bed of copper was, on May 8 1821, buried beneath weeping willows.

According to Dr. Antommarchi Napoleon's height was 5 feet 6 and 22/25 inches,[1] 'neck short, hair light chestnut, top of head to chin seven inches 6 lines; chest wide, well-formed, hands and feet rather small.

'I felt a curiosity to examine the head of this great man, according to the criminological system of Drs. Gall and Spurzheim. The following are the signs which were most apparent on it:

(1) organ of dissimulation; (2) organ of conquest; (3) organ of kindness and benevolence; (4) organ of imagination; (5) organ of ambition and lure of glory.

Of the class of intellectual faculties, I found: (1) the organ of individuality, or knowledge of individuals and things; (2) the organ of locality — of the relation of space; (3) the organ of calculation; (4) the organ of comparison; (5) the organ of causality — of the faculty of induction — of a philosophical head.

After Napoleon's death, at eleven minutes to six in the evening of May 5 1821, Antommarchi had performed a post mortem: 'I detached the heart and stomach and put them in a silver vase filled with spirits of wine.[2] The valet-de-chambre dressed the Emperor in his usual clothes: drawers, white kerseymere breeches, white waistcoat, white cravat and over that a black one fastened behind with a buckle, the riband of the Grand Cross of the Legion of Honour, the uniform of colonel of the *chasseurs de la garde* — green with red facings — decorated with the Order of the Legion of Honour, and of the Iron Crown, long riding boots, with small spurs, and lastly a cocked hat.

Napoleon's grave was in the Valley of Silence, about three miles from Longwood. He had chosen the secluded spot himself, near a spring of whose waters he had often drunk. The Emperor had frequently rested under the weeping willows that shaded the fountain.

The exhumation began at one o'clock in the morning of October 15, by the Royal Engineers of the British garrison. First the iron railing enclosing the grave was removed, and then the six-inch stone slab covering it. This gave access to a stone vault fourteen feet deep, six feet wide, and ten feet long, partially filled with earth, beneath which had been placed a layer of ordinary cement. On removing this a layer of heavy stones bound by iron clamps was encountered, the removal of which took five hours. Under this was disclosed the lid of the stone sarcophagus that enclosed the coffins. This sarcophagus was carefully raised from the grave by means of a crane, and conveyed by the soldiers of the 91st Regiment to a tent near at hand, the Abbé Coquereau meanwhile reading the Requiescat. In deep silence the four enclosed coffins of mahogany, lead, mahogany, and tin were successively raised, and the body of Napoleon was disclosed to view.

An English writer — whose modesty has deprived us of his name — described the scene.

The anxiety with which those present waited for the moment that was to expose to them all that death had left of Napoleon, could not be described by even an eye witness of the scene. Notwithstanding the singular state of preservation of the tomb and coffins, they could scarcely hope to find anything but some misshapen remains of the least perishable parts of the costume to evidence the identity of the body. But when the satin sheet was raised, an indescribable feeling of surprise and affection was exhibited by the spectators.

The Emperor himself was before their eyes. The features of his face, though changed, were perfectly recognised — the hands perfectly beautiful — his well-known costume had suffered but little, and the colours were easily distinguished. The uniform of the Chasseurs of the Guard was easily recognisable, though the epaulettes had lost their brightness, as had some of the small decorations placed on the breast. The attitude itself was full of ease, and but for the fragments of the satin lining, which covered as with a fine gauze several parts of the uniform, it might have been believed that Napoleon was before them.

'At this solemn moment,' says the Prince de Joinville, 'at the sight of the easily recognised remains of him who had done so much for the glory of France, the emotion was deep and unanimous.' All were visibly affected, and many burst into tears.

General Bertrand and Marchand, who had been present at the interment, pointed out the different articles which each had deposited in the coffin; and it was even remarked that the left hand, which General Bertrand had taken to kiss for the last time before the coffin was closed, still remained slightly raised.

After an inspection lasting only two minutes, the coffins were closed, carefully re-soldered, and placed in a magnificent ebony sarcophagus (brought from France), which was protected by an oak casket.

The sarcophagus was finely polished and bore upon the top in letters of gold the single word NAPOLEON. Within it had been placed a lead coffin, upon which were engraved branches of laurel and arabesques in bas-relief, with the words, *Napoleon, Empereur et Roi, Mort à Sainte Hélène le V Mai, MDCCCXXI.* A magnificent violet-coloured velvet pall, edged with ermine, studded with Napoleonic bees, and adorned with the Imperial eagle and the letter N in silver brocade, had accompanied the sarcophagus from France.

At half past three in the afternoon, amid torrents of rain, the coffin was placed upon a funeral-car drawn by four horses, and over it was thrown the velvet pall, the corners of which were held by Gourgaud, Arthur Bertrand and Marchand. The Emperor's remains were placed on board *La Belle Poule,* which left Jamestown on October 18 and entered harbour at Cherbourg on December 2, 1840.

The anonymous writer describes how
At Annières, a small village two miles below Courbevoie lay the massive and gorgeous vessel which had been built to convey Napoleon's remains from Vale-de-la-Haie. A receptacle for these had been raised on its deck in the form of an Egyptian temple. This magnificent and expensive piece of craftmanship was not used for the purpose it was destined for, its great weight rendering it impossible it should be towed up by any steamer on the river, in time for the translation to take place on the 15th instant. But the vessel formed part of the convoy from Annières to Courbevoie, and had a magnificent effect. The cortège proceeded slowly to Courbevoie, a small village about four miles from Paris, situated on one of the delightful eminences which diversify the left bank of the Seine, at a short distance from Neuilly.
On December 14, Leon stood below Courbevoie to watch the solemn arrival of the body of the father of whom he had glimpsed so little in life.
William Makepeace Thackeray was moved to exclaim:
They say that on the passage of Napoleon's coffin down the Seine, old soldiers and country people walked miles from their villages just to catch a sight of the boat which carried

his body, and to kneel down on the shore and pray for
him . . . Something great and good must have been in this
man, something loving and kindly, that has kept his name so
cherished in the popular memory, and gained him such
lasting reverence and affection.

When the *Dorade* reached Courbevoie it was about three-thirty in
the afternoon and the sun was going down behind Mont Valérien;
on one side the islands of Neuilly, on the other the hills of
Courbevoie.

It was on the landing stage at Courbevoie that Napoleon's body
rested once more on the soil of France. The decorations on the
quay and at the head of the bridge of Neuilly could not be
completed in time for the ceremony. The wind was so piercingly
cold that the workmen were unable to raise to the top of the
rostral column of Notre Dame de Grace a ball of the world, six
feet in diameter, and a huge eagle which was to crown the whole.

During ten days, [observed a witness] and up to the 14th,
Paris and its vicinity were enveloped in a dense fog; but, as if
on purpose to give brilliance to the spectacle, the sun made
his appearance on the morning of the ceremony, and shone
throughout the day. It has been truly remarked that you
scarcely meet with a Parisian who lived in the time of the
Empire, who does not, when speaking of Napoleon, add,
'How fortunate he was in all his fêtes! It never rained on a
fête day of the Emperor.' His good fortune in this respect
continued beyond the grave, for there never was a lovelier
frosty day than the 15th, and a hundred times during the
ceremony did standers-by hear some remnant of the old army
exclaim, in Napoleon's words at Friedland, 'Tis the sun of
Austerlitz'!

And Thackeray records:

Hundreds of people were marching to and fro, laughing,
chattering, singing, gesticulating, as happy as Frenchmen do
— there is no pleasanter sight than a French crowd on the
alert for a festival, and nothing more catching than their good
humour . . . Itinerant merchants were shouting out lustily
their commodities of segars and brandies, and the weather
was so bitter cold that they could not fail to find plenty of
customers.

The morning was excessively cloudy, the thermometer marking
twenty-two and a half degrees Fahrenheit below zero; but notwithstanding this, long before daylight all Paris was on the move.

Gradually, the windows of the houses adjoining the Rue Point de l'Etoile, the stages in front of or connected with them, the sloping embankment on the south side of the road, and the walks and roadway became crowded, and then commenced the *industrie de circonstance,* for which the Parisian hawkers and pedlars were famous. Independently of barrows laden with *gâteaux de nanterre,* and other cakes of indescribable qualities, all of them, however, saturated with lard, there were portable kitchens in full swing, getting up potatoes and sausages in such an inviting way, that they had all disappeared by noon. There were, besides, lemonade sellers, and to the annoyance of the cafétiers, brandy-merchants.

So far the creature comforts. Then came the intellectual broadsheets — some coloured, some plain — with all manner of representations of the Emperor, ascending to or seated in heaven, surrounded by his Old Guard, or emerging from his tomb at St. Helena, which were thrust before every passer-by, and eagerly purchased. Another set of merchants sold, for three sous each, gilt or plated medals, commemorative of the occasion, to which an *immortelle* was fastened by a piece of black ribbon. Others had everlasting flowers of all colours, but mixed with black. These were earnestly sought after, in order to be worn in the button-hole. Lastly a man drove a roaring trade with little knots of black crèpe, to be similarly worn, or for passing round the arm. While this was going on in the streets, the restaurateurs, so renowned for the glories of the French cuisine, and wine — at six sous the bottle — were crowded to overflow. All the world was excited, busy, bustling, hurried, or otherwise occupied.

The newspaper *France* treated the whole proceedings as a *coup de théâtre.* But Napoleon would probably have approved; for he once observed; 'Noisy festivals are a necessity. Blockheads love noise, and the multitudes are blockheads.

On December 16, 1840, Thackeray rose,

At a very early hour on this eventful morning, while the keen stars were still glittering overhead, a half-moon as sharp as a razor beaming in the frosty sky, and a wicked north-wind blowing, that blew the blood out of one's fingers, and froze your leg as you put it out of bed.

It was said in the newspapers that Lord Granville had despatched circulars to all the English residents in Paris, begging them to keep to their houses. The French journals announced this news, and warned us charitably of the fate intended for us . . .

Fancy then, that the guns are fired at Neuilly, the body
landed at day-break from the funeral barge, and transferred
to the car; a huge juggernaut on four wheels of an antique
shape . . . At the head of the procession the Gendarmerie of
the Seine, with their trumpets and colonel; the mounted
Municipal Guard, with their trumpets, standard, and colonel;
two squadrons of the 7th Lancers, with colonel, standard and
music; the Commandant of Paris and his staff; a battalion of
infantry of the line, with their flag, sappers, drums, music,
and colonel.

His Royal Highness the Prince de Joinville; the five
hundred sailors (from *La Belle Poule*) marching on each side
of the car.

The base of the chariot rested on four massive gilt wheels. It was
twenty-five feet long and six feet high, and presented the form of
a parallelogram, with a semi-circular platform in front. On this
stood a group of four genii, supporting the crown of Charlemagne;
at the four angles were four other genii, in relief, who held
garlands with one hand, and with the other the trumpet of Fame.
Above were fasces, in the middle eagles, and the cypher of the
Emperor surrounded with crowns. The base and its ornaments
were covered with burnished gold.

The pedestal was covered with gold and purple cloth, with the
cypher and arms of the Emperor. On both sides hung two velvet
imperial mantles sprinkled with bees.

Fourteen caryatides supported an immense gold shield loaded
with fasces and javelins. An antique sarcophagus lay on the shield
and in the centre on a rich cushion rested the sceptre, the hand of
justice, and the Imperial crown, studded with jewels.

Thackeray is inspired to render in fanciful and poetic paraphrase Dr. Guillard's description of the Emperor after he had
rested nineteen years beneath a nameless stone in Rupert Valley:

His Majesty, the Emperor and King, reclined on his shield
with his head a little elevated. His Majesty's skull is
voluminous — his forehead broad and large. We remarked
that His Imperial Majesty's brow was of a yellowish colour,
which appearance was also visible about the orbits of the
eyes. He kept his eyelids constantly closed, by which we had
the opportunity of observing that the upper lids were
garnished with eyelashes. Years and climate have effected
upon the face of this great monarch only a trifling alteration,
— we may say indeed, that time has touched his Imperial and

Royal Majesty with the lightest feather in his wing. In the
nose of the Conqueror of Austerlitz, we remarked very little
alteration, — it is of the beautiful shape which we remember
it possessed five-and-twenty years since, ere unfortunate
circumstances induced him to leave us for a while . . .

Vive l'Empereur! The soldier of Marengo is among us
again. His lips are thinner perhaps than they were before; —
how white his teeth are! You can just see three of them
pressing his upper lip, and pray remark the fulness of his
cheeks, and the round contour of his chin. Oh, those
beautiful white hands! Many a time have they patted the
cheek of poor Josephine, and played with the black ringlets
of her hair. She is dead now and cold, poor creature; and so
are Hortense and bold Eugène — 'than whom the world ne'er
saw a courtier knight ' as was said of King Arthur's Sir
Lancelot. What a day it would have been for these three,
could they but have lived until now, and seen their hero
returning! . . .

Where's Ney? His wife sits looking out from M. Flahaut's
window yonder, but the bravest of the brave is not with her.
Murat, too, is absent: honest Joachim loves the Emperor at
heart, and repents that he was not at Waterloo. Who knows
but that at the sight of the handsome swordsman those
stubborn English *canaille* would have given way? — a king,
Sire, is, you know, the greatest of slaves — state affairs of
consequence — His Majesty the King of Naples is detained, no
doubt. When we last saw the king, however, and his Highness
the Prince of Elchingen, they looked to have as good health
as ever they had in their lives; and we heard each of them
calmly calling out 'Fire!' as they have done in numberless
battles before.

Is it possible? Can the Emperor forget? We don't like to
break it to him; but has he forgotten all about the farm at
Pizzo, and the garden of the Observatory? Yes, truly; there
he lies on the golden shield, never stirring, never so much as
lifting his eyelids, or opening his lips any wider.

O vanitas vanitatum! Here is our sovereign in all his glory;
and they fired a thousand guns at Cherbourg, and never
awoke him!

The great Imperial chariot moves on. The cords of the pall
are held by two Marshals, an Admiral, and General
Bertrand . . . Hush! The enormous crowd thrills as it passes,

and only some few voices cry *'Vive l'Empereur!'* Shining golden in the frosty sun, with hundreds of thousands of eyes upon it, from houses and house-tops, from balconies black, purple, and tricolours, from tops of leafless trees, from behind long lines of glittering bayonets, under schakos and bearskin caps, from behind the line of the National Guards again, pushing, struggling, heaving, panting, eager, the head of an enormous multitude stretching out to meet and follow it. Amidst long avenues of columns and statues gleaming white, of standards, rainbow-coloured, of golden eagles, of pale funeral urns, of discharging odours amidst huge volumes of pitch black smoke.

The fifty foot high carriage was drawn by sixteen black horses, yoked by fours, and so caparisoned as only to show the extremity of the feet. The caparisons were cut in the shape of those of the tournament horses of the middle ages, and in cloth of gold. The manes were adorned with gold tresses and white plumes; and valets, dressed in the livery of the Emperor, led the horses.

Here were, in all their variety of uniform (some of them approaching to the grotesque, and others to the acme of military costume) the soldiers of Hoche and Marceau, of Moreau, Jourdan, Massena, Augereau, Lannes, Kilmaine, Davoust, Ney, Berthier, Lasalle, Murat, Bernadotte, Bessières, Kléber, Kellerman. Here were represented all arms — of the Imperial Guard, Horse Grenadiers, Cuirassiers, Dragoons, Lancers, Hussars, Chasseurs, Grenadiers, Fusileers, Chasseurs à pied, Pontoneers, Marines, Guides, and even Mamelukes.

Among the glorious débris of the Grande Armée were the Polish Lancers of the Guard; and a *chef d'escadron* of the Mamelukes of the Guard — on whom every eye was turned. The general belief was that this individual was the favourite Mameluke of Napoleon; but he (Rustam) is, we believe, dead. At all events, his desertion of his Imperial master, as it was deemed, would have prevented his figuring today among those whose presence proclaimed their undying attachment to him. There were also one or two of the Red Lancers of the Guard. They tended to vary a scene which the monotonous red and blue of the National Guard and troops of the line had begun to render painful to the vision.

At length the chariot arrived, preceded by a charger magnificently caparisoned, and led by two servants of the deceased Emperor in state livery. Shouts of 'Long live the Emperor!' rent the air, and contrasted strongly with the cries of 'Down with Guizot!', 'Down with the English!', and 'Down with Palmerston!' raised by students, but which were not in any single instance responded to.

Medical and law students who had been denied participation in the procession, nevertheless accompanied the cortège as far as the Place de la Concorde, and then ascended the Rue Royale and the boulevards. Singing the *Marseillaise* they reached the Ministry of Foreign Affairs, where they yelled: 'Death to Guizot! Hang him from a lamp post! Chuck Guizot in the Thames! Long live Thiers!'

Napoleon's famous war-horse Marengo had long since passed on, but the bridle, saddle and spurs borne by the charger that followed the Emperor's body were his own. Then came the Commission of Saint Helena, the Marshals of France, and the Eighty-Six Eagles, representing the eighty-six Departments of the Kingdom. His Royal Highness the Prince de Joinville and his staff preceded the funeral car, which was guarded by five hundred seamen who had accompanied the remains of Napoleon from St. Helena. Marshals Oudinot and Molitor, General Bertrand, and Admiral Roussin, all on horseback, held the cordons of the pall.

At two o'clock the funeral-car reached the gateway of the Hôtel des Invalides, where it was met by the Archbishop of Paris, attended by sixteen acolytes and accompanied by his bishops and clergy. There the coffin of Napoleon was placed upon the shoulders of thirty-two of the Emperor's Old Guard. Preceded by the Prince de Joinville and his suite, and accompanied by Generals Bertrand and Gourgaud, the remains were conveyed across the Esplanade and the Cour d'honneur of the Invalides in the presence of more than thirty-six thousand people.

Louis Philippe received Napoleon's body at the entrance to the Invalides.

'Sire,' said the Prince de Joinville, 'I present to you the body of the Emperor Napoleon;' to which the king replied: 'I receive it in the name of France.'

Inside the Invalides Louis Philippe said to Bertrand: 'General, I charge you to place this the glorious sword of the Emperor upon his coffin;' and, holding out the famous black tricorne, 'General Gougaud, place on the coffin the hat of the Emperor.' The cortège then moved to the catafalque to the music of Mozart's Requiem.

Thus was fulfilled the Emperor's wish, when he rested finally beneath the gallery adorned with Simart's ten white marble reliefs depicting the chief civil events of his reign: the Reformation of the Public Administration; the Restoration of Public

Order; the Promulgation of the Code; the signing of the
Concordat; the Execution of Public Works, the Protection of
Commerce and Industry; the Foundation of the University; the
Administration of the Finances; the Institution of the Council of
State; and the establishment of the Legion of Honour.

From the great host of generals who witnessed the Emperor's
return, however, one of Napoleon's companions of St. Helena was
absent. From his second exile — at the side of a later Bonaparte —
General Montholon had written to Marshal Soult, an old comrade
of Waterloo:

Citadel of Ham, December 1, 1840

Monsieur le Maréchal,

To accompany to their last abode the mortal remains of the
Emperor is a right which I would claim if I were free, and
which I implore as a grace, now that I am a prisoner. I intreat
you to accede to my respectful and pressing prayer. Deign to
allow me to fulfil the pious and filial duty, and I pledge
myself by oath that the same sentiment of honour and
fidelity which led me to St. Helena, and bound me there
while the Emperor lived, and which threw me on the coast of
Boulogne, will induce me to return to the walls of Ham
immediately after the funeral ceremony.

At almost the very moment — on October 7, 1840, when *La Belle
Poule* was dropping anchor off St. Helena to bring home the body
of his exiled father — Leon's 'little cousin' was entering the
fortress of Ham, on France's bleak northern marshes as a prisoner.

Prince Louis Napoleon Bonaparte, 32 years old, had left his
friend Orsi's house, at 18 Stockbridge Terrace in Pimlico, on
August 4, to board the paddle steamer *Edinburgh Castle* at
Gravesend. His intention was to invade France!

The previous evening Prince Louis had appeared at a dinner in
Gore House, Kensington, wearing a black satin neckerchief secured
by a large spread-eagle in diamonds clutching a thunderbolt of
rubies. He had mystified Lord Blessington's guests by inviting
them to drink with him at the Tuileries 'this day twelve month.'

At 1 Carlton Gardens, Dr. Conneau had prepared Imperial
proclamations on a printing press in the basement:

Soldiers:

France was destined to take orders and she obeys. You are
the nation's élite and they treat you like a vulgar rabble. You
have sought the resting-place of the eagles of Arcole, of
Austerlitz, of Jena. Here they are! I restore them to you!

Louis's invasion force numbering fifty-five persons received 100 francs apiece for their services. On August 6 the *Edinburgh Castle* anchored off Pointe aux Oies, near Wimereux; and with Montholon and Parquin Prince Louis led his party ashore at three o'clock in the morning. At five o'clock they had reached Boulogne, a distance of six miles.

The prince's invading force handed out their rousing pamphlets to such early risers as they found along their route, and presented five franc pieces to a crowd of vagabonds who had placed themselves at the head of the company.

At Boulogne the Strasbourg fiasco of four years ago was re-enacted. In their barracks the men of the 42nd Regiment of the Line — just getting out of bed — were startled by the sudden appearance of Louis and his troupe. An officer offered resistance, whereupon the prince drew a pistol and fired; but his shot went wide and hit a soldier, who died later in the day.

The Imperial force withdrew and attempted to suborn another guard post, without success. They found other entrances blocked; and decided to withdraw into the fields where they brought up at the Napoleon monument. The door at the base was broken open and a member of the party climbed the stairs to plant a flag on the summit. To Louis's nicknames was added that of 'The Child of the Column'.

Montholon and Parquin, who had made for the harbour, were arrested by a police superintendent — while the *Edinburgh Castle* had already been seized by the Lieutenant of the Port. Hunted by the National Guard, the prince's party made for the shore, where Louis managed to regain the small landing boat. But under musket fire the craft capsized and he was captured.

'The poor wretch is in a sad state,' wrote *The Times* correspondent; but the local French press took a more cynical line.

On August 12, *Le Boulonnais* listed the contents of the *Edinburgh Castle:*

Five swords, two sabres, three pistols, and a sword-stick, but not a single musket. It had been reported that the money on board amounted to half a million francs. There were twenty-one napoleons, six sovereigns, two five franc pieces, three two-franc pieces, one one-franc piece, and a little medal inscribed *Perruques perfectionées.*

There were nine horses, one live eagle (which had never left the boat), two new carriages, new uniforms, twenty-four hampers of wines and spirits, regimentals, about twenty-four hampers of 'excellent' wine, beer, ginger-beer, soda-water and brandy, a lady's *nécessaire*, an album containing Prince Louis's views of Arenenberg, and *'Distances érotiques'*, written, according to the Boulogne reporter by the prince.

The crew were nineteen in number. Then there were three grooms — the Comtesse d'Aspell's groom, the prince's and his valet. In the trunks and carpet-bags there were fine evening clothes which, according to the reporter, were to have been worn at a magnificent ball at the Etablissement des Bains in the evening of the 6th. 'Folly and deception,' is the verdict of the *Boulonnais*.

The eagle — which was probably a vulture — had been tendered by a London urchin on the quayside before the main party embarked; and Parquin immediately purchased it as a happy omen. To induce the bird to flap symbolically about his head, Louis Napoleon secreted a piece of bacon in the band of his hat. After the prince's capture the vulture was consigned to the Boulogne abattoir; but happily it escaped and fetched up in a coal merchant's house at Arras. The bird's owner, the tragi-comic Colonel Parquin, died in prison at Doullens.

From his fortress on the Somme estuary, Prince Louis Napoleon heard of the homecoming of the Emperor's remains, and wrote:

To the Manes of the Emperor, Citadel of Ham, 15 December, 1840.

Sire, You return to your capital, and the people in multitudes hailed your return; whilst I from the depths of my dungeon can glimpse but a ray of that sun which shines upon your obsequies!

With compassion mingled with disapproval George Sand wrote to Louis Napoleon quoting Falstaff, 'God save thee, my sweet boy.'

But all was not gloom in the castle of Ham. Montholon and Conneau were there. And the prince conducted experiments in a well-appointed chemical laboratory. To help Louis with his washing, the prison governor allowed visits from a local girl, Eléonore Vergeot, who, although given the soubriquet *La Belle Sabotière* was in fact the daughter of a weaver and not a clog-maker. The prince tutored the beautiful Eléonore; and in return she helped him to make his bed — and ultimately shared it. A police report of 1843 confirmed that the authorities winked at this liaison, which was blessed by the birth of two sons: Alexandre Louis Eugene was born on February 25, 1843, and Alexandre Louis Ernest on March 18, 1845. In the tradition of most official bastards, Louis's two sons entered government service. Eugène was sent as a diplomat to Russia where he ran off with the mistress of the French ambassador. He was posted as consul to Zanzibar, and in 1869 received the title of Count d'Orx. Alexandre Louis Ernest became a Collector of Taxes and married in Mexico. His arms bore the motto *semper recte*. On June 11, 1870, he was created Count de Labenne, a title which derived — like that of Eugene — from properties settled on the brothers in the *Landes,* the ancient Gascon territories bordering on the bay of Biscay.

One of Louis Napoleon's female visitors, however, was compelled to remain without the 15th century walls of the fortress of Ham; for after an arduous journey to visit her hero, she could only gaze on the future Napoleon III distantly, from the edge of a moat. The woman was to form a bizarre link between the sculptor of the Napoleon Column at Boulogne, Prince Louis — and his cousin Leon.

She was denied entrance to the castle and in her agitation she made her way to one of the towers which Louis Napoleon was known to visit. He had been informed of her coming and stood by a window which looked out on to a piece of water. The actress stood motionless, and in order that the prisoner would know she had come only for him, she sang with all her soul the *Lisette* by Beranger. The singer has described how, at the end of the aria, she blew a kiss to the prisoner who waved three times with his handkerchief as the early morning sun lit up his pale heavy features. When she met him later, in London during her season at St. James's Theatre in King Street, Louis Napoleon showed her on his watch chain the religious medal she had left for him at the castle gate.

The woman who had been denied access to the prison of the future Emperor of France was Virginie Déjazet. Born in Paris in 1798, she first appeared on the stage at the age of five in a one-act vaudevillle by de Ponet at the Théâtre des Capucines; and was a member of the Gymnase Dramatique in 1823 when the sixteen year old Leon made his abrupt exit from that theatre. It was during those fading days of the reign of Louis XVIII that she began her famous series of rôles in male costume.

Described as a great actress in modest parts, a mélange of finesse and seduction, of grace and mischief, she created a very personal style which subsequently bore her name. One of her great successes was in *Bonaparte at Brienne,* in which she played the 14 year old Napoleon at boarding school. 'Mademoiselle Déjazet personified another face of comedy,' observed Henri d'Almeras, 'the familiar and unaffected side. A great lady; she was never afraid of portraying — both on stage and a little in her private life — the most exquisite of *grisettes.*'

She was an ardent admirer of Napoleon, and Arthur Bertrand is said to have written especially for her the account of his return to St. Helena. He had been born on the island during the Emperor's exile; and it was in the carriage of his father, General Bertrand, that on June 29, 1815, Napoleon left Paris for the last time. The day after Arthur Bertrand met Djazet — on June 22, 1834 — his mother, Countess Bertrand, had sent a lock of Napoleon's hair to her son's future mistress.

The occasion of Déjazet's introduction to Leon was a cottage at Seine-Port, an arrondissement of Melun on the right bank of the river near Fontainebleau, which the actress was in the process of buying. The vendor was Bossio — the sculptor of the statue of the Emperor atop the Grande Armée column on the cliffs above Boulogne.

The exiguous fragment of correspondence that has survived shows that the transaction followed the usual unhappy course of Leon's business dealings.

In a letter dated Friday, July 29, 1841, Arthur Bertrand complains to Bossio.

> Yesterday I wrote to Count Leon. Last night I dropped in on him to leave your note personally, and asked him to be sure to let you have a reply before mid-day today. I do not know if you have seen him, or if his representative has called on you; but I admit to you that the promise he made to Mlle. Déjazet — so far as I know anyway — has not been fulfilled.
>
> I saw his agent yesterday and he indulged in small talk for an hour by way of refusal. I hope that Mr Quin or yourself can settle this matter. I believe the purchase of this property is a mistake which is going to cause Mlle. Déjazet much trouble. I shall have the pleasure of seeing you today, or of sending you a note.

Déjazet wrote to Arthur Bertrand from Boulogne where she was appearing in a play:

> What you say about Count Leon surprises and angers me. After all, I was not the one who asked him to do this for me — he practically threw it into my lap; and here he is today asking for a guarantee! Offer him an assignment of the box-office takings for four months; but if you can do something elsewhere, don't hesitate to rid me of this gentle-

man, who has already caused me so much trouble that I
cannot bring myself to feel the slightest gratitude.

Besides — what I have been told about him explains his
lack of good faith. No one likes him; and one can't even
make allowances on account of his birth. On all sides I hear
them saying, 'Ah! Count Leon — he's a bad lot!'

You ask me to keep my good temper; what do you think I
stand to gain by losing it?

If I write to him I shall be too frank to hide my
annoyance. That is why I came away without seeing him. If
he gets me out of a jam I shall be obliged to thank him, and
you have no idea what that would cost me. I hope to God
you will be successful elsewhere, then I shall be delighted to
write and tell him what I think.

In spite of the impression given in her letter, Virginie Déjazet was
by no means in dire straits.

Just three months before writing to her lover she had been given
a contract by the Comédie Francaise which assured her an annual
salary of 20,000 francs until April 7, 1844. And she was continually pressing Bertrand who was a confirmed gambler for the 500
francs he had owed her since 1840.

The circumstances surrounding Leon's transaction with the
actress are tantalisingly obscure; but de Mauvières certainly had
property in the Melun region: for at the family council of March
25, 1812, the baron is cited as the owner of the estate of Marcilly
in the Melun arrondissement of Evry-les-Châteaux, Seine-et-Marne,
which he was obliged to mortgage as a guarantee to the court
when he became Leon's guardian.

Leon *was* in dire straits. He had apparently no more success in
the arcane world of French immovables than he had when treating
with horse traders or art dealers; or in the export to London of oil
lamps, 'superior to those named Carcel.' He did possess, however,
the Bonaparte talent for writing letters, and he continued to
bombard the survivors of Waterloo with appeals for aid; which one
of them at least was unable to resist.

Baron Gaspard de Gourgaud, born in 1783, was Napoleon's
aide-de-camp from 1811 until he accompanied the Emperor into
exile on St. Helena. He returned from St. Helena in 1818 — three
years before Napoleon's death — for reasons which are somewhat
obscure. Nevertheless, while on the island General Gourgaud was
the repository of some of Napoleon's frankest confidences. He had
saved the Emperor's life when it was threatened by a Cossack

lance; had carried pistols for his son at Vincennes; and his debt to
the Emperor was yet uncancelled. Between 1840 and 1845
Gourgaud lent to Leon various sums totalling 650 francs.

The unfortunate baron now had Leon for a neighbour, and
from a house a few doors away in a street off the Chausée d'Antin
he continued to receive importunate letters. In a note written on
Friday, July 25, 1845, from No. 3 Rue Joubert, Leon alludes to
the protracted legal actions in which he is claiming a share of the
dowry given to his mother by Napoleon:

My dear General,

I have been to your house several times and it is only
today that I learn of your illness. Although I believe your
health gives no cause for alarm I should be grateful for a
word of reassurance.

You have been exceedingly generous towards me; since the
return of the Emperor's remains to France you have
advanced me on three occasions a total of 650 francs. For
that I shall always be grateful; for in this century of
selfishness and depravity you have shown yourself noble and
good to me. I thank you for it with all my heart.

My mother could not have behaved more unkindly
towards me. By means of one ruse and subterfuge after
another she is dragging out the case. Knowing my circumstances she is trying to starve me into submission; but thanks
to God, if you do not abandon me I shall triumph over all
obstacles, and emerge triumphant from this battle which has
been going on since 1840.

In order to retrieve some pieces of documentary evidence
which a business man by the name of Justou was witholding
from me illegally it was necessary to use force. Because of
this I was summoned to the police court. I could not deny
the evidence and I have been fined 110 francs. My dear
general, I do not have this money and I count on your help.
You will see from the enclosed paper that my personal
liberty is at stake.

Please allow me to see you for a moment tomorrow,
Saturday, so that I may shake your hand. For if I am truly in
need of money, you cannot prevent my seeing you and
showing you all my gratitude for your many kindnesses.

With all my heart and soul, dear General,

Yours, Comte Leon.

While Leon was having recourse to begging letters, his mother,

Eleonore, and the Count de Luxbourg had been entertaining the
beau monde. The youthful Ferdinand von Strantz — who later
became director of the Berlin State Opera — wrote: 'At the home
of the Bavarian Minister, Count de Luxbourg, where Jenny Lind
was entertained, I met the celebrated singing teacher, Professor
Manuel Garcia, whose famous pupil she was.'

On March 20, 1846 Leon addressed the citizens of St. Denis
who, as children years before celebrated him with fireworks:

Leon, natural son of the Emperor Napoleon, to the citizens
of the arrondissement of St. Denis.

A child of Paris, you are well acquainted with my birth; it
is glorious and I have preferred to fight face to face against
my adversaries' scandalous and unceasing chicaneries of every
sort, rather than soil it by rallying to a Government that
inspires in a man of integrity only scorn and mistrust.

My dear fellow citizens, it is the earnest wish of several of
my old comrades of the St. Denis battalion — which I had the
honour of commanding — that I should offer myself for your
votes. I accept this candidature with gratitude, and I would
like to tell you in a few words the line of action I propose to
take should you deign to honour me with your confidence.

Since I lived among you, dear fellow citizens, you have
been aware of the unswerving aim of my researches and of
my studies — the wish that lies nearest to my heart — the
assurance of the material and spiritual well being of the
people.

Great things have been achieved in the past few years;
there remain no less great things to accomplish.

I will cite only one of these — which to my eyes embraces
all the others: to bring down the cost of living to a normal
level, in such a manner that a man's normal wages will suffice
to maintain himself and his family.

This is a complex question: the solution demands above all
the suppression of gambling in stocks and shares, which
throws away capital diverted from agriculture and industry
into the pit of unproductive speculations.

This, then, my dear fellow citizens, is the order of my
ideas and one which — if you will charge me to represent you
in the Legislative Assembly — I shall strive after by developing our institutions.

Count Leon, former Commandant of the National Guard
of St. Denis.

To attract to himself the votes of the burgesses of the royal
northern suburb of Paris, Leon did not appeal like his father to the
sentiment of *la gloire;* but to a matter which rarely exercised the
Emperor's attention — the price of bread. Just two months after
his address to the electors of St. Denis, an event occurred which
was to have a profound effect on Leon's future finances: his
cousin, Louis Napoleon, escaped — after six years' imprisonment
from the fortress of Ham. The prince's continued detention must
by now have been proving an embarrassment to Louis Philippe.[3]

On Monday morning, May 25, 1846, Louis Napoleon shaved off
his moustache and blacked his face with burnt-cork. Putting on a
blue workman's blouse, and sabots — obtained for him by Charles
Thélin — he removed a bookshelf from his library and hoisted it
on to his shoulder to conceal one side of his face.

At 6.30 a.m. a party of workmen arrived at the castle; and in
order to leave the coast clear for the escape, Charles Thélin took
the men away for a drink. As Louis passed the first sentry, he
allowed his pipe to fall and stopped and knelt down to pick up the
pieces. But the officer of the guard was reading a letter and paid
no heed to the 'workman' carrying a plank of wood. The prince
crossed the courtyard in front of the Governor's windows and
approached the castle gate. Here the soldiers, especially the
drummer, eyed him several times. The gate was opened by an
orderly; and Louis passed through, hiding his face from two
workmen just entering, who exclaimed, 'Oh! It's Berthoud.'

Once outside the fortress Louis strode off briskly along the St.
Quentin road, where he was overtaken by Thélin in a cab. The
prince got rid of his labourer's blouse and the two walked into St.
Quentin where Louis Napoleon boarded a train for Brussels. The
faithful Dr. Conneau remained at Ham and reported the prince
sick to give him time to reach the Belgian frontier.[3] A few days
after his escape Prince Loius put up at the Brunswick Hotel, 52
Jermyn Street.

Leon, meanwhile, was being housed and fed by the wife of an
old general who, as Mâitre Crémieux declared in December, 1846,
'could not forget what she and her husband owed to the memory
of the Emperor.' Crémieux, the celebrated advocate, after lengthy
proceedings managed to secure a small alimentary pension for

Leon, who had been so munificent with his mother and her family during the days of his youthful affluence. The measure of Crémieux's triumph can only be appreciated by reference to that Civil Code which at the instance of Napoleon had compounded the difficulties of the illegitimate child.

CHAPTER 9

An Affiliation Order against a Mother

Leon was now thirty eight years old and still casting around for the means to survive. On October 22, 1845, he brought an action against his mother in the vacation court of the Civil Tribunal of the Seine for a maintenance allowance of 6,000 francs a year.

The correspondent of the *Gazette des Tribunaux* recorded the customary shock of recognition:

> Count Leon is present at the hearing, and seeing him one is struck by the resemblance of his features to those of the Imperial head. Viewed especially from the side his face, of severe and formal cast exactly recalls the profile of Napoleon.

Leon's birth certificate was to be read out so many times that all Paris must have had it by heart:

> Monday, 15 December, 1806, Leon, of male sex, born 13th of this month, at 2 a.m., Rue de la Victoire No. 29, in the Mont Blanc District, son of Mademoiselle Eleonore Denuel, of independent means, aged twenty, and of an absent father.
>
> The witnesses were Messieurs Jacques René Marie Aymé, Treasurer of the Legion of Honour, and Guillaume Andral, doctor of medicine at the Imperial Hospital of the Invalides.

The mis-spelling of Eleonore's surname, the omission of her other names, and the error in her age were to be vital issues in her denial of Leon's claim to an alimentary pension.

The court room echoed to the most illustrious names of the Empire as letters were read from General Bertrand, Count de las Cases, and Marchand — all companions of the prisoner of St. Helena.

In the distribution of a sum of 700,000 francs destined by the Emperor to satisfy the bequests known as the 'legacies of conscience', a sum of 300,000 francs was to be left to 'the ward of the father-in-law of de Meneval — Baron de Mauvières — called Leon.' This sum was to be employed, in buying in the very year of Napoleon's death, a parcel of land for the young Leon.

Napoleon's thoughts on the future career of Leon, who was at the time of his father's death fourteen years old, are contained in the often-repeated Article 37 of the instructions dictated on St. Helena: 'I should not be sorry if little Leon were to enter the magistrature, if that were to his taste.'

Now the magistrature had the task of mediating between the Emperor's mistress of 1806 and her son. Eleonore was not in court. She was at her home in Mannheim where her husband had been director of the state theatre. Her lawyers had twice succeeded in postponing the case and Maître Delorme who requested a third adjournment was in very deep water. His was the classic nightmare of the junior counsel holding the fort for his master in a superior court and on an issue about which he had slight notion how to proceed. Unlike most pupils in his dilemma, Delorme was devastatingly frank about his abilities.

'The postponement that I beg of the court,' he pleaded, 'is justified by the state of the affair and by my own personal position. It is Maître Marie's task to appear for the Countess de Luxbourg. Count Leon's demand for a maintenance allowance conceals a grave question of status with which it is not mine to deal — lacking as I am the experience and eloquence of Maître Marie.'

Delorme submitted that the question of Leon's capacity must be argued before his request for an alimentary pension could be entertained — and that in any case the question of status was not proper to a vacation court. He then asked to see the documents on which Leon's claim to be the son of the Countess de Luxbourg was based, maintaining that any document of title should in itself be a complete proof of Leon's affiliation; and that furthermore the lady named in the birth certificate as Leon's mother did not correspond with the Countess de Luxbourg in name, quality or age.

The Bonaparte family itself had never worried over much about such details. At his wedding, Napoleon — like Lucien before him — borrowed his brother Joseph's birth certificate and Josephine that of her sister Catherine. (The British Navy was at the time effectively guarding the true documents in Corsica and Martinique respectively.) Thus at their marriage Napoleon gained a year and Josephine lost four.

Me. Delorme, having somewhat mastered his diffidence, went on to give a summary of Eleonore's marital adventures.

'Mlle. Louise Catherine Eleonore Denuelle de Laplaigne was married first to M. Revel. In the month of May 1806 she applied

for and obtained a divorce. M. Revel — her divorced husband —
brought an action in respect of the birth certificate produced
today by Count Leon. As his birth could be ascribed to a period
when the marriage still subsisted, M. Revel, profiting from the
scandal, brought an action for disavowal of paternity in the Court
of Cassation. The court refused to entertain the case and noted
simply that Count Leon was not the son of M. Revel. Thus only
one issue was determined — that the birth certificate now
produced by Count Leon does not prove the relationship he claims
today.

Me. Delorme ran out of law and repeated his arguments about
the inconclusiveness of Leon's birth certificate. However, he again
betrayed his real reason for requesting a postponement when he
concluded, 'The case will benefit by the delaying of a decision
until after Me. Marie has been heard.'

It seems that Master Delorme was not temperamentally suited
to the highly-charged atmosphere of the *salle des pas perdus,* for
on at least one occasion he resorted to extra-legal remedies. Leon
and he were to meet again in a much more direct encounter.

In contrast to Me. Delorme's uncertain style, Leon's counsel —
Maître Nogent Saint Laurens — began smoothly: 'May I be
permitted to declare at the outset that only the urgency of this
matter prevented our acceding to the adjournment requested by
an absent colleague.' Sweeping aside the doubts cast upon the
birth certificate he said, 'It is impossible that the Countess de
Luxbourg should have given a mandate to dispute Count Leon his
quality as her son.' But she had!

He described the objections to Eleonore's description on the
birth entry as 'puerile chicaneries' and with crushing logic
continued, 'It will be remembered that M. Revel, the first husband
of the Countess de Luxbourg, formulated a claim for disavowal of
the paternity of Leon. That alone proves the truth of the birth of
Count Leon, for it is quite true that one can only disown the child
of one's wife — and M. Revel was the husband of Eleonore
Denuelle!'

He alluded to the pending case referred to by Me. Delorme in
which Leon was claiming part of the capital investment settled on
Eleonore through several intermediaries by Napoleon at the time
of her second marriage:

'It was incontestably in her capacity as mother of Count Leon.'

Me. Boudin then produced a touching letter which witnessed
above all to the regard in which Leon was held by his grandmother

and aunt. 'The day before yesterday,' said Me. Boudin, 'I received from Mannheim a letter from Mme. de Laplaigne, the mother of the Countess de Luxbourg and grandmother of Count Leon. This letter, addressed to myself, was enclosed in an envelope in which the sister of the Countess de Luxbourg had written these words: 'I beg you M. Boudin, advocate of Count Leon; to be so very kind as to give him the enclosed letter from my mother. It is essential that he should receive it. Accept my thanks in advance. Yours, Zulma de Laplaigne".'

Eleonore's mother wrote as follows:

My dear grandson,

It is my duty not to leave you in ignorance of the fact that since she returned from Paris your mother is — in spite of what I have written — sweet, always attentive, tender with her sister, and has had her eyes opened on the troubles of the past. It is to be deplored that among us — even in the school where I placed her — there have always been flatterers.

I count on the largeness of your heart to understand that these my thoughts are prompted only by a desire for the truth, and by my sorrow at the state in which I see your mother.

Adieu my grandson, Your affectionate grandmother, Widow Denuelle de la Plaigne.

The court decided that following the submission of M. Royer, *Avocat du Roi,* the birth certificate and other documents did indeed furnish proof that Leon was the son of Mademoiselle Eleonore Denuelle de Laplaigne, Countess de Luxbourg, and having regard to the urgency of the request for a maintenance allowance ordered the case to be argued. Me. Nogent Saint Laurens, in the absence of substantive evidence for the Countess de Luxbourg, summarised Leon's case, and the court ordered her to pay him a living allowance of 6,000 francs a year.

Eleonore, however, did not allow the matter to rest there. She made default in payment, and another court held that the first tribunal was not competent to rule on Leon's status.

A huge crowd was assembled in the second chamber of the Royal Court of Paris on February 12, 1846, to see once again the classic features of Leon as he sat outside the bar. He had come to claim a portion of the dowry settled on his mother in 1808 by the Emperor Napoleon.

The celebrated advocate Maître Crémieux described Eleonore's second marriage on February 1, 1808 to a M. Augier de la

Saussaye, infantry lieutenant. 'The powerful and invisible hand which had presided over this union assured to the bride as a dowry the income for life from Government stock amounting to 22,000 francs. But the donor — wishing to remain anonymous — made the necessary capital available through a Sieur Henry, a confidential agent attached to the household of Murat.

'This investment was at first acquired and registered in the name of M. Henry, who immediately transferred it by marriage settlement to Mlle. Denuelle, wife of M. Augier. It is evident from the conditions which accompanied the registration of this investment that after the death of her father and mother and of her husband the 22,000 francs, non-transferable and not subject to seizure for debt etc., must belong to Count Leon and in the case of his earlier death should return to the State.

'In fact, in order to guarantee the execution of these terms, M. Henry had signed a declaration in favour of a person whose name remained blank, thus proving that the investment capital belonged to this unnamed person whose name would be added at the appropriate time and place.

'M. Augier de la Saussaye is believed to have perished in the disastrous campaign of 1812. In 1814 Mme. Augier, now a widow, entered upon a third marriage, this time to the Count de Luxbourg, and has lived with her husband in Mannheim ever since.

'During these nuptial peregrinations what became of young Leon? He had as guardian the Baron de Meneval and for tutor Monsieur Vieillard, who is today a member of the Chamber of Deputies. One day he escaped their surveillance to go off and join his mother. This was in the month of January, 1823.

'Some years later M. de Meneval, yielding to the entreaties of the mother and to pressure from the son, consented to release of his ward a year before his majority.

'We must admit that Count Leon foolishly dissipated and squandered his youth. But it is hardly up to Mme. de Luxbourg to reproach him with this; for if he was prodigal he was always generous to her and to all the members of her family, right up to the day when his fortune had melted away.'

Maître Crémieux came now to the episode of Eleonore's mysterious dowry in which Napoleon had covered his traces most thoroughly by using as intermediary Prince Murat, Aymé the Treasurer of the Legion of Honour, and finally a man of straw — M. Henry, a jurisconsult of Paris.

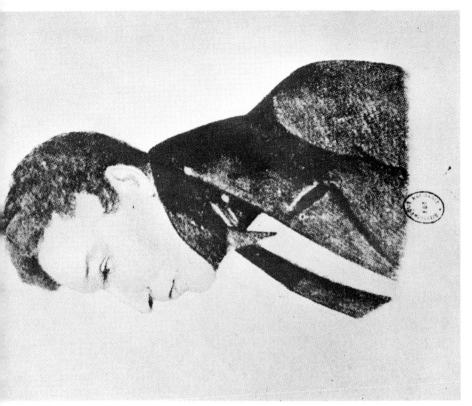

Profile sketch of Count Leon. Compare the profile with that of the Antommarchi death mask of Napoleon (*facing page 97*)

Count Leon at the age of 27, wearing the uniform of a major in the National Guard of St. Denis

Baron de Méneval. *After a lithograph by Auguste Bry*

Baron Claude-François de Méneval, private secretary to Napoleon, and later guardian to Count Leon. *From a miniature*

'On the death of M. Henry an action took place between his heirs, the de Luxbourgs, Eleonore's mother, and M. Aymé, Baron de Chevaillière on the validity of the settlement made by Henry.' The hearing of the dispute with Henry's heirs had taken place at Château-Thierry, a small town near Soissons and Rheims, where fourteen years previously Napoleon had met Blücher in one of the Emperor's last battles before abdication and Elba.

Me. Crémieux described how Leon had handed over to one of the most honourable members of the Paris bar – Masson – a sum of 25,000 francs, to buy-off Henry's heirs and to reimburse Baron Aymé his costs.

Leon's magnanimous gesture seems to have been in vain, for on August 30, 1828 – Leon was then twenty one – the Tribunal of Château-Thierry declared that M. Henry had furnished no funds for the purchase of the Government stock of 22,000 francs and that his heirs had no claim to the investment.

Leon, however, had paid the 25,000 francs to Eleonore on condition that his name would be inscribed as beneficiary of the reversionary investment. It seemed to him unnecessary to receive a written declaration to this effect, since at that period Leon and his mother were living in perfect harmony.

Nevertheless on various pretexts Eleonore had subsequently dishonoured her undertaking. It was objected that the original registration of the investment contained a part share in favour of Eleonore's second husband, Augier, and that because his death had not been proved no change could be made in the particulars inscribed.

In view of the fact that to deprive Leon of his claim Eleonore had been brazen enough to invoke the possible survival of her second husband it is not surprising that Leon accused her of bigamy! It was further objected that the widow – of the doubtfully-departed Augier – having re-married, the consent of her new husband, Count de Luxbourg, was necessary to any re-arrangement of the terms of the dowry.

Eleonore was in effect saying, 'The death of my late husband has never been proved; but even if he is dead I need the consent of my present husband!' Augier's death had in fact been certified by a French court of law. The French Treasury had added to Leon's agony by maintaining that the stock was not transferable and that on the death of the beneficiaries named and in the absence of any children of Eleonore the investment would revert to the State. Leon was not considered to be the child of his mother!

To overcome all these obstacles Eleonore at length agreed some three years later on June 17, 1831, to transfer to Leon the right to part of the capital investment — 16,000 francs. This agreement was subject to the consent of the Count de Luxbourg. He never gave it.

The years rolled on. When Leon was thirty three years old, on May 9, 1840, Eleonore, subject always to ratification by her husband acknowledged and declared that she had always regarded Leon as being entitled to the capital investment of 22,000 francs. Leon, recklessly assuming that this time the de Luxbourgs would keep faith, assigned the right to 3,000 francs of his reversionary interest to a Monsieur Daublaine. The Treasury refused to sanction the transfer.

Leon then once more requested his step-father to honour the agreement. Upon the Count de Luxbourg's final refusal Leon angered by the twelve-year delay and the abuse of his generosity, summoned Eleonore and the Count before a police court. He accused them of converting to their benefit securities which were his property, and by fraudulent means obstructing the performance of a contract freely and legitimately entered into. Eleonore and her husband replied with an action for malicious prosecution. This case did not materialise and Leon dropped his complaint.

Maître Crémieux tersely describes the final rupture: 'But our adversaries became annoyed and all relations between the parties ceased. The Count and Countess de Luxbourg abrogated their agreement of June 17, 1831. It was necessary to sue.'

He insisted that faced with the facts it was impossible to doubt that the intention of the donor was to secure the capital of the investment for the child — the reason for the gift. Mme. de Luxbourg had admitted so herself in her letters.

Maître Crémieux pointed out the only logical reason for the blank in the marriage settlement. It was not intended for Henry, a mere figurehead, nor was it for the benefit of Baron Aymé, who had merely channelled the funds to Henry. For who else could it be intended if not for the child of Eleonore and the shadowy donor — the Emperor?

But this is the year 1846. Louis Philippe is now on the throne of France and another Bonaparte is in England plotting his overthrow. The judges are royal judges. They are not prepared to defy the Treasury. It is arguable that but for the intervention of a government department the Bench would have upheld Leon's right to have his name endorsed on the deed as ultimate beneficiary after the death of his mother.

Maître Marie resumed his case. He had learned not to leave his brief again to Delorme, and today he appeared in person for Eleonore. He argued cogently against the transfer of any part of her interest in the 22,000 francs to Leon. Whether or not he was her son did not affect the matter. If Leon had a right it was a right in expectation that he would exercise after his mother's death. Here he read out the conditions laid down in the original settlement. It demonstrates in an impressive manner the care with which Napoleon had assured the finances of everyone who might in the slightest degree be concerned with Leon. While he had himself stipulated that Eleonore was to have no hand whatsoever in his son's upbringing he nevertheless made dispositions which envisaged the disregard of his wishes. In 1808 when he settled the dowry on the young Eleonore and her lieutenant, Napoleon was thirty nine years old, at the height of his powers, and for four years the crowned master of France. It must have appeared to him then that the empire he had founded would endure for a thousand years.

Me. Marie read out the terms of the investment:

Five Per cent Consolidated

I the undersigned, Secretary of the Great Book of the National Debt, certify, that Mme. Denuelle de la Plaigne, Louis Catherine Eleonore, the independently maintained wife of Pierre Philippe Augier, is the donee of Jean Claude Henry by a marriage settlement; subject to the following conditions and charges;

That the accrued dividends shall be inalienable and drawn by her against her own receipts, without need of her husband's consent for any reason whatsoever;

The same Mme. Augier is responsible for paying to her father and mother, Dominique Denuelle de la Plaigne and Francoise Caroline Sophie Coupries, 4,000 francs annually from the accrued dividends of the present inscription. . . .

In the case of Mme. Augier's earlier death without children, her husband will take annually 6,000 francs which on his death will revert to M. Henry the donor . . .

On the death of all the foregoing the capital and income of the stock will revert to M. Henry . . .

Neither M. nor Mme. Augier may dispose of all or any part of the investment to the prejudice of M. Henry's right to the reversion.

Inscribed in the Great Book of 5 per cent consolidated for
a sum of 22,000 francs with enjoyment from 22 September,
1807.

Paris, 24 February, 1808.

'As you see,' went on Maître Marie, 'this donation contains no
dispositions direct or indirect in favour of the young Leon, who
was then aged two. Why?

'The reason is simple. He who held himself responsible for
securing to the mother a comfortable standard of living took it
upon himself to provide for the present and the future of the
child. And at that period he was already thinking of creating for
him the brilliant rank which had already belonged in earlier
centuries to the bastards of our former kings.

And it is a fact that the Emperor — in so far as events permitted
him — did assure to Count Leon a position. At his majority he was
granted 36,000 francs. Further, he was to inherit a substantial part
of the four million francs bequeathed by the Emperor. However,
the funds charged with the satisfaction of these legacies proved
irrecoverable.

'On the death of Henry his heirs wished to speculate on the
superficial authority with which the deceased had been invested.
They claimed a reduction of the dowry. Whom should they sue —
Count Leon?

'No. They were not concerned with him but with Mme. de
Luxbourg, and with her husband whose consent was necessary.
Thus the judgment of Château-Thierry which has been raised here
was for the sole benefit of the Countess. Count Leon had no part
in it.

'The result of the decision was to wipe out the right of reversion
to Henry or anyone else. But the condition of non-transferability
remained, and with it perhaps the Treasury's objection to any
future transactions.

'It is true that at the time of the case of Château-Thierry Count
Leon enjoyed good relations with the de Luxbourgs. He asked
them for the investment capital and they showed themselves
well-disposed. So the agreement of 1831 was drawn up in his
favour — albeit under certain conditions. It is true also that he
paid out 25,000 francs to satisfy the claims which arose during the
suit . . .

'Nine years went by, and in 1840 Count Leon brought an action
against Mme. de Luxbourg for the capital of the income to be
made over to himself. He knew that his mother had married again

in 1814 and that M. Augier de la Saussaye had perished in 1812. By a harmful presumption — which rendered his mother flagrantly guilty of the crime of bigamy — he joined in an action that same Augier, who, he claimed, was a warder in the salt mines at Tobolsk (in Siberia!). This demand was negatived by a judicial declaration that the unhappy Augier had died in hospital at Marienbourg.

'If therefore Mme. de Luxbourg has not been arraigned as an arch-criminal it is not the fault of the man who calls himself her son. I shall not speak of the complaint which he had the temerity to bring in 1840 against the Count and Countess de Luxbourg. On better advice he dropped the accusation.

'What then remains? Only the deed signed by Mme. de Luxbourg on 9 May, 1840, without her husband's consent. But this agreement was never ratified by Count de Luxbourg.'

The court dismissed Leon's claim to the dowry; Eleonore, however, not content with her success, defaulted in payment of the 6,000 francs maintenance allowance and another court decided that the first tribunal had not been competent to declare Leon her son!

And so — in the first days of a Paris summer — M. d'Herbelot, the President of the fifth chamber of the Civil Court of the Seine, arranged his robes and listened to yet another recital of Leon's early life.

On June 26, 1846, M. Mahon, the *Avocat du Roi,* opened the case:

'A child was born at 29, Rue de la Victoire on 13 December, 1806, whose life for a long time was a mystery, but who from his cradle was surrounded by the most lavish care and became the object of the most powerful protection. This child is today Count Leon who seeks the aid of justice to obtain food; and who claims it from the Countess de Luxbourg by maintaining that he is her son. Mme. de Luxbourg disputes his claim by stating categorically that she is not his mother, and you have to decide this question of affiliation.

'According to his birth certificate, Count Leon was born of Eleonore Denuelle and of an absent father. Nevertheless he received from his birth an endowment which guaranteed to him a brilliant future. He was given stock in the National Debt and on the canals valued at 36,000 to 40,000 francs.

'The mighty eye which watched over the existence and the education of Count Leon lost sight of him only at the hour of death. The Empire had fallen; Napoleon was dying on St. Helena, when on 24 April, 1821, by a sublime effort, he drew up with his own hand the testament of his wishes. The codicils added to his will were for him the accomplishment of a great duty — he declared so himself — and when he wrote them he was hoping to be obeyed.

'At every stage of his life Count Leon was treated with interest and regard by the highest personages of the Imperial epoch. You have seen the letters from King Joseph, Prince Lucien, Cardinal Fesch, and former officials of Napoleon. And now the testimony of the executors of the will is submitted for your consideration.'

M. Mahon went on, 'You will see that the Emperor did not limit himself in any way to creating an income for Count Leon. He had scanned his whole future, and without prejudice to the nature of his abilities or the desire to interfere brusquely with his wishes, he had nevertheless mapped out his career.

'Let us permit ourselves one regret. Count Leon is today in distress. The legacies charged on the Empress [Marie Louise] and Prince Eugène [de Beauharnais] have proved irrecoverable and the 40,000 francs of stock inscribed on the day of his birth have been foolishly dissipated.

'Why is it that with such prospects of success he did not follow the advice he received? Why did he not understand that a wise and industrious life was not only a pledge of fortune and contentment, but an Imperial and sacred duty? And how has he fallen into the cruel straits in which he finds himself? Unhappily in his youth he did not understand that passions and flatterers always conspire against those whose existence is assured; and Count Leon, from illusion to illusion, from error to error, victim of his misadventures, victim perhaps of too much vanity, is today reduced to receiving his crust of charity from a few old friends.

'In this deplorable condition he appeals to the ties of blood and is obliged to prove them. Since they are disputed, let us before examining the defence she puts forward make known to you the Countess de Luxbourg.'

After a recital of Eleonore's matrimonial history, the *Avocat du Roi* continued, 'In 1828, Mme. de Luxbourg and Count Leon were surprised by a quite unexpected claim. Henry, the fictitious donor of the settlement of 1808 having died, his heirs — whose situation after his death was extremely modest — bethought themselves to attack the income settled on Mme. de la Saussay (Eleonore) claiming he had paid her in excess of the sums laid down. They demanded the greater part of the income from the 22,000 francs.

'In order to reach a settlement with the Henry family, Count Leon paid over to Maître Masson, former dean of the Paris bar, a sum of 25,000 francs for the benefit of Mme. de Luxbourg; and indeed we have before us a receipt bearing her signature certifying that she had received the sum from one Delpech, and a quittance for an identical amount signed by Maître Masson on behalf of Count Leon.[1]'.

M. Mahon turned to the disputed circumstances of Leon's birth.

'In opposing the claim for declaration of maternity, Mme. de Luxbourg evidences a decision given by the Tribunal of the Seine under Article 342 of the Civil Code to reject a demand which if judgment were given against her would charge her with a maternity which, having regard to the peculiar circumstances, would saddle her with adultery.

'To appreciate the meaning of that decision you ought to know that during the Restoration and shortly after the death of the Emperor, Revel, with the clear object of scandal recalled the existence of his marriage with Mlle. de la Plaigne.

'Working from the date of his divorce — 24 April, 1806 — and revealing the date of the birth of Count Leon from public documents to be the 13 December following, he relied upon Articles 312 and 314 of the Civil Code.

'At the instance of Revel a Monsieur Denuelle (it was in fact Dominique Denuelle — Eleonore's father) had been appointed ad hoc guardian of Leon, in order that Revel could bring an action for disavowal of paternity under Article 318 of the Code.

'Then — in order to create a bigger stir and to bring to light facts which are today notorious but at that time were unknown — he brought into court the Baron de Mauvières, the two witnesses to the entry of birth — M. Aymé and Dr. Andral, — all the members of the family council, who had confided the wardship to the former notary of Napoleon, and finally the Count and Countess de Luxbourg. The Baron de Meneval — Leon's guardian — intervened in the suit.

'A superior will had fixed the obligation of Baron de Meneval to his ward. If Count Leon's advocate is to be believed on this point, the mother of this child was forbidden to have anything to do with his education. He was to be kept away from her influence. She was forbidden to leave any imprint upon his character or his manners.

'You can understand therefore how M. de Meneval grasped the surest means of rejecting Revel's suit for denial of paternity, at the same time leaving to Leon the means of deciding his parentage. So it was on his demand that the Tribunal of the Seine — under the Presidency of M. Moreau of venerable memory — dismissed Revel's claim — because it did not prove the identity of the mother with the woman he had married.'

M. Mahon struggled through a morass of legal issues that Balzac in his most inspired moments could never have conjured up.

'If the court had decided in 1822 that Mme. de Luxbourg was positively not his mother, we would today be unable to escape the consequences of that judgment. But it ruled on the facts put before it while reserving to Count Leon the right to produce later — if he obtained them — the proofs of maternity that were missing at that time. And it limited itself to declaring that the birth certificate could not of itself furnish *prima facie* evidence in support of Revel's request for denial of paternity.

'Countess de Luxbourg's second objection can not succeed any better than the first. Her case is as follows:

'Under Article 315 of the Civil Code a child born before the three hundredth day after the dissolution of the marriage belongs in law to the husband. In other words it is assumed to have been conceived in wedlock.

'Count Leon having been born 223 days after the pronouncement of the divorce would, then, be a legitimate child in the eyes of the law — if he were the son of Revel.

'But as he claims a natural relationship he recognises himself to be by that sole fact a child conceived in adultery; and Article 342 forbids him in consequence to seek maternity.'

It must surely now have seemed to a casual observer either that Leon did not exist — or that he had been born without parents!

But the *Avocat du Roi* had only fairly begun. 'Gentlemen, we do not admit of such reasoning. We would be making a bizarre application of Article 315 — created in the interests of the legitimate child — to discover in it a presumption of adultery. And to maintain today that because he was born 223 days after the divorce the child was necessarily conceived during marriage is to apply in the most erroneous manner the presumptions consecrated in the Civil Code.

'What, in fact, do Articles 312 and 314 say? They say first of all that a child can be born alive after 180 days — or six months after conception. They then add that gestation can extend as far as 300 days — that is to say up to the expiry of the tenth month. And do not think that these presumptions are completely arbitrary — far from it! They rest on the laws of nature. Before drafting Articles 312 and 314 the legislature consulted specialists, accepted their advice, and — being unable to determine in a precise manner the date of the ever-problematical conception — fixed the intervals by acute observation of physiognomy.

'In so far as concerns Count Leon the date of conception can therefore be referred to the month of February. But it could also date only from the month of June. And since the marriage was dissolved before the end of April, adultery could not then be established and the request for maternity might be admitted.

'Calculated on these principles the question of maternity will cease to be a problem. Armed with the most numerous and conclusive documents we are not afraid to proclaim with Count Leon's advocate that Mme. de Luxbourg is his mother and we will prove it in an incontestable manner from her own letter.'

The *Avocat du Roi* read once more from Eleonore's correspondence.

'We ask you, gentlemen, in the face of these letters is any doubt possible? Yet Mme. de Luxbourg has the nerve to make a formal denial of her maternity, and goes so far as to say that there is no similarity between Eleonore Denuelle the mother of December 13, 1806, and Louis Catherine Eleonore Denuelle de la Plaigne, wife of M. Revel.

'Confronted with a birth certificate, the focus of public attention, and after all the vows she has made in writing, she is not afraid to stoop to deception. Gentlemen — this is not what you understand by the duties of motherhood.

'That a woman should yield to seduction is a fault that neither the aura of greatness nor the allure of youth can warrant. Nevertheless it is a fault that thirty-two years' repentance might have banished. But that this woman can reject a son who appeals for maternal help, refuse him bread when he is in need, and when he is homeless withhold shelter — these are sentiments that we dare not justify.'

M. Mahon, the *Avocat du Roi,* sat down. What influence his speech had on the judges we do not know — only that they declared themselves as follows:

'We declare Count Leon to be born of Mme. Louis Catherine Eleonore Denuelle de Laplaigne, today Countess de Luxbourg, and this conforms with the birth certificate of December 15, 1806. The court orders that the present judgment be inscribed in the margin of the entry of birth.'

The Count and Countess de Luxbourg were ordered to pay Leon 4,000 francs a year. So he succeeded in claiming a maintenance allowance — though much reduced — from his mother and stepfather. Equal to £4,000 in today's purchasing power, the sum was not inconsiderable even in the Paris of Louis Philippe; but to a Bonaparte it was a mere pittance.

There still remained the question of Leon's claim to the government stock. It turned on the transferability of the 22,000 francs investment.

On December 28, 1846, Maître Crémieux once again related the history of Leon in the Royal Court of Paris.

For a third time he read out the letter written by Eleonore after her re-union with the sixteen year old son whom, on the orders of Napoleon, she had not seen for fifteen years.

Mannheim, January 20, 1823

I little thought when I left Paris that I would be writing today with my son at my side. But since Providence has guided his heart and his steps towards his mother you will easily feel how I received him. If Leon had been entrusted to a wise tutor who had inspired him with high and dignified conduct; who had won his confidence by instilling into him simple and lofty thoughts, he would still be with you. But treated almost as a stranger by his Mentor — who ought rather to have been his friend — he responded accordingly, and crossed only feeble barriers to rejoin a mother who lives only for him, and has no other object — no other care — but his happiness.

It was not from you, monsieur, that Leon wished to flee; because he has spoken only with the highest esteem of his guardian, and if he had one regret it would be to have caused you pain. But he knows your paternal heart too well not to be persuaded that putting yourself in his place and consulting such a good and sensible mother as Mme. de Meneval, you could not do other than excuse him — which is not to condemn M. Vieillard, who simply had not the experience to penetrate to the depths of his pupil's heart. I received a letter from him yesterday and no doubt he will have informed you of Leon's departure.

My husband, who is as much attached to my son as if he were his own, entirely occupied with his education has already fixed an hour of the day for each lesson and chosen the best professors in every discipline that we have here; who are renowned throughout the country, and who, out of devotion to my husband are more than zealous in teaching my son who, keeping you informed of all his activities, will take pleasure in writing to you often. He flatters himself with the hope that in a few days he will be able to come to you again, monsieur, adorned with all the charms which a virtuous soul and a refined education endow. His mind nourished by study will give birth to no more chimeras, and his lessons filling every minute of the day will make him forget idleness, the begetter of all vice.

His leisure hours will be devoted to his mother, who, feeling all the joy of having her son close to her after such a long and painful deprivation, will be devoted wholly to forming his heart and his mind. Yes, monsieur, from today this is my unique study . . . Not that he was less dearly loved than I love him; but as a tree separated from its roots perishes in a strange earth, so a son can have only one mother, only one heart: the heart of her who is able perfectly to understand him.

Leon, striving ever more each day by his application to his studies and to himself, thus guarantees it. And we, increasing our care and friendship for him, hope that you will not withdraw your paternal kindness; and that in continuing to watch over his fortune — as until now you have done with such fervour — will not refuse to send each year the sum of 10,000 francs, for the payment only of his teachers and his upkeep, since in my home his unnecessary expenses will be much curtailed.

Comtesse de Luxbourg.

Maître Crémieux concluded: 'Count Leon was then in a situation of the most brilliant fortune. He had 27,000 livres a year, and he was happy to spend some of it on his mother. In this way he laid out 10,000 francs on diamonds which she purchased from various jewellers.

'He bestowed his benefits in particular on one of his aunts [Zulma de la Plaigne]. And to Revel who was in a situation of the most profound wretchedness he allowed a pension of 2,000 francs a year which he paid up to 1835, the year in which Revel died. I have in my brief the receipts for all these payments. Then, surrounded by flatterers, urged on by bad advice, he soon dissipated his fortune.

'It is quite an ordinary story; but what is not ordinary about it is the conduct of his mother. At present Count Leon is quite without resources and since commencing this action he has been maintained by the wife of one of the Emperor's old generals who has not forgotten what she and her husband owe to his memory.'

In spite of the richest eloquence of the Paris bar, Leon's claim to the investment was dismissed.[2]

Maître Marie's unfortunate pupil Delorme had been given the unglamorous job of attending to the details of Leon's successful claim for maintenance. The negotiations becoming acrimonious, Delorme quarrelled with an official of the court; but it was upon Leon that he vented his wrath in a violent assault. Delorme was prosecuted, and on March 13, 1847 sentenced to fifteen days imprisonment plus a fine of 100 francs, which on appeal was increased to 1,000 francs!

The de Luxbourgs would have been better advised to settle out of court, for theirs was a Pyrrhic victory. On October 1, 1847, the King of Bavaria relieved the Count de Luxbourg of his functions as Envoy Extraordinary and Minister Plenipotentiary to the Court of Louis Philippe and ordered his recall.

Eleonore was a bad payer. She had delayed satisfaction of the earlier judgment awarding Leon 6,000 francs; and in spite of the allowance of 4,000 francs Leon was still in straitened circumstances. In 1840 he had battened on to General Gourgaud whom he assisted during the elections of 1834, and whom he was still tapping.

CHAPTER 10

An Open Letter to the Prince President

A fortnight before the abdication of Louis Philippe, Leon wrote to Gourgaud:

Paris, February 7th, 1848.

General,

The reply you gave me — through your servant — to my letter of January 25th last, which I sent by hand of M. Charbonnel, and its tardiness — which I was given otherwise than to expect after the hopes you raised when I told you personally of my difficulties — have placed me in a most embarrassing position.

M. Caillieux insisted that either I pay him or leave his house at once. A few minutes afterwards I was turned out with nothing but the clothes on my back. He has heartlessly retained my trunk in which I kept all my papers and effects, as well as a valuable painting of the Emperor at Waterloo.

I have found a room at 9, Rue Joubert, thank God; but because of my shortage of money I have been unable to move in a bed to sleep on. For the time being I am sleeping in a miserable furnished room at 20 sous a day where I am wretched. I come to beg of you, my dear General, to be so kind as to lend me a little money to buy a bed, and I will repay it as soon as I am able. I would be most grateful for it.

I beg you to accept, my dear General, the sincere expression of my affection and my highest esteem.

Count Leon.

P.S. I should be happy to see you again, and I beg you to tell me at what time I may call upon you.

This time the patient Gourgaud did not delay his reply; for that same day he scribbled in the margin of Leon's appeal: 'Sent 40 frs. 7 February, G.'

Leon's legitimate relations continued to leave a fast-changing world. Joseph Bonaparte, his surprised host of Denham, had died in Florence on July 28th, 1844; while his uncle Louis, ex-King of Holland, survived Hortense by ten years and died at Leghorn of a

brain haemorrhage on July 25th, 1846. Alexandre Walewski
helped to redress the balance by leaving the family mistress — the
actress Rachel — with a son, whom he later adopted and placed in
the French consular service.

Louis Napoleon, living temporarily in St. John's Wood, had just
completed the installation of his mistress, Miss Howard, in
Berkeley Street. Although he had inherited 1,200,000 francs and
his father's estates in Civitanova worth 624,000 francs, the
prince's gambling was taking effect; but — unlike Leon — he
hedged his bets and was provided with a standing credit of £2,000
by Baring's. In February 1847 Louis Napoleon wrote to his
confidant, Narcisse Vieillard, Leon's old tutor, to report that he
had moved into 3A King Street Houses, happily situated near
Almack's, Christie's, and the St. James's Theatre — where he saw
Virginie Déjazet. Louis was too close to Crockford's, however, for
a member of that club swindled him out of £2,000. Toying with a
fund-raising venture for the Nicaraguan canals, he had tried to
raise money without liquidising his railway shares. After
prosecuting the dishonourable member unsuccessfully at Bow
Street, the prince was reimbursed by Crockford's manager.

Although it was Louis Napoleon's proud boast that 'all the
Bonapartes were dead and it was I who re-tied the cord,' his uncle
the indestructible Jerome continued to tap his son-in-law, the
brutal Count Demidoff, to the tune of 40,000 francs a year — even
after Princess Mathilde and the Russian had separated.

In Tallahassee, Florida, on April 5, 1847, Leon's infant
companion, Achille Murat, who had shared with him the ministrations of Mme. Loire their nurse, died; and on December 18, in
Vienna, Marie-Louise was re-united with the Emperor she had
deserted thirty years before.

Louis Philippe abdicated on February 24, 1848. Because his
reign had been relatively tranquil and he had given to the people
of France eighteen years virtually undisturbed by military
adventure, he had earned the soubriquet 'Napoleon of Peace'. But,
as the Napoleon of Austerlitz had remarked, 'Government ought
to be a continuous demonstration.' The domestic monarch with
the green umbrella was rejected by a generation which had not
known the horrors of Borodino; and the leader of the romantic
movement, Lamartine, declared, 'France is bored.'

An orderly crowd of people had marched to Guizot's Paris
home on the night of February 23; but a few hotheads clashed
with troops and a Corsican sergeant panicked and fired. The

National Guard joined the subsequent uprising and the king fled to Vincennes.

Leon quickly entered the arena and on March 20, 1848, he again harangued the people of St. Denis: 'Under the fallen Government I never wished to receive anything; its corrupt and corrupting principles angered me . . . You will never see me vote the re-establishment of any dynasty in France.'

On the same day, Leon's little cousin in King Street was also writing a letter, to *The Times* asking the editor to print without attribution a denial of the prince's intention to stand for a place in the National Assembly.

France, however, was not alone in her political upheavals. In Austria and Hungary, and in Germany and Italy, revolution flared. There was a gold rush in California; and after the U.S. — Mexican war that state was incorporated into the Union together with Texas and New Mexico. The *Communist Manifesto* appeared, and John Stuart Mill's *Principles of Political Economy*. Metternich fled to England where, during the Chartist demonstrations of April 10, 1848, Louis Napoleon was sworn in at Marlborough Street police station as one of Lord John Russell's special constables.

Disdaining a common truncheon, the prince patrolled Piccadilly between Park Lane and Dover Street carrying a light, gold-headed cane. Declaring to his American publisher-friend, Palmer Putnam, 'The peace of London must be preserved,' Louis Napoleon took into custody a drunken old woman.

A fortnight later, on April 23, 1848, three of the Emperor's nephews were returned to the Legislative Assembly: Jerome's son Prince Napoleon — 'Plon-Plon'; — Caroline's son, Lucien Murat; and Prince Bonaparte — Lucien's son Pierre, 'the Corsican wild-boar', who had once set fire to the Castel' Angelo.

Louis Napoleon had crossed to France three days after the February revolution — and had been politely invited to leave. On June 4 he was chosen as their deputy by four departments; but the law proscribing the Bonapartes had not been repealed and he would not enter the Assembly.[1]

Leon once more reached for his pen. In an open letter to Louis Napoleon he wrote:

At the approach of the new elections which without doubt are again going to open to you the doors of the National Assembly; at an hour when the new republican institutions of France appear to be consolidating themselves, and are calling upon all citizens to co-operate by their intelligence and by

their labour to the solution of the immense problem of the
spiritual and material well being of all classes of society, I
must inform you of my thoughts on the organisation created
by the immortal days of last February and the part you must
play, by bringing to your notice the matters which, until
today, have prevented my taking up any kind of stand; and
the trend of thought on which I have based my personal
attempts to pay my debt also to society.

So far as concerns me personally, since I left St. Denis —
where the Government of Louis Philippe persecuted me even
to the extent of my functions as a major in the National
Guard — slander has never ceased to portray me, at every
turn, in a false light.

In spite of his three-cornered dispute in 1834, Leon continued
consistently to solicit the votes of the people of St. Denis; and just
as consistently they elected someone else. His attachment to St.
Denis may be explained by the fact that it lay beyond the
jurisdiction of the Parisian *recors*. Leon's experience of these
bailiffs' men and process-servers had not been a happy one.
Presumably the debtors' usual sanctuary of Batignolles was not to
his taste.

Having disposed of the National Guard in a few lines, Leon
believes it expedient to clear the tables completely by rationalising
the duel on Wimbledon Common which had taken place just eight
years previously.

'In the month of March, 1840,' Leon continued, 'I went to
London for the purpose of finding out from Joseph and Jerome
Bonaparte the testamentary dispositions that His Eminence
Cardinal Fesch had made in my favour.' Apart from a few pictures
and *objets de vertu*, Leon seems to have received nothing from the
cardinal, who left 50,000 francs to the illegitimate Jerome
Patterson — a sum which 'Bo-Bo' had no difficulty in collecting.
Leon was likewise ignored by Mme. Mère, whose estate at her
death on February 2, 1836, was valued at some two million francs.

It is probably true that Leon came to London not to pick a
quarrel with Louis Napoleon but to collect money — always a
question of the highest priority — and to become accepted by the
family. It is more than possible that had Leon been treated less
like an outsider he would have responded like Aesop's Man in the
Cloak. His half-brother Alexandre Walewski was *persona grata*,
though illegitimate; and even Leon had never equalled the excesses
of his Roman cousins. He is most probably sincere when he writes:

Louis Napoleon. *After a photograph taken in 1849*

Louis Napoleon (later Emperor Napoleon III) working in his laboratory in the prison at Ham.

After an engraving by Philippoteaux

Le Comte D'Orsay

Eleonore Vergeot, mistress of Louis Napoleon, and called 'La Belle
Sabotière'
After a portrait painted c. 1840 by one of the officers of the prison of Ham

I also wanted to tell you about the great things which were occupying my time, in the belief that they would find entry to your thoughts. But malicious talk had preceded me; I could do nothing; you regarded me as your enemy and it sufficed little to precipitate a duel between us.

How I should have regretted it. It would have become my life's sorrow. Divine Providence did not allow that duel to take place; and in the middle of the distress occasioned me by those painful events, I received from M. Guillaume Coëssin that precious letter which acquires an important significance for today, since it proves that my life at that period was employed otherwise than you believed.[2]

Leon's favourite uncle was Lucien, whom Mme. Tussaud described as 'the finest looking man of the family; rather above middle height, and having good features; his manners elegant. He has given proofs of a highly cultivated mind; and at the critical moment, at St. Cloud on the 9 November, his eloquence, firmness, and presence of mind were highly serviceable to the cause of his brother Napoleon.'

Lucien's compassionate interest in his nephew may have been prompted by recollections of his own wayward sons. At all events, Leon, whose literary excursions always contain a generous sprinkling of quotations whatever their relevance, now interposes a brief note with which he was entrusted by his uncle *after* his encounter with Louis Napoleon:

Prince Lucien Bonaparte who, as President of the Five Hundred, protected the Emperor at the moment when he was being outlawed, adjourned the session, and by this action saved his life, remaining faithful to republican principles never wishing to accept a post under the Empire, was the only one of the Emperor's family who welcomed me to London with kindness. He lavished upon me every proof of interest and friendship, encouraged me in my plans, inspired in me the fondest hopes, and at the moment of my departure from London gave me, for one of his cousins this short letter:

London, March 19, 1840.

My dear Cousin,

I am giving to my nephew, Count Leon, these few words which will afford you the benefit of making the acquaintance of a person who is dear to us . . . You may have confidence in him. My wife is better. I have written to her

concerning her silence towards you, and I hope
it will end. Believe me, my dear cousin, in my
good wishes.

Your devoted,

Prince de Canino.

Having disposed of the unpleasantness at Wimbledon, Leon feels at
liberty to get down to the serious business of running the Second
Republic.

Today times have changed. The Republic has been proclaimed in France; your duty is to serve it without any
ulterior motive. Twice you have been called to represent the
nation by the wishes of your fellow citizens: twice you have
refused to take your seat. In the opinion of the majority you
were wrong. Nevertheless the little group of people who are
given to reflection saw in your refusal motives only of
prudence and wisdom, inspired by the vexed state of the
parties.

If the new elections at present taking place result in your
recall it is my belief that you must place yourself without the
slightest hesitation at the head of your fellow citizens. It is
by making yourself known by great actions; by your
devotion to the true interests of the whole people and of
France that you must aspire naturally to the highest
functions of the Republic, and even to attain to the
Presidency — which in my view must be the noblest of your
ambitions.

The word *republic*, which literally means a 'public thing' —
the common good abrogates to this concept alone all the
duties of the true republican — is epitomised in the subordi-
nation of the individual to the happiness of everyone. The
Presidency is in the final resort merely elected royalty,
accessible to the most worthy, the most honourable and the
most able whatever their birth and fortune. Its riches must
consist of labour organised on new bases; and it goes without
saying that the economy can only prosper by the regulation
of all earnings from the salary of the highest official to the
wages of the humblest labourer.

If intrigues, lies, venality and abuse of position, and all the
evils of the monarchy were to be perpetuated, *republic* would
be a vain word; and France would merely be taking a step
backwards. Without virtue the republic cannot exist.

After his essay on the meaning of a republic — the conclusion of

which reads almost like a paraphrase of the thirteenth chapter of
Paul's letter to the Corinthians — Leon goes on to refer to one of
his father's speeches:

> You will find the complete expression of these opinions in
> the address given to the assembled clergy of Milan. I enclose a
> copy of it in the assurance that you will find it of great
> authority. The noble sentiments which it expresses, and the
> eternal truths which it contains, must serve as a rule of
> conduct for all who presume to govern the people. I myself
> have found it a source of great instruction.[3]

Leon concludes his advice to the imminent Prince-President with
the words:

> Such then are the principles which must form the basis of
> your future conduct. It is in the light of this the purest, the
> most lofty and the one true philosophy, that you will
> succeed in holding yourself inviolate against the dangers of
> seduction, and that you will be truly useful to France, your
> country. Any other course would be at your peril and you
> would be lost beyond recall.
>
> If I am mistaken and I do not enjoy your comprehension;
> and should you be unhappy enough to reject these high ideas
> which are now engaging my attention, and which I now pass
> on to you, I can but pity you with all my heart. Nevertheless
> I shall persevere in the path which I have elected to follow,
> and say with M. Coëssin:
>
> *Let evil turn and devour all that is his.*

On September 17, 1848, Louis Napoleon was returned by the
voters of Paris, Corsica, the Yonne, the Charente-Inférieure, and
the Moselle, and ten days later he took his seat in the Chamber of
Deputies. A law providing for the direct election of a President by
the votes of the people was passed by the Assembly on October 9,
and two months later the French people chose Louis Napoleon.

In the late summer of 1848 Leon's importunities at 30 Rue
Joubert, had recommenced with a letter of August 20 to
Gourgaud:

> My dear General,
>
> As I mentioned in my last letter dated 28 February, I have
> been obliged to quit M. Cailleux's house and move to a room
> with a few bits of furniture at 9 Rue Joubert. I have been
> unable to pay the rent for the April quarter, and my room
> has been taken and my furniture detained until I am able to
> pay the six months rent totalling 125 francs.

I have therefore been forced to move into a small furnished room at 63 Rue de Provence, Cité d'Antin, as I was advised to do by the late General Fournier.

Since the days of February, and in my eager anticipation of the arrival of Prince Louis Napoleon, it has been my desire to accept nothing from the Republic. I have been unable to get a sou from anyone; I am unable even to pay the two months rent for my furnished room, and in this unhappy plight I come to you again, my dear General, that you might help me. I shall be most grateful. If you will receive M. Charbonnel, the bearer of this letter, he can explain to you my affairs and my circumstances. I am ill and unable to leave the house.

Accept, my dear General, the homage of my most sincere affection,

Count Leon.

After forty years Leon had come full circle. He was now living in squalor a few steps from the mansion where Caroline Murat had cradled him in Imperial splendour. Evil had certainly devoured all that was Leon's.

Shortly before his death Napoleon had written, 'I bequeath to the King of Rome all my campaign beds.' These included the folding copper couch on which the Emperor was laid at St. Helena, and the heavy iron *lit de campagne* with a green canopy which, in its black leather case, had travelled with him from battle to battle.

Leon demanded but one bed; and in his despair was moved to liken himself to the Galilean who had no resting place. On February 7, 1848, he had begged the price of a bed from the long-suffering Gourgaud; and in the following November he was still seeking a provider of that most necessary French *meuble*. His search ended near his favourite café in an L-shaped arcade off the Boulevard Montmartre.

It is said that Nathan Rothschild made a fortune after the battle of Waterloo simply by leaning against a pillar in the Stock Exchange, the first one on the right from the entrance in Cornhill.

One late autumn day in 1848 a certain Sieur Bernard was using a column in the Paris Bourse for a similar hopeful purpose when he was approached by Leon. The meeting resulted in the classic relationship of the provincial and the man-about-town. Like so many of Leon's friendships it ended in a court of law; and all because he wanted a bed like his illustrious father's. Perhaps he had seen it on his visit to London among the relics brought from Paris by Marie Tussaud — the iron bed on which Napoleon had dreamed his conquests.

Bernard, forty-seven years old and a native of Lyons, was living on the Champs Elysées. Leon, five years his junior, was sharing a flat with one Doctor Comet on the Boulevard des Italiens.

The case came before the 8th Chamber of the Tribunal Correctionel de Paris — the magistrate's court — under the Presidency of M. Turbat. Bernard brought an action against Leon for the fraudulent acquisition of an iron bedstead and repayment of a debt of 700 francs; and Leon replied with a suit for defamation and malicious prosecution.

A shopkeeper named Monsieur Henri was the first witness. He described how the two friends visited his establishment in the Passage Jouffroy, a new arcade between the Boulevard Montmartre and the Rue Grange-Batelière.

'About two and half months ago M. Bernard came into my shop with Count Leon to select an iron bedstead. M. Bernard said to the Count, "Here's a design that should suit you. I knew we would find a likely one here because I've already bought similar ones for other people". Nothing was decided on that day, however, and the gentlemen left. Later M. Bernard came back by himself and said, "Well now! The iron bed is quite suitable for the gentleman. Your bed has been sold. Let me have your assistant to take it away." M. Bernard went off at once with my lad and the bed was delivered.'

The President of the Court asked, 'Who was to pay for it?'

'M. Bernard — he was the only one I knew and I sold the bed on his sole responsibility.'

'And what happened when you came to be paid?'

'M. Bernard asked for a bill so that he could get payment from Count Leon. Then he came back and said he was unable to obtain the purchase price: "Go and see him yourself," he told me. When I sent my boy with the bill Count Leon asked to see me; so I went round myself. He received me very politely and said that it was not necessary to negotiate with me as he had settled the matter with M. Bernard. So I went to see him. "What are you playing at," I said. "Count Leon has sent me back to you because you have settled up with him. Are you going to pay me for my bed"?'

Bernard took the witness stand and went into great detail about the circumstances of his dealings with Leon. He had lent him various sums totalling 700 francs for which he received an IOU.

Maître Lachaud, Leon's advocate, addressed the court.

'According to Bernard, Count Leon tried to induce him to loosen his purse strings by talking of a pension he was to receive from the President of the Republic. I ask permission to produce two witnesses who will testify to the truth of the allegation put forward, but which — I repeat — was not made to M. Bernard by Count Leon.'

Two witnesses were heard on this point: Monsieur Godot, Secretary-General of the Prefecture, and Porix-Livernois, an official of the household of Louis-Napoleon Bonaparte, President of the Republic. Their testimony confirmed that the President of the Republic had shown much concern over Count Leon and had made known his intention of granting his cousin a pension. If the present circumstances had not yet permitted the fixing of it with certainty, the witnesses were in no doubt that the President's wishes would be put into effect.

'But what motives obliged you to lend money to Count Leon whom you hardly knew?' asked the President of the court.

'I would not say that I was naïve enough to believe all the tall stories he told me,' Bernard replied. 'Certainly not — consequently it was in vain that he told me he was going to be named ambassador to Russia; that the Government were afraid of him; that they wanted to send him away; that if he desired to go to Rome he was assured of a high position with his cousin Pierre Bonaparte — the chief of the revolution — but that he preferred to stay in Paris. Anyway — all this was hardly likely to persuade me.'

During this part of Bernard's statement Leon shrugged his shoulders and smiled.

'But I had a certain enthusiasm for him,' Bernard went on, 'because of his birth; and I felt myself completely disposed to be of service to him, at the same time setting a limit to the loans which I found to be rising too steeply.'

Passing on to the acquisition of the iron bedstead he declared that after refusing several times to pay him for it Leon had spirited the bed away from his room.

'You are wrong,' Leon put in, 'the bed is still with me.'

Bernard then launched into a detailed account of the scene in which he claimed to be Leon's victim and said that his Imperial friend had treated him like a moneylender in the street, and assaulted him.

'We will hear witnesses on that point,' the President said; 'but I think I ought to read a letter which you addressed to Count Leon and which you left completely unsealed with his *concierge*.' The President then read out the letter which was expressed in the most injurious and defamatory terms and which gave an unflattering description of Leon.

A Maître Rozet then intervened to say that to his understanding the price of the iron bed must not be joined with the 700 francs owing to Bernard, as this loan had been made the subject of a special settlement to be executed later. In his opinion there was not a scintilla of fraud in that matter. Another acquaintance of Leon spoke about the unedifying spectacle in which Bernard had involved Leon. After describing two earlier scenes — both equally deplorable — which Bernard had precipitated that same day at Count Leon's he went on, 'Count Leon and I went into the Passage Jouffroy to have dinner when Bernard arrived on the scene, came up to us on the Boulevard Montmartre and shouted at the top of his voice, "Give me back my bed I tell you! Are you going to give it back to me?"'

'Count Leon asked him to go away; but he only shouted the louder.'

'Provoked beyond measure, Count Leon said, "If you don't go away I shall give you a thrashing." At once Bernard let out a dreadful yell: "Thief! Murderer! There's the thief, there's the assassin!"'

The President asked the witness, 'Had there been an assault by Count Leon?'

'Not even a gesture,' Doutre answered. 'He went on shouting, "Help me sovereign people! I place myself under the protection of the people." Then, pointing out Count Leon to a crowd of more than three hundred people who had gathered — "This is Count Leon, he's my robber, he's my murderer! Arrest him!" All the same, he went and hid in the crowd as if he were seeking protection.

'Count Leon did not budge,' went on the witness, 'but merely turned round and slowly crossed the boulevard. We called a cab and went to the police station where our complaint was taken down.'

Maître Lachaud asked on behalf of Leon: 'And the crowd did not urge Count Leon to teach Monsieur Bernard a lesson?'

'I actually heard the crowd shouting, "Aren't you going to sort this hooligan out then?"' replied Doutre.

Doctor Comet — who sub-let a part of his flat at 9, Boulevard des Italiens to Leon — described how he saw Bernard one day at the apartment. He had told the doctor to be careful of his tenant, who he made out to be a thief and a trickster. Bernard told him that he had lent money to Leon and even showed him the acknowledgment he had received for it. 'Indeed,' Dr. Comet had replied, 'then that proves that you are either his friend or a moneylender.' At this remark the court was again filled with laughter.

'Did you know that Bernard had left an open letter with the *concierge* telling her to give it to Count Leon?' asked the President of the Court.

'I learned about it from the *concierge*,' answered Dr. Comet, 'who told me in confidence.' Here the courtroom again exploded into mirth.

'And it is more than likely that she had read the letter,' observed the President.

'I don't know about that,' said Dr. Comet, 'but she told me that Bernard had said to her: "Here, this is for your cheat." Later, when I was at the Bourse, I met M. Bernard who again regaled me with slanderous remarks about Count Leon.'

Monsieur Turbat, the President, asked Leon if he had any observations to make on the charge of false pretences.

'None, Monsieur le Président. I will only say that the acquisition of this iron bed was in my eyes nothing more than a simple purchase for which Bernard and myself would settle up later.'

The President then asked, 'Why did you not return the bed?'

'I was no longer able to do so from the moment I was accused of having stolen it. I am concerned above all that justice should be done in this respect; but I must admit that I never had any intention of keeping it. It is still new and unpacked: I have never used it. I shall return it this evening — and I wish to state that I am proceeding with my action for defamation against Monsieur Bernard.'

Maître Lachaud concluded for Leon by requesting damages of 10,000 francs against Bernard.

After hearing Maître Desmarets, Bernard's advocate, and the submissions of the Avocat de la République, Avond, the Court found that the charge of false pretences had not been proved and dismissed Leon from the case. Bernard was sentenced to ten days in prison and fined 50 francs for defamation; but Leon did not receive a sou in damages.

On July 27, 1849, Bernard's appeal was heard in the Cour d'Appel de Paris, Chambre Correctionnel, under the Presidency of

M. Delshaye. The proceedings proved even more hilarious than the hearing in the magistrate's court.

Not content with the decision of February 21, Leon had hauled the unfortunate Bernard before the Tribunal de Police Correctionnel and obtained for him another fifteen days in jail plus a further fine of 50 francs. But Leon was no more successful than before in his attempt to obtain damages — a crucial point, having regard to his state of perpetual financial embarrassment. After the appeal court had heard a summary of the hearing in the Tribunal Correctionnel, Maître Morise, for Bernard, decided that the best policy of defence was to attack. 'In a matter of this nature an appreciation of the respective characters of the two parties is assuredly of great importance. As to that of our opponent I shall not say one word. I shall leave the judges to their memories and content myself with proving that the man at the bar of the court for whom I speak is more honest before the law than he has been ajudged. I have a handful of testimonials signed by the most honourable names. As I wish to spare the Court's valuable time I shall content myself with reading two letters addressed to M. Bernard on the occasion of this case. One is signed by M. Rapetti, a professor at the Collège de France; the other is from M. de Gasparin, a former Minister of the Interior. It is sufficient to cite these names; all comment would be superfluous.'

Maître Morise read the two letters, which confirmed Bernard to be a perfectly honest man, of good and generous character, but possessed of an easy-going nature which rendered him always the dupe of scoundrels and tricksters. They spoke also of Bernard's passionate admiration for the Emperor, and a sort of cult which he indulged for anything in the slightest degree relating to him.

'These documents give you the key to this case,' he finished, and went on to describe the fateful encounter. 'One day Bernard was leaning against the pillars outside the Bourse when a person approached him mouthing imprecations against "that den of thieves" where a good man could not be found. Bernard attempted to bring him round to more rational sentiments. He wanted to show him that a financier might perhaps retain some human emotions.

'The stranger had burst out, "If that were so, why am I — the son of the Emperor — not surrounded by riches? Yet not one of those men of money has a desire to help me; and the *Son of Man* has nowhere to lay his head!" '

Bernard's counsel continued: 'I would not have the temerity to affirm that the meeting had been planned. Whatever be the case one must recognise that Count Leon could not have spoken to a better listener. Bernard took him home and lent him 200 francs.

'The following day Count Leon again sought out the precious man who had so generously obliged him and said that the Emperor's family were disposed to grant him a pension; and that in a few days he would repay the loan and any that he might receive in the future.

'For three months Count Leon met Bernard every day as he left the Bourse, and every day Bernard took him out to dinner. We must explain that Bernard is not rich — far from it — and his daily meal on which until then he had been spending 1 franc 25 centimes now cost him 2 francs 50. Each evening after dinner they went to the café in the Passage Jouffroy and Bernard paid for the beer and cognacs that his illustrious companion put away. It frequently happened that the waiter when making up the bill added to it a grog or so that Count Leon had consumed during the day and had not paid for, Bernard settled for the lot and had to tip the waiter into the bargain.'

After the hoots of laughter which greeted this episode had subsided, Maître Morise went on, 'Bernard's friends — decent chaps who unlike him were not afflicted with this Imperialistic fetish of which you are aware — often said to him: "Be careful, this man's using you as a milch cow — and to add insult to injury he's taking a rise out of you." Bernard had replied: "Can I refuse anything to the son of the Emperor?" '

At this the whole courtroom dissolved in mirth.

Whether or no this was the effect intended by the shrewd Maître Morise he gallantly persisted, 'Things came to such a pass that he was completely taken for granted; and Count Leon would say to him in restaurants, cafés and shops, "Be quiet, Duroc!" to the great amusement of the people about.'

At the mention of Leon's astute use of the name of Napoleon's parsimonious comptroller of household there were further outbursts of laughter. 'Nevertheless, the day came when Bernard began to open his eyes. He wanted to settle up with Count Leon — who did not welcome this proposal one little bit. "You are asking me for what I owe you? Very well, monsieur, I will give you a receipt." And indeed Count Leon made out this piece of paper in which he acknowledges a debt of 750 francs to my client.'

There was renewed laughter as the advocate held up the slip of paper and said, 'Monsieur Bernard's security!'

It must have appeared to Leon and his counsel that their case was dissolving under the wit of Maître Morise, who had by no means exhausted his satire. 'Some days passed during which Count Leon cold-shouldered Bernard. He said to him one day, however, "Bernard you are treating me badly. You have asked me for money. The Emperor would never forgive Duroc for that. But I am a decent fellow and I shan't hold it against you." '

Here laughter again broke out and Maître Morise came to his main theme as he continued to quote Leon. 'Let us forget the past. I have seen an iron bed in the Gallery Jouffroy that I need very much. You won't refuse me the 120 francs they are asking for it?'

The Passage Jouffroy contained not only a furniture shop; it also held the café in which Bernard tempered the December nights to his Imperial companion. No doubt he was aware of the double danger: what he did not spend in the shop he would lose in the bar.

So Bernard positively did refuse a 120-france bed as the price of their reconciliation. It was not the first time he had bought furniture for his friend. He remembered particularly well a bed in mahogany. Leon had re-sold it with such verve that his *concierge* had taken him for a second-hand dealer.

Bernard was definitely not prepared to make this new sacrifice. 'Very well,' Leon said, 'we won't speak of it again. But just let us go and see the bed. That won't commit us to anything and it will give us a walk.' Bernard could not fault this suggestion and they merely had a look round the shop. The bed was really well-designed and most comfortable. And there the matter ended.

Maître Morise was now at the heart of the matter. 'Some time later Bernard was taken aback to see the shopkeeper arrive with a bill for 120 francs. The bed had been delivered to Count Leon for the account of M. Bernard and now it was a question of paying for it. Bernard protested and argued with all his might. The shopkeeper became angry and declared that if he did not pay at once he would take action against him as the perpetrator of a fraud, or at least as an accomplice. Bernard resigned himself and paid — always in his rôle of Duroc.

'Bernard complained to the local police superintendent who sent one of his men round to Leon's apartment. With a princely panache rarely seen these days, Count Leon simply showed the policeman to the door, and threatened to break Bernard's neck — Empire style. . .

'In the afternoon Bernard and Leon met on the boulevard. A dispute arose and Monsieur Leon raised his fist to punish the rascal who had made so bold as to accost him. Bernard — in the throes of excitement — shouted. "It's not enough to steal from people, you've got to kill them! Robber! Murderer!" '

Bernard's counsel explained that this was the incident which gave rise to Leon's complaint of defamation. Committing the offence with which he reproached his opponent, he alleged that Bernard was an infamous moneylender who charged 200 per cent. 'Really gentlemen, this transcends in a spectacular manner the right of a person well endowed with wits to take advantage of a man who has hardly any at all.'

Here Maître Morise drew the Court's attention to the scene in *Le Bourgeois Gentilhomme* where Vicomte Dorante points out the munificent M. Jourdain to the Marquis de Dorimène with the words: 'He is a rather ridiculous bourgeois as you can see.' Bernard's advocate commented: 'At least he did not take upon himself the liberty of declaring: "He is a moneylender who lends at twenty per cent." '

'For his part Bernard made an accusation of false pretences against M. Leon and the magistrate's court rejected this complaint. So this poor Bernard — abused, almost assaulted, almost robbed — is condemned to twenty-five days in jail as a slanderer and a malicious prosecutor!

'Both sides have appealed against the judgment. The accused assumes the duty of establishing that the circumstances necessary for false pretences are present in this case. But even should the wisdom of the gentlemen of the court decide otherwise, the facts would still demonstrate what manner of slanderer and malicious plaintiff Bernard is. After all — this method of getting money or furniture daily by taking advantage of the lack of wits of this innocent Bernard is but a venial sin — pure pleasantry. These are the amusements of princes. Fine! But if Bernard was deceived by all this and frankly categorized the method by means of which he was parted from his money, this is an error of judgment which cannot render him liable to penalties by which the law punishes a malicious complainant — who must of necessity have acted with a desire to harm and in the full knowledge that he was furthering a slander.'

Maître Morise had almost reached the end of his peroration and he concluded, 'As for the defamation, it just is not possible that a creditor who is threatened in the street with a stick and who cries

"Stop thief!" and "Murderer!" should be considered a slanderer. It is clear that the defamatory words were mutual. Assuredly if all things were equal Bernard's case would be much more favourable than that of Count Leon. Taking into account the mutual wrongs, I hope that the Court will at least dismiss both parties and throw out their several complaints.'

Unfortunately for Bernard his advocate did not have the last word and Leon's counsel was soon to dispel the amused sympathy of the courtroom for the forty-seven year old provincial from Lyons.

Maître Lachaud declared himself for brevity: 'I hope the Court will allow me five minutes on this affair which a vain attempt has been made to puff-up. This will suffice me to establish the facts.

'My opponent really has too brilliant an imagination and the speech he has made to you is quite amusing and well turned. I am certainly not complaining about it, because it has given me a great deal of pleasure to listen to my colleague; and if it pleases Monsieur Bernard to have himself proclaimed through his advocate the most half-witted and ridiculous of men I shall not presume to stand in his way. I leave him completely free to make of himself a laughing-stock.

'The fable is an ingenious one: M. Bernard in adoration before Count Leon because he is the son of the great Emperor, pouring out upon him homage and money to the amount of 750 francs; paying everywhere with a touching and awesome obeisance, the Duroc — it is my opponent who says it — the Duroc of the son of the Emperor! I might almost say to M. Bernard that if all this is true then he is not right in the head —'

'It *is* true!' interjected Maître Morise.

'You say so? Splendid! Regrettably I have another tale to tell,' went on Maître Lachaud. 'Monsieur Bernard is not the enthusiastic adventurer you have been shown; neither is he the generous soul whose liberality was honoured just now. I know that he has a vice — an habitual vice.

'He is a gambler — a most assiduous gambler on the Bourse. And now, gentlemen, do you believe that I need tell you more to make you understand Bernard's passion for Leon?

'It was at the end of November that the loans began. The elections of 10 November were not far ahead. Count Leon might soon be a well-placed personage; and men of the stock exchange sometimes have such extraordinary hopes and extravagant ideas!

'Let us then, I beg of my colleague, restore the brains and the

good sense of his client; and instead of a dolt let us make of him —
a speculator.'

Maître Lachaud examined first of all the charge of false
pretences. He maintained that nothing was more incredible.
Bernard himself bought the bed. He had it delivered to Count
Leon's flat. No trick was employed, Count Leon had returned the
bed — a fact evidenced by the shopkeeper's receipt. If he had not
sent it back sooner it was because he could not have it removed
while he was being reproached with having obtained it
fraudulently.

Finally, after examining the grounds of the two judgments
against Bernard, Maître Lachaud declared the circumstances to be
self-evident.

'There is no doubt,' he finished, 'that by reason of the facts
there exist some extenuating circumstances in favour of M.
Bernard. I acknowledge this. But I believe the Court has exhausted
all possible indulgence and that M. Bernard can not be treated less
severely.'

The Avocat de la République while asking for the conviction of
defamation to be upheld, at the same time appealed to the widest
indulgence of the Court.

After a lengthy retirement the Court confirmed the two
verdicts, but quashed the prison sentences and reduced the two
fines to 50 francs for each offence.

Once more in the limelight, Leon sought a wider audience.
Turning his back on the Palais de Justice he again looked westward
along the left bank of the Seine — to the Palais Bourbon.

CHAPTER 11

Leon and the Second Emperor

Leon had begun the year 1849 with a letter to the newly-elected Louis Napoleon, who he considered, on attaining high office had not given sufficient thought to his cousin's financial problems.

'Patience is a great virtue,' wrote Leon on February 4, 1849:

For over twenty years I have proved that I possess it. This is all most serious, Monsieur le Président; and you will not forget it! The glorious blood of the Emperor runs in my veins; and his nephew is Head of State — am I to obtain reparation and justice?

But the Prince-President was concerned with ultramontane things. Charles-Louis-Napoleon-Bonaparte inherited from his grandmother Josephine, and Hortense his mother, sexual ardour and compassion; but while there is some doubt whether the blood of the Bonapartes ran in his veins, his life was bedevilled by a slavish imitation of the Emperor. Half a century after the long-haired young general Napoleone Buonaparte had invested Venice with the forces of the Revolution, the thirty-nine year old Prince-President sent another army into the unhappy peninsula. On July 3, 1849, Garibaldi's infant Roman republic was crushed; and the Pope — who had fled the chair of St. Peter disguised as a parish priest — was restored to his worldly dominions.

The following month a generous Leon again put his pen at the service of Louis Napoleon and addressed the people of Rome, exhorting them to put off the spirit of revolt with which France had inspired them, in order to make themselves worthy to receive the true spirit of peace. 'Go into your temples,' he adjured them, 'and pray to God to give you this new spirit.'

While 'Duroc's' appeal for the price of a bed was being entertained by the criminal division in Paris, Leon made his periodical declaration to the French voters. This time, however, he looked beyond the walls of St. Denis.

Under the imposing superscription, *Citizen Leon, ex-Count Leon, son of the Emperor Napoleon, Director of the Pacific Society, to all the electors of France in the forthcoming elections,*

Paris, 20, Rue Saint-Thomas-du-Louvre, 22 July, 1849, Leon
declared: 'I have lived in poverty for over fifteen years; I know the
sorrows of the poor man. I shall be faithful to his cause.[1]

The following day Leon became an advocate in his own cause
when he approached General Gourgaud on a new tack: 'In 1833
[sic], at the time of my duel with Captain Hesse, you assisted me.
You subsequently declared before the Court of Assize that you
had given me your aid out of respect for the memory of the
Emperor. . .'

Like the poor, Leon's creditors were always with him, and in
September, 1849, he was concerning himself with a prosaic issue
quite uncharacteristic of the *fils ainé* of a warrior's family –
although it could never be alleged that the Bonapartes were
indifferent to wealth. During Napoleon's worst moments after
Waterloo, he never lost sight of the millions of francs in gold coin
which he had stored away in kegs in the cellars of the Tuileries;
and indeed he was only reflecting his mother's canny attitude. 'So
long as it lasts. . . ' was Madame Mère's sceptical comment on the
family's good fortune.

Leon addressed a petition to the Legislative Assembly on the
urgent necessity of granting a suspension of seizures of real
property.

Citizen representatives,

I think I ought to call your attention to the pressing need
for the passing of a law which will – for a period of one year
at least – grant a postponement of all seizures of land.
During the year following the revolution of February, 1848,
capital disappeared almost totally from the market: houses
could not be found for sale at any price; creditors holding the
first half of the value of goods kept as security dared not
provoke a foreclosure because they feared the valuation
would be too low to compensate them.

Creditors with a high degree of priority profited from the
improvement in the financial state of the country by going
ahead with a large number of foreclosures on properties
valued at less than half the prices they would have fetched
before the February revolution. This has resulted in very
heavy losses for the people concerned.

Fathers of families who had placed their savings in
mortgages to the value of half the price of the goods thus
encumbered have lost sums which they had put by for their
old age, or with the object of setting up their children. Entire

families who were living an honourable existence on land inherited from their ancestors have been made destitute by the unconscionable seizures of which they have been the victims; and they have been thrown into the depths of misery.

The magistrates have groaned under the harsh necessity of lending their assistance to judgments which deprived so many citizens of their capital.

Leon's blood-curdling appeal to the legislature nevertheless strikes a curiously modern note:

If parliament does not place a check on these disasters, the prospect of the enormous benefits which might result from buying houses will attract much capital in that direction; and industry — deprived of such capital — will languish for a long time in the crisis through which it is passing.

There are many moneylenders who before the February revolution advanced capital against land, since they considered the property was worth double the money they lent. Because this land has suffered a temporary diminution of half its value, is it just to allow these moneylenders to become the owners by valuing the property at one half the price they themselves placed on it in better days?

How can this plunder be permitted when one considers the fact that the property will in all likelihood very soon recover its original value; for all things lead us to the hope that tranquillity will soon be completely restored throughout the country. And since the country relies heavily on landed property in difficult times, it is only fair that it should come to its aid — at least by lightening the burdens it has imposed upon it.

A postponement of one year would perhaps suffice to allow landed property to recover from the shocks it has received.

The Chamber remained unmoved by this carefully researched and documented prayer — in which Leon cited decrees as early as the thirteenth century; and so, on October 25, 1849, he turned once more to his cousin the Prince-President to obtain from England Napoleon's will of St. Helena. But Louis Napoleon was in the middle of a drastic change of his ministers and the matter of the Emperor's bequests was put off for another four years.[2]

The Prince-President continued to enjoy the confidence of the French voters; and in March 30, 1850, Leon begged permission to congratulate his cousin on his sweeping victory. But the great doors on the Rue du Faubourg St. Honoré opened only to emit an icy blast:

Private Office of the President of the Republic, Elysée Palace,
30 March, 1850.

Sir,

The President of the Republic would have liked to receive you in audience and to accept from you in person the expressions of devotion that you have given him in writing; but engagements many and serious have prevented him. He nevertheless wishes that you should be aware how much he appreciated your gesture and the thought that inspired it. He asks me to inform you of this and of his regrets.

Mocquard, Private Secretary.

Encouraged by Mocquard's reply, which he interpreted as evidence of Napoleon III's 'benevolent disposition' towards him, Leon requested an audience of his uncle, Prince Jerome Bonaparte, now Governor of the Invalides, and spoke to Jerome's aide de camp — Lt Col. Dame. 'I hastened to lay before the Marshal the subject of our discussion,' wrote Dame on June 4, 1850.

M. le Maréchal replied that you know the motives which prevent his receiving you, that these motives still exist; that in addition he is unable to be of service and that he does not wish to depart from his self-imposed principle of remaining aloof from all matters not connected with his official duties.

In the silver boudoir of the Elysée Palace on the night of December 2, 1851, a little group of excited men stood with Louis Napoleon as he opened a drawer of his desk and drew from it a folder marked *Rubicon*. The coup d'état had been planned meticulously — even regimental drums were to be slashed to prevent the sounding of an alarm.

On December 3, 1851, Napoleon III was dictator of France. The Second Empire had virtually begun.

Leon issued his own proclamation three weeks later from his house at 18, Quai de Sèvres on the Ile-Saint-Denis. 'My dear Comrades,' he began:

Great things have been accomplished since I ceased to command your brave battalion. You will remember where my sympathies lay, and all that I was happy and proud to accomplish when I had the good fortune to march at your head. In the memory of this is all my glory and all my pride.

By calling to power Prince Louis Napoleon Bonaparte, the

whole of France has desired to hallow the revivifying principle of order, of liberty. Prince Louis is the true tradition.

We on our part have all co-operated in this great national demonstration; let us continue our work. What France desired in 1848 she in fact still desires: to have done with the epoch of revolutions and internal dissensions; to re-establish peace and order on an unchanging and sacred equilibrium — and for all factions to give way before this great principle.

Such was the mandate that we confided to Prince Louis Napoleon. Has he betrayed it? No! Prince Louis Napoleon remains faithful to his great mission and worthy of his illustrious origins.

NAPOLEON!

It is no longer a name, it is a symbol! It is no longer a word, it is a flag!

If in the past we have given our admiration, let us have confidence in the future. That great voice, which has filled Europe with its glory, cannot fall beneath anarchist conspiracies. It is not only France which is called upon to safeguard the honour of that name; it is God — and God is the people! In a letter which I addressed to Prince Louis Napoleon in 1849, I wrote these sacremental words:

The eyes of the whole world are upon you; France is waiting!. . . He also is waiting! . . . He has waited a long time! The parties are combining; but they do not declare themselves! They have at last made up their minds; they have shown themselves for what they are — treacherous — and united for the purpose of snuffing out liberty and the great principle of order. Louis Napoleon has outwitted them and shown them to us in all their hideous nakedness . . .

All honour to him! Honour to his heroic courage which is not only touched by genius, but by the sublime! . . .

Let us all unite to bestow upon him the palm of saviour of France, of protector of civilisation and restorer of liberty! . . . Yes, my friends, let us unite to prove once more that France is the foremost nation in the world, and that it is she who gives the watchword to the entire universe.

Let us all vote for Louis Napoleon Bonaparte.

Count Leon, former Major of the National Guard of St. Denis

While France was still in a state of political ferment, Parisians were flocking to see Eugène Labiche's new play *The Italian Straw Hat*;

and at the Great Exhibition of 1851, held in Paxton's Crystal
Palace at Hyde Park, French *haute couture* earned 350,000 francs
and its country's only gold medal — with the help of the
twenty-five year old son of a Lincolnshire solicitor named Charles
Frederick Worth.

Baulked in Paris, Leon's thoughts turned to Rome 'the refuge of
the Bonapartes,' where he had once been well received: 'I wished
to undertake the journey to Rome, to regularise my life in my
relations with the Church.' Accordingly he wrote to yet another
general of Empire — Count Roguet, aide-de-campe to Prince Louis
Napoleon, now President of the French Republic.

'As you were one of the glorious and faithful companions of His
Majesty the Emperor Napoleon, my august father,' wrote Leon in
his letter of May 25, 1852,

> you will be not at all surprised that I see in you a natural
> protector at the side of Prince Louis Napoleon of whom you
> are the devoted friend. I intend to go to Rome and submit to
> the Holy Father the work to which I am devoting my time.
> When I was rich I had friends and a banker. Today I no
> longer have a banker; and those who gloried in my friendship
> and were proud to call themselves my friend have disap-
> peared and withdrawn themselves from me. I feel therefore
> that there is now only one person who, in his capacity of
> nephew of the Emperor, can furnish me with the means to
> accomplish the design which has become the unique pre-
> occupation of my life.

Leon described the provisions made by Napoleon during his
lifetime and after his death.

> You will see, General, from the letters of General Bertrand,
> M. de Las Cases, M. Marchand, and from the notarial
> declaration of General Montholon, that at the moment of his
> death on St. Helena, the Emperor left to me substantial sums.
> Right up until this very day I have claimed my rights. I
> received no assistance whatsoever from the Government of
> Louis-Philippe, who always held against me the letter that I
> sent to General Excelmans.[3]
>   Today I go to Rome to determine and accomplish my
> destiny. I want Prince Louis to learn from you, General, that
> I am his best friend, and that it lies with him and him alone,
> to render to me the justice and the reparation which are my
> due.

General of Division Roguet replied personally from the Elysée on

May 31, 1852, to say that he was entirely at Leon's disposal and that he had placed his letter before Louis Napoleon.

A week later Leon was told by Mocquard's secretary, Sacaley, 'The Prince has given a favourable reception to your request for funds to enable you to go to Rome. Would you accordingly let M. Mocquard know how much money you will need.'

This temporising note from Leon's little cousin, transmitted through two intermediaries, raised his hopes inordinately and he rushed for pen and paper. 'Before leaving for Rome,' he wrote on June 11, from St. Denis, 'I should like to pay off some debts, and for this purpose I need 20,000 francs . . . ' Leon was also tactless enough to mention the question of the Mosel forests and the Emperor's bequests and he turned the sword in the wound by adding, 'In going to Rome to visit the Holy Father and accomplish a great work of the future, the son of His Majesty the Emperor Napoleon could not request less of Prince Louis Napoleon Bonaparte, President of the French Republic.'

The President was quite capable of giving nothing at all to the son of the Emperor. In recollecting the occasion Leon naïvely observed, 'But to my great astonishment, I received no further response and was unable to make my journey to Rome.'

A few days before Louis Napoleon made his triumphal tour of the French provinces at the conclusion of which he was proclaimed Emperor, Leon asked the abbé Orsini — afterwards Chaplain of the Invalides — to intercede for him with the prince. The abbé was warmly received by a preoccupied Prince-President who said to him: 'Tell Count Leon not to worry; I shall see to his problem as soon as I can.'

Leon, now forty-six was still scribbling away at his pamphlets on the Île St. Denis when, on November 2, 1852, Louis Napoleon announced the complete restoration of the Empire. A month later to the day he was proclaimed Napoleon III at the Hôtel de Ville and simultaneously a new French Constitution was approved. In the Assembly there was one dissenting vote — that of Narcisse Vieillard.

Leon hastened once more to congratulate his cousin; but the entrée to the Tuileries — like that of the Elysée — remained closed. Louis Napoleon — who had pardoned so many offences in others — refused to forget the farce of Wimbledon Common; and Leon was twice refused an audience.

I have been to see my mother the Countess de Luxbourg, accompanied by Mlle. Zulma de la Plaigne, my aunt [wrote

Leon to Gourgaud] and in her presence my mother said to
me that she had met M. Mocquard, His Majesty's secretary.
My mother wished to know why the Emperor would not
receive me, and M. Mocquard gave her this reply: 'Madame,
the Emperor remembers the London duel; he is unable to
forget that Count Leon came to London to kill him, and as a
consequence he will never see him.'

Eleonore had come upon the Emperor's secretary in the Bois de
Boulogne, and he confirmed that it was purely the recollection of
the duel of 1840 that had moved Napoleon III to reject Leon. 'His
Majesty,' said Mocquard, 'will never receive him. Advise your son
of this.' It is to Eleonore's honour that she persisted in her efforts
to obtain Leon's rehabilitation at Court. To this end she enlisted
the aid of a certain general. 'Tell the Countess de Luxbourg,' said
Napoleon III, 'that I shall put no obstacle in the way of her son in
his just claims upon the State; but let us leave it there, general, I
am unable to forget the incident in London.'

The new emperor, with the assistance of his 'faithful servant'
Persigny, and the President of the Senate — Troplong — obtained a
Civil List of twenty five million francs — equal to that of the
Bourbons and twice the amount of money granted to Louis
Philippe; and Leon's 'just claims' were received at the Tuileries.

During his campaign of 1849, Louis Napoleon had run up debts
amounting to half a million pounds; while Leon's obligations
amounted — by Bonaparte standards — to a derisory, 7,026 francs.

The account books of the Tuileries Palace tell the story:

Count Leon, a personnage who may perhaps be considered a
member of the Imperial family — a pension of 6,000
francs . . . On 7 July, 1853, Count Leon, basing his claim on
Imperial decrees of 30 April, 1808, and 31 May and 29 June,
1815, annulled by the Restoration, put in a claim for
872,670 francs allegedly granted to him by Napoleon I from
the proceeds of the sale of wood from the state forests in the
Department of the Moselle . . .

On the eve of Napoleon III's marriage, Cardinal de Bonald sent a
message to Leon by way of Charbonnel — who had twice been to
Rome for consultations with the Holy See — to say that he ought
to go himself to Rome, furnished with a letter from the Archbishop of Paris.

'For the past year I have been making preparations for this
journey,' wrote Leon, to His Highness Monseigneur Sibour, Archbishop of Paris, on March 12, 1853.[4]

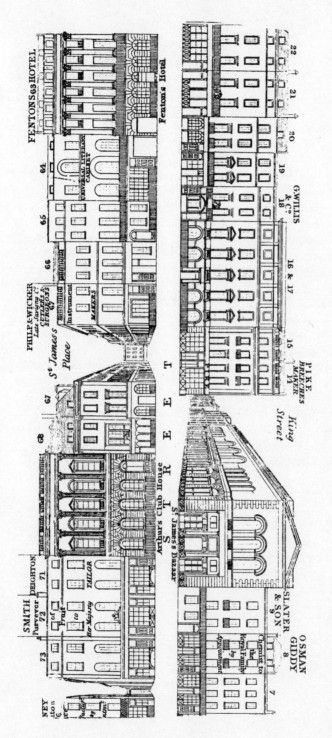

Plan of St. James's Street, showing Fenton's Hotel

168

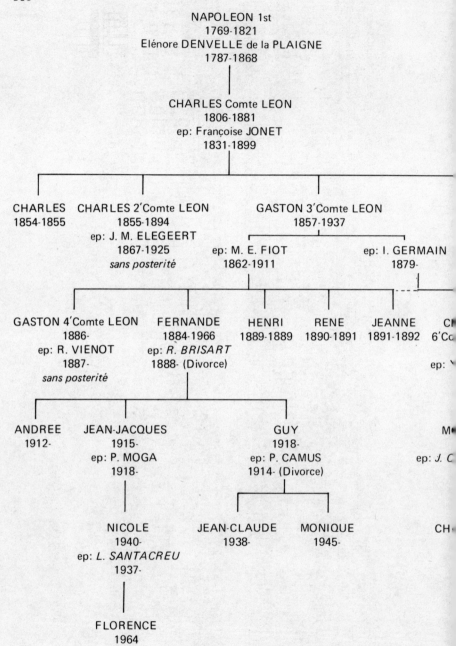

NAPOLEON 1st
1769-1821
Elénore DENVELLE de la PLAIGNE
1787-1868

CHARLES Comte LEON
1806-1881
ep: Françoise JONET
1831-1899

CHARLES
1854-1855

CHARLES 2′Comte LEON
1855-1894
ep: J. M. ELEGEERT
1867-1925
sans posterité

GASTON 3′Comte LEON
1857-1937

ep: M. E. FIOT
1862-1911

ep: I. GERMAIN
1879-

GASTON 4′Comte LEON
1886-
ep: R. VIENOT
1887-
sans posterité

FERNANDE
1884-1966
ep: *R. BRISART*
1888- (Divorce)

HENRI
1889-1889

RENE
1890-1891

JEANNE
1891-1892

CI
6′Co

ep: '

ANDREE
1912-

JEAN-JACQUES
1915-
ep: P. MOGA
1918-

GUY
1918-
ep: P. CAMUS
1914- (Divorce)

M

ep: *J. C*

NICOLE
1940-
ep: *L. SANTACREU*
1937-

JEAN-CLAUDE
1938-

MONIQUE
1945-

CH

FLORENCE
1964

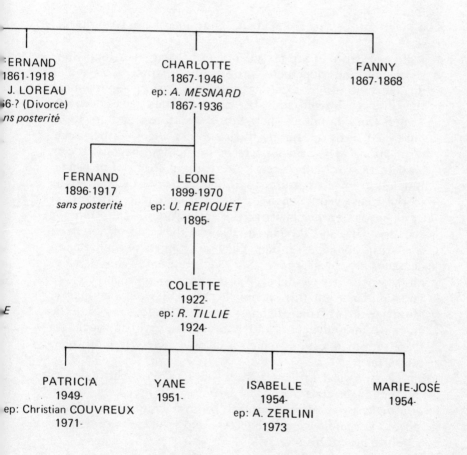

ERNAND
1861-1918
J. LOREAU
66-? (Divorce)
ns posterité

CHARLOTTE
1867-1946
ep: *A. MESNARD*
1867-1936

FANNY
1867-1868

FERNAND
1896-1917
sans posterité

LEONE
1899-1970
ep: *U. REPIQUET*
1895-

COLETTE
1922-
ep: *R. TILLIE*
1924-

PATRICIA
1949-
ep: Christian COUVREUX
1971-

YANE
1951-

ISABELLE
1954-
ep: A. ZERLINI
1973

MARIE-JOSÉ
1954-

Count Leon's family tree

When I wished to enter into relations with Christian Rome to accomplish my high mission, Cardinal Bonald observed, 'Count Leon is a natural child; but, after all, the Church can take care of that. He should apply to the *Nunciatura*.' In 1850 Monseigneur de Falloux, a Roman priest and brother of the former minister, sent and told me, 'What is Count Leon doing in Paris? Cardinal Fesch's will was published in Rome, not Paris; if he comes to Rome we will do something for him.'

'Although my origins are evident,' continued Leon without bitterness,

I did not wish to lay myself open in Rome as an impostor, since no legal document proves my filiation. Today this difficulty no longer exists: at the request of the Government the Emperor's will and its secret codicils have been returned from London. Their terms are known and are to be published. I figure among them and my august father made dispositions in my favour which for me have become a new legal birth. I no longer fear to arrive unrecognised in Rome. But before my departure, I am unable to remain indifferent to the great events which are about to take place: the arrival of the Holy Father in Paris; the coronation of the Emperor Napoleon III, and the inauguration of the tomb of Napoleon the Great, my august father. Filial piety and above all religion demand my presence at this sad ceremony. This is why, Monseigneur, I have believed it my duty to approach you for your guidance on this solemn occasion. I would be happy, Monseigneur, if Your Highness would deign to accord me the grace of an audience, in order to explore with thoroughness these serious questions which I am able merely to indicate in this letter.

From Christ's vicar in Paris Leon received a short shrift delivered by his canon-secretary, the abbé Dedoux: 'Monseigneur the Archbishop of Paris is not in a position to give Count Leon the advice he needs. The audience he requests would serve no purpose and he asks you to accept his regrets.'

However, at the urging of the abbé de La Bouillerie, Vicar-General and subsequently Bishop of Carcassonne, Archbishop Sibour agreed to receive Leon at four o'clock in the afternoon of March 19, 1853.

Whether by accident or design, the letter notifying him of the appointment was wrongly addressed and did not reach Leon until four days after the date fixed for the audience. He was again obliged to postpone his journey to Rome.

Wearying of the arid phrases of the Church's civil servants, Leon now approached the Minister of War, Marshal de Saint-Arnaud.[5]

'I submitted your request for a private audience to the Emperor without delay,' replied de Saint-Arnaud; 'but I can only indicate to you his attitude since requests for audiences must be submitted to His Majesty through the Grand Chamberlain. However, the Emperor's response leaves me in no doubt that if you made an approach of this kind it would be turned down.'

Leon's correspondents had not learned that when they in their turn indulged in name dropping this was merely a signal for the indefatigable petitioner to probe yet another postern in the walls of the Tuileries.

He accordingly applied to the Duke de Bessano, and received nothing more than a formal acknowledgment from Chauveau, the Grand Chamberlain's *chef de cabinet*.

It is ironic that in that very month of July 1853, when Leon's claim for almost a million francs was finally received at Court, the benefactor of his darkest hours, Gaspard Gourgaud, baron and general, died.

While awaiting his new-found riches, Leon decided to enter the world of industry. Napoleon once remarked, 'The old nobility would have survived if it had known enough to become master of writing materials'; but the fact that they were prolific writers did not ensure the survival of the two emperors. Leon, however, besides his steady output of pamphlets and letters, decided to provide a more basic service to the cause of literature — by supplying its raw material.

CHAPTER 12

The Children of God and the Ink Factory

'To organise productive works in order to afford the French people the means of earning their living by their labour,' Leon, on March 26, 1849, founded the *Society Pacifique*.

In a pamphlet entitled: *Work of the Children of God, Gathered together in spiritual families*, he sets out his views on politics, social ideas, and religion. 'It remains for me to say to what high order of ideas I belong, and what have been my preoccupations since the year 1840.'

He goes on to describe a watershed in his life, when — in 1838, at the age of thirty-one he met the founder of the Societies of Children of God.

Providentially I made the acquaintance of M. Francois-Guillaume Coëssin. I grasped the full significance of the labours of the future which occupied his life, and I have consecrated to them the remainder of my own.

From that time onwards I occupied myself seriously in regulating my whole existence by reference to the church and to the government. If I have not yet succeeded in this, it is totally contrary to my will.

The son of the Mayor of Lisieux in Normandy, Coëssin was born on November 7, 1779, at St.-Germain-de-Montgomery in that region. Early in life he became imbued with revolutionary fervour and gave himself the name of the Roman hero Mucius Scaevola.

At the age of twenty he sailed to Sinnamary in French Guyana to found a Utopian republic. The project collapsed and at the beginning of the Empire Coëssin returned to France. He took rooms in the vicinity of the Ecole Polytechnique near the Boulevard St. Germain and interested himself in the study of advanced science.

The French Government subsidised his invention of a submarine but the trial of the vessel at Le Havre ended in a fiasco. He then turned to the world of nature and undertook experiments on animals with a view to the mutation of species.

Having returned to the fold of religion, as he stated, through scientific research, he founded in 1810 at the age of thirty-one a community at Chaillot known as the Maison Grise. The rules of the 'Grey House' were spartan; but it was rumoured that while his disciples mortified their flesh Coëssin maintained himself comfortably on their devout contributions.

Napoleon's police began to take a lively interest in the society, and the Prefect himself — Rhéal — investigated the Maison Grise. After half an hour in the master's presence, however, the police chief was completely won over, and thenceforth gave the establishment his protection.

This would seem to confirm the judgment of Madame de Genlis. In her memoirs she says:

I have never known a man who in conversation on the great subjects of religion and politics possessed an eloquence as strong and captivating as that of M. Coëssin.

The philosopher transferred the activities of the Grey House from Passy to Thernes, north-west of the Champs Elysées, where he established his company at the Rue de l'Arcade in a large mansion surrounded by an extensive park. Here — to gain more adherents — the mystic abandoned asceticism for a more permissive community to which women were admitted. The Arcady of Thernes dissolved with the Empire.

Besides the celebrated lamps with revolving base 'superior to those named Carcel,' Coëssin invented a pump for raising water, and a pneumatic irrigation spray. About the year 1820 he was invited to visit Holland by the Netherlands Government and put before them his plans for draining the Lake of Haarlem; but after discussions with the Dutch authorities this grandiose project never left the paper stage and Coëssin returned to Paris.

Madame de Genlis, the friend of Voltaire and one time governess of Louis Philippe, believed that after having been a philosopher 'in the bad sense,' Coëssin had become a true believer and very devout. Certainly he gave shelter to Leon when he was in the utter depths — and with little hope of any recompense. Leon seems never to have forgotten this kindness and returns time and again to the theories of Coëssin, who, he declared, had predicted the revolution of 1848. 'The lofty conversation of this man of genius and perusal of his books have left me in no doubt as to the events that have lately been accomplished and as to the future.'

For Leon the Rue de Clichy was the Damascus road. But his enthusiasm for the prophet was by no means universally shared. Madame de Genlis who received the visionary occasionally at her salon thought he was too ultramontane. 'His enemies call him a hypocrite, but I am certain that he is quite convinced of the truth of religion; he has the kind of faith that throws out great flashes of light ... It was her understanding that Coëssin entertained the hope and intention of being elected to the papal chair on the death of Pius VII.

The writer 'Alexandre Erdan' — Alexandre André Jacob — is unable to make up his mind about Coëssin. He concludes that the philosopher is a 'politico-religious half-breed,' but he cannot decide whether he was motivated by conviction or by calculation.

Coëssin — whose spiritual centre of gravity lay firmly across the Alps — was greatly attracted to religious orders, particularly the Society of Jesus; according to Erdan his mysticism was akin to that of the Middle Ages. When Johann Kaspar Spurzheim visited Paris Coëssin lost no time in calling upon him. In accordance with his practice, the German phrenologist examined the bumps on the prophet's skull and observed: 'It is a pity that religious orders have been dissolved — you would have made an excellent Jesuit.'

In 1818 Coëssin visited the Vatican and seems to have established good relations with the Curia. Like the Vicar of Bray he survived the Restoration and prospered. In one of his books he relates that while in Rome he heard a voice that spoke very distinctly in his ear.

Coëssin preached that humanity, which had passed through the three conditions of savagery, slavery and mercantilism, was about to enter the fourth state of peace, happiness and contentment, of which the moving spirit would be the love of God.

He described the fourth stage, which was to follow the publication of the *Nine Books*, and the establishment of the 'spiritual families,' in highly mystical terms. It was to be for him an era of universal piety: the contemporary tendency towards industrialisation would be replaced by that of religion.

'Industrialism,' said Coëssin, 'creates men to be the makers and consumers of calico. . . God creates men, says the Christian, to get to know him, to love him and to serve him . . . '

Coëssin manifested the greatest repugnance for the English laisser-faire industrialism of the early nineteenth century. He saw it as a transient state; a period of intestine war, and — almost a paraphrase of Hobbes — a time in which men, like wild animals, were abandoned to their natural lusts.

He reproaches the mercantile system with having only one slogan: respect for persons and property. 'If all men believed in

Jesus Christ,' says Coëssin, 'the laws of property and of inheritance would be without motive and without an aim.' In the organisation of the spiritual families private property is excluded.

The institution of the spiritual family consisted in subordinating the carnal system of the human family to the organisation of Christian benefits under the *wholly spiritual* patronage of Coëssin. Upon entering his community, disciples were obliged to take vows of poverty and obedience.

Erdan tartly comments that Coëssin was like many another abbot — poor and humble as an individual, but very rich as the superior of the community.

He kept a good table at 290 Rue St. Honoré — where he manufactured his patent lamps — and there professed no enthusiasm for the mortification of the flesh and the contemplative regime.

This was in stark contrast to the asceticism of the early days in the Grey House on the plain of Passy. In 1810 he was preaching that the severity of his diet had for its aim the raising of man to the highest degree of Christian perfection. Said Coëssin, 'The need of food is in truth the seal of our earthly imperfection and the shameful results of the digestion are the permanent stain flowing from the original sin.'

Now in his new home, close to the Court of the Tuileries, the prophet was spreading the doctrine of spiritual strength through joy. 'The sumptuous regime of the spiritual families,' said the rule, 'provides for everything in the nature of lodging, clothing and food in a most generous measure; and consideration, delicacy and respect for the conventions in general, *carried off with a degree of elegance,* are elements absolutely indispensable to the community.'

The revolutionary young socialist of 1799 had become the mellow philosopher of 1829.

Coëssin's little band of Christian hedonists continued to flourish into the reign of Louis Philippe.

Article 10 of the regulations for the spiritual families ordered: 'We will pray in assembly morning and evening; hear together the first mass of the parish; make our communion on Sunday in memory of Saint Joseph and the Holy Virgin — patrons respectively of the several spiritual families (of which Paris was only one); finally — before the evening prayer — we will read from some pious book approved by the church and universally estimed by devout persons, and afterwards the life of tomorrow's saint.'

Posterity's title for Coëssin might well be 'tomorrow's saint.'

The faithful of the Rue St. Honoré were able to buy from the master useful articles and devotional books — no doubt at a privilege discount:

1. *First Bulletin of the Children of God gathered together in spiritual families,* by F.-G. Coëssin, founder of the said families.

2. Continuously on the presses — new edition of the *Nine Books,* a work printed in 1809, that is to say anonymously for 21 years — by F.-G. Coëssin.

3. Hammocks, or *lits Americaines,* suitable for the use of the spiritual families.

4. New lamps with revolving base, invented by F.-G. Coëssin, superior to those called 'Carcel' . . .

5. Pneumatic sprays, invented by F.-G. Coëssin . . .

Coëssin's ideal was the supremacy of the sacerdotal power. Under the rule of the spiritual families, the holy corps of pontiffs would possess the absolute direction of the 'thinking force' of society, in the same way as the monarch possessed the executive power.

He explains, 'The body executive and the pontifical body might be represented in the form of two pyramids, of which one would have its base on earth and the other in heaven. And these two pyramids would be so shaped that in being joined together they would form the cube which is the most solid and immovable structure . . .'[1]

Coëssin had selected four points in Europe for the four degrees of perfection to which the members of the spiritual families must attain. The first, or expiatory, degree had its centre in Paris, the second degree, the purgative, was to be at Lorette, the third or illuminative degree at Rome, and the fourth, the degree of union with the Creator, had its 'provisional' headquarters at Monte Luco.

When in 1809 the thirty year old visionary completed the first volume of his writings, entitled the *Nine Books,* he sent a copy to Napoleon by way of the Emperor's *maître de chapelle* — Leseur. Bonaparte sent back the reply, 'Tell the author that I have read his books three times in succession; but he is going to have a deal of trouble to see the handsome ideas of which he writes realised in his lifetime.'

Forty years on the Emperor's son was still trying to achieve the earthly paradise — the headquarters of which was to be in his father's honeymoon villa, the hôtel Bonaparte at 60 Rue de la

Victoire, at the other end of which (at No. 29) Leon was born.

'In 1849,' writes Leon,

I laboured to found a fellowship under the title of the *Société Pacifique,* which had for its aim broadly to respond to the real needs of the people. The deed constituting this society was legalised in the chambers of Maître Aumont-Thiéville, the Paris notary. It was in some sort a transition to the *Great Work of the Children of God.*

I laid out a substantial amount of money and I had won the sympathies of the administrative authorities. But the time was not yet ripe. I dropped this plan . . .

To finance his Peaceful Society — which was to include the setting up of 'economical kitchens' — Leon offered for sale shares at five francs each. However, contributions to the equivalent of this sum might be given in goods or in labour.

Leon must have been among the first operators in the field of mail order religion, for he says, 'the director of the society counts on the assistance of all men of goodwill to help him to carry on his publications by sending him a postal order for five francs.'

'If I have any ambition, it is to prove by the facts, that the Catholic religion — Roman and Apostolic it goes without saying — is the only one which provides the means of realising the sublime motto written on the flag of the Republic: *Liberty, Equality, Fraternity.*'

Under Louis Philippe republicanism had again become fashionable; but after the seizure of power by Louis Napoleon Leon would write of the glories of monarchy.[2]

On June 28, 1849 — three months after he had founded the *Société Pacifique* — Leon applied to the National Assembly for a subsidy of one million francs for his new body, at the same time promising to devote this immense sum[3] to the extinction of poverty. It was also his intention to publish a bulletin which would afford free discussion of ideas for the improvement of the constitution of the Republic!

French Governments rose and fell; revolution was succeeded by elections and a coup d'état was confirmed by a plebiscite; Napoleon III was now dictator of France, and still Leon published his utopian blueprints and made the Paris notaries fat.

In his pamphlet *The work of the Children of God gathered together in Spiritual Families,* Leon explains:

The Children of God, of whom it is spoken in the Holy Scriptures, namely in the Second Chapter of the Book of

Job, and in the First Chapter of the Gospel of Saint John,
have been predestined from all eternity, from the beginning
of the world unto the consummation of the ages — Book of
Genesis.

Monsieur F.-G. Coëssin conceived the idea of regularising
this work by organising the Children of God into spiritual
families on the model of the human family. A few persons of
goodwill having spontaneously joined him, he published on
September 29, 1829, the first Grand Bulletin of the
Children of God gathered together in spiritual families
addressed to the Children of God scattered across the face of
the earth.

The books of M. Coëssin, which we took to Rome and
deposited at the Monastery of the Holy Apostles on 10 April,
1850, by order of His Eminence Cardinal Orioli, Prefect of
the Holy Congregation of Bishops and Clergy, contain all that
is necessary for organising the spiritual families, which are a
social institution developed from the concept which
invariably accompanied the formation of religious orders, but
executed on a more general plan.

Leon continues to use the royal plural — a device which conceals
the fact that it was Charbonnel alone who went to the Vatican:

We were authorised to proceed to its realisation under the
direction of the bishops in a letter from R. P. Vaures,
Canonical Counsellor, dated at Rome, 26 June, 1850,
deposited in the papers of Maître Berceon, Paris notary, by a
deed legalised on 30 May, 1851.

Vast agricultural and industrial operations were commenced by M. Coëssin in 1830, and continued with our
co-operation up to his death. We shall resume the work in
such measure as the holy families increase.

Today (May 25, 1853) we have founded an ink factory
at No. 27 Quai de Seine, on the Isle of St. Denis, and on 23
July last we published a circular entitled: *The Christian
Organisation of Work.*

We have re-published this prospectus in order that no one
may be mistaken as to the true aim we have set ourselves in
all our labours.

Obliged by circumstances to suspend these first trials, I
waited until the day when time was available to act
effectively in developing the *Great Work of the Children of
God gathered together in spiritual families,* of which M.

Coëssin sowed the seeds. To this effect, on 1 February, 1855, in the chambers of Maître Berceon, Paris notary — who received the will of M. Coëssin — I legalised a deed, together with M. Joseph-Jean-Baptiste Charbonnel, man of letters, to lay the foundations of the Commercial Company of the Children of God, and we have published the statutes and general plan of the Spiritual Families under the title of *Prolégomènes.*

Among the great enterprises that we are in the process of realising there is one above all which interests the population in the highest degree. It is the re-afforestation and general reclamation of all the uncultivated lands of France, for which we published the prospectus on 22 November, 1854, and which was referred to the Council of State by order of the Emperor. This vast operation is under consideration.

If it is now asked — what is the Work of the Children of God gathered together in spiritual families, we reply plainly that it is the most general and radical work that has ever been conceived — and that can ever be conceived — by Catholicism, since it is the exact realisation of the reign of Jesus Christ — of the reign of God — on earth. The future, at a more or less distant time, will prove it!

It is not by working upon the masses that this reign can be established; it is in extracting from the masses methodically and progressively what they embody of the highest, the noblest and the most pure, in order to organise it as a living preface to the ultimate social form of which human nature is susceptible. In fine, it is in leaning upon the immovable rock of the Catholic Church, Apostolic and Roman, and under the efficient Imperial French Government, that this last great peaceful attempt may be made, and of a surety crowned with success. The facts speak loudly enough that the day has come openly to rally ourselves to the tree of life.

Like his master Coëssin who was able to modify his views in the light of changing circumstances, Leon — six years after the formation of the Pacific Society — now solicited contracts from the armed services. In the Crimea an Anglo-French force was waging war on the Czar in defence of the Moslem Turks; and when the armies became bogged down in the severe winter snows, Victor Hugo scathingly described Napoleon III's early reign as '*l' Empire qui recommence par 1812*'.

On February 12, 1855, Leon wrote to his cousin the Emperor,

enclosing a copy of the deed-prolegomena of his new *Commercial Society of the Children of God*:

The Ministry of State has informed me through M. Charbonnel that the petition and prospectus sent to Your Majesty on January 2nd were commanded to be laid before the Council of State. I make it my duty to send you a printed copy. At the same time we are busy manufacturing a covered hammock which was ordered by the Minister of War on January 25th last. We are able to offer a complete hammock with a new suspension system by which it may be hung in barrack rooms and thus serve as an excellent bed for the soldier. A model of the submarine which formed the subject of the Minister of Marine's letter to us of 29 December is also being prepared.

I hope, Sire, that Your Majesty will deign to look upon these divers projects with a favourable eye, and encourage me in the pious scheme of the work of the Children of God; and that Your Majesty will be the first shareholder in the Commercial Society of the Children of God.

No. 27 Quai de Seine, Île St. Denis.

Leon received an acknowledgment three days later from the *chef de cabinet* of the Ministry of State and Household of the Emperor, and his letter and its accompanying prospectus were duly pigeon-holed.

On the anniversary of the death of Napoleon, May 5, 1855, Leon read in the *Moniteur Universel* an announcement which must have seemed like the fanfare of a golden age. It was the publication by the Minister of State, M. Fould, of the dispositions of the Emperor's will. Perron, head of section at the Ministry and secretary of the Will Commission, informed Leon that the sum of 255,319 francs allotted to the 'ward of the father in law of Meneval' was to be converted into shares at three per cent of which he was to enjoy the annual income, and the capital of which would devolve upon his half-brother Count Colonna Walewski, the Minister of Foreign Affairs.

'It has given me much joy to learn of the decision of the Minister of State regarding the execution of the legacies in my favour made by my august father Napoleon Ier,' wrote Leon to Walewski on September 6, 1855.

I am happy to see that his wishes have been religiously honoured and that restitution to the family is a sacred principle. The Commission has allotted me 255,319 francs of which 210,000 francs at three per cent. will furnish me with an annual income of 10,000 francs which will pass to you should I die without issue, and 45,000 francs will go to satisfy diverse creditors; but only through the medium of a liquidator, my advocate Me Boudin. His integrity is above reproach; but there are certain debts of honour and of heart which can only — and must only — be settled by myself; otherwise I should offend the just susceptibilities of certain creditors who for me are somewhat above the ordinary. I have no doubt you will be considerably affected by these considerations, and if you will tell me at what time I might see you to discuss the matter I have no doubt we shall reach a solution which will satisfy all the demands of heart and family.

To Leon's astonishment his half-brother did not reply, and so, a fortnight later he sent off a reminder. Primly he began:

It is none of my business and I shall make no further inquiries to find out what has prevented your replying to my letter. It would nevertheless give me much pleasure to discuss this matter with you, because I believe such things ought to be settled within the family without the intervention of a stranger. If you are unable to spare me a moment, please inform me accordingly and also tell me if I must arrange for Me Boudin to dispose of the matter.

Walewski was prompted to reply in his own hand; and he seems to have taken personally Leon's allusion to 'debts of honour and of heart,' for on September 20 he wrote, 'I regret that my duties do not permit me to receive you at the moment. As for the paltry loans I was happy enough to be able to make, do not give them a thought, I beg you; there will be time to settle up later.'

It is a measure of Coëssin's influence upon Leon that more than twenty years after their first meeting he is still promoting — and in the minutest detail — the teachings of the Norman mystic.

French public opinion was divided on the functions of the Pope, Pius IX, and to the spate of pamphlets Leon contributed a substantial tract of his own.

The solution of the human problem, [he writes] is to revive the memory of the most outstanding Christian philosopher, who was the contemporary of the Great Man [Napoleon].

And since it is a constant that all true philosophers have by the genius and veracity of their writings always influenced human progress by preparing the great social transformations

of the future, how could we hesitate today to fulfil our
mission and proclaim this incomparable philosopher, the
memory of whom is still so much alive in the sanctuary of
Christian Rome — Monsieur Francois-Guillaume Coëssin, who
died at 9 Rue Monthabor, Paris, on 14 September, 1843.

Today in Paris his memory is all but forgotten. His tomb is
destroyed and his mortal remains scattered. Nevertheless, he
was known to the whole of the intelligent world, including
M. Emile de Girardin himself. His door was open to all. By
his words and his writings he communicated to men the
whole of his thought. But because it is purely Catholic,
everyone with the exception of a very small number reviled
and spurned him; and he died alone, in the arms of religion.

Without a great deal of subtlety Leon now directs attention to
himself:

However, he left conscientious heirs and executors, faithful
and devoted to his entire thought. And — we are not afraid to
say it — only this concept is today capable of giving to the
Napoleonic idea the complete potential of realisation that is
desirable — even possible . . .

The *Neuf Livres* had a magical attraction for Leon and it is he who
drew attention to the fact that his father, the Emperor, had read
the work three times in succession:

In his first volume, the *Nine Books*, printed for the first time in
1809, M. Coëssin applied himself to writing the metaphysical
history of man, and all the phases through which the human
species must necessarily and unfailingly pass until it is regenerated
by the doctrine of Christ.

And considering in particular each epoch of civilisation
and all the phenomena it produced, he has proved mathematically — by theoretical science and rigorous observation —
certain laws of creation: (1) that the condition of savagery,
which is the primordial state of man, corresponded to the
system of the family, and that the religion of that time was
the love of the creature, and consequently the exclusive love
of self; (2) that the family concept must give birth to the
system of slavery, in which religion is the law of fear; (3) that
the mercantile system, which has in a singular manner
furthered the emancipation of the human race, must of
necessity replace the system of slavery, and that the religion
of the mercantile epoch was the regard for person and
property; (4) the mercantile system will inevitably give place

to the regime of regulated pontifical Christianity which will be the ultimate — since it will be the divine — order, in which love of the creature and of self, the law of fear, will give way to the law of love, that is to say to the love of the Creator or of God and of other men, who are our brothers.

Following upon this Coëssin-like preamble, Leon nears his climax in which he supports Napoleon III, but at the same time puts in an encouraging word for the pope — the keeper of the *Nine Books*.

In this last society, which is closely deduced from the preaching of the Gospel, the pontifical body and the whole of the clergy and of religious orders in general will possess nothing in the temporal sphere. All riches belong to the Monarch, who is chief of the corps executive and of the workers and who is charged with supervising and providing for the real needs of the corps pontifical and clergy, and those of the executive body.

But all the laws and regulations of the temporal government are to be submitted to the control of the corps pontifical in order to verify that they contain nothing contrary to the doctrine, and consequently to the eternal laws of the Creator — that is to say that they are not tainted with atheism.

From this order of things clearly stems the precise and radical solution of the problem of the division into spiritual, temporal or material: since the Monarch — with the body of executors — being united to the Pontiff by the sacred bonds of doctrine clearly becomes the executor of the will of God manifested by he who is the pope; and the sovereign Pontiff himself, who is the unique representative of God on earth, accomplishes his divine mission by rendering to Caesar that which is Caesar's and to God that which belongs to God.

M. Coëssin gives to this latter form of government — the only true one — the name of *scientific, regulated, pontifical Christian monarchy,* and his books contain all the general rules for its organisation.

The *Syllabus of Errors* in which Pius IX dismayed even his most friendly critics, showed how little he had taken to heart Leon's thesis on his spiritual and temporal powers. Fortunately Leon had incorporated in his pamphlet other of the prophet's ideas. He writes:

In his *Spirit of Conquest and Usurpation in the Mercantile*

System, printed in 1814, M. Coëssin proves by the logic of fact and by the observation of men and things, that the mercantile — or competitive — system, is just as much a usurpation as the system of war, and like it will only result in raising up one or two nations above the rest by monopoly, and then in its culminating development encompass the ruin of all, by unerringly bringing about universal impoverishment.

But, as industry and the fundamental needs of men — even their most outlandish requirements — have very positive limits, there will come to pass and — in a time that is not so far off as may be imagined — everything that I have indicated above. I mean that bankers and merchants will become the princes of the earth — one moment before its complete annihilation and their own; and the world will come to know whether their domination — short as it will be — is preferable to that of the sword.

Leon's next excursion into the field of Coëssin's politico-economic ideas may have been influenced by his lack of success in selling the mystic's patent oil-lamps in London for he says:

M. Coëssin goes on to blame admiration for the English or American system as a false sentiment, because the system is founded on heresy.

He then demonstrates that to return to the past is an impossibility and goes on finally to show how the hostile attitude of the clergy towards the Revolution and their pretensions to recovering the riches of which they were deprived are the greatest obstacles to the establishment of religion in France. He counsels the Roman Church to resign herself to what has been done and to confine herself to saintliness and the spreading of the doctrine that she preaches; a form of government which — by its resemblance to herself more closely as the days go by — will end by possessing the same steadfastness, and thus make Rome the centre of religion and the fine arts; of literature, high politics and the sciences.

Thus Catholic thought joins hands with the Napoleonic idea. The one embraces all the true spiritual needs of the people; the other their material interests.

And so the alliance of these two powers is an absolute necessity since France is the eldest daughter of the Church, and because she has received the mission to spread the good news — the Gospel — in every way.

The works of M. Coëssin are deposited at Rome in the Sacred College where we placed them in 1850. They have been examined and perfectly understood. But in view of the gravity of the political situation the Holy Apostolic See has not believed it timely to deliver a definitive judgment on them, and has limited itself to charging us verbally and in writing to press on and hold ourselves in readiness to return to Rome when the time is ripe.

While Leon was writing these — his final views — on Coëssin, Napoleon III was at the centre of one of the greatest crises of his career. For a decade France was to be split by the controversy over the temporal and spiritual powers of the pope, and the extent of his worldly dominions.

Leon waited in vain for his summons to the Eternal City; but he was used to waiting. In the meantime he continued to make unwelcome propaganda for his Imperial cousin, whose modest pensioner he continued to be:

. . . The programme from Saint Helena to Ham lives on in all its power and in all its splendour in the words of M. Coëssin:

And I perceived that since heroes stand always in the presence of these great thoughts, all peoples and all individuals who refuse to share therein must be devoured.

CHAPTER 13

The Intendant's Daughter of St Denis

At the Town Hall of the 18th Arrondissement on June 2, 1862, Leon married a girl twenty-five years his junior with whom he had been living for six years. Françoise-Fanny, born in Brussels on January 14, 1831, was the daughter of Maximilien Jonet, Leon's estate manager at St. Denis.

To marry for love was not a Napoleonic weakness. 'What matter if our wives are ugly so long as we have beautiful mistresses,' said the Emperor to his indomitable brother Lucien, and afterwards remarked: 'Of all my brothers he is the one who possesses the greatest talents. A dreadful thing — to go and marry a working-class girl, a pretty Parisienne!' The youngest Bonaparte, Jerome, being a minor was forced by Napoleon to repudiate his American wife, Elizabeth Patterson of Baltimore, who retreated to Camberwell where she gave birth to their son Jerome — 'Bo-Bo' — bastardised by Imperial command.

It is therefore to Leon's credit that he regularised his relations with his young mistress. He knew the unnatural existence that awaited the natural child.

On September 4, 1862, Leon wrote to his mother-in-law of two months, *Ma bonne mère*,

My wife and I have just received news of your health and it is causing us much concern. Do not lose heart; but look well after yourself.

You know, since I last saw you a great change has taken place in the situation of your daughter — my good Fanny. She has become my beloved wife and my lovely children have become my children. Circumstances outside my control have prevented my coming to see you. But do not accuse your daughter; she is not ungrateful. In a few days we will come altogether, with my little Charles, to embrace you and my dear little Gaston. At the moment I have a little pain and my left ear is sore. My wife is applying linseed poultices every two hours and I think they will do it good. My little Fernand is very well, but his nurse has been rather off-colour this week.

Madame Duhay has just arrived and asks me to give you her regards.

Leon hazards a new familiarity with his mother-in-law:

We are coming to see you soon. Take good care of yourself, my good Josephine. Do not forget that I think a great deal of you: I have the most ardent desire to improve your situation as soon as I am able. Until then look well after my dear little Gaston. And accept, *ma chère et bonne mère*, with the wishes that I make for your happiness, the most sincere assurance of all my affection.

Leon's style here — as in other of his writings — seems to be influenced by St. Paul:

Lots of good wishes to Laporte. Eugène could well have come to see me. I regret very much my poor Lowe; she was very old and very ill. Perhaps now she is happier. I recommend to you my poor companion.

And thus there had appeared in the letters with which Leon importuned his rich and legitimate acquaintances two new topics — his marriage and the future of his children. His correspondents, however, remained unmoved.

While Françoise-Fanny was within a fortnight of delivering her first-born, Leon had noticed a happy announcement in the press which provided him with the cue he was badly needing; and on October 12 he wrote to his little cousin,

I have just experienced the great joy of reading in my newspaper — *La Patrie* — that Her Majesty the Empress is in the fifth month of her pregnancy. Permit me, Sire, to lay at your feet all the happiness that I feel at this most interesting announcement. I sincerely hope that Providence will watch over them both and that you will have a Prince. With the whole of France I rejoice.

Among the correspondence received at the Tuileries there was also a letter from M. Louvet, a deputy and Mayor of Saumur, suggesting that Eugénie should wear the Virgin Mary's Girdle. This relic, lodged in the church of Puy-Notre-Dame, had been donated by William IV, Duke of Aquitaine on his return from the Crusades. It had been worn most successfully by Anne of Austria, said M. Louvet, when she gave birth to Louis XIV at St. Germain-en-Laye in 1628.

Leon's first child, Charles, was born on October 25, 1855, at St. Denis; and during the following months he sent out many begging letters; but in spite of his pleas for a starving brood and a yet unsanctified Françoise-Fanny, he failed to raise the wind.

In August Napoleon III had turned down a request for 3,000 francs. He was much too busy showing Queen Victoria and Prince Albert round the Paris Exhibition; and although she had received a rapturous Cockney welcome at the Bricklayer's Arms railway station in the Old Kent Road the previous April, the Empress Eugénie was making the first few weeks of her pregnancy an excuse for disregarding protocol and wilting at St. Cloud. She was to survive for another sixty-five vigorous years.[1]

The year following the birth of Leon's first child saw a curious incident at St. Denis. Leon had given refuge at his property on the Quai de Seine to the distinguished Spanish liberal Sagasta who was on the run from the authorities in Madrid. It was not long before the French Government traced his sanctuary, and a police inspector with several officers was despatched to interrogate and if necessary to arrest Leon's guest.

'Who is there?' asked Leon when the *agents* demanded entry.

'The Commissaire and the police.'

'I don't give a damn for the Commissaire and the police!' shouted Leon.

'We have come to arrest Señor Sagasta.'

'He's not here!'

'We saw him go in.'

'Impossible!'

'In that case permit us to search the house,' said the inspector.

'Oh no you won't by jingo!' shouted Leon from the window. 'If you try to get in I shall let the dogs make a meal of you!'

The Commissaire did not insist; and Leon eventually let Sagasta out by a rear door.[2]

Leon's second child was born in the Marais. The formerly aristocratic Paris suburb centred on the elegant Place Vosges had long been deserted by the nobility, and poor families now occupied its crumbling mansions. Gaston Leon saw the light of the Second Empire at 163 Rue St. Antoine, far from the Grand Boulevards, on June 1, 1857, and his birth was recorded at the Town Hall of the unfashionable 12th Arrondissement.

Napoleon's will of St. Helena was finally executed on June 12, 1857, and although Leon had benefited substantially, the Second Emperor had interpreted its dispositions to the ultimate advantage of the son of Marie Walewska. Leon was prompted to write a warm family letter to his Polish half-brother. 'I have called several times at your office,' he wrote to Alexandre Walewski, 'without the benefit of seeing you:'

I wanted to ask you to obtain for me an audience of the Emperor. I have long felt the desire to express to His Majesty my gratitude for the kindnesses he has shown me, in the measures taken for the execution of the will of the Emperor Napoleon Ier. But I did not wait on these matters before imparting to His Majesty the admiration inspired in me by the glory of his achievements and the assurance of my devotion to his person. Nevertheless my heart is yet unsatisfied; I feel I have another duty to fulfil. I have deeply regretted the insinuations which were directed against me in 1840 and above all the duel which followed them.

I have most cruelly expiated this wrong by the deprivation, for many a long year, of being admitted to the honour of the presence of His Majesty. I hope, my dear Walewski, that the generosity of the Emperor will pardon me this fault that I would like to repair by placing my life at his service. My duty is to serve the Emperor. This cry from my conscience leaves me no peace. I have enough strength and energy to fulfil worthily any task confided to me. My devotion to the Emperor and to his dynasty will never fail. I beg you to be, my dear Walewski, the interpreter to His Majesty of my sentiments and of my wishes, and I pray he will grant the audience I crave.

To this letter from the Ile St. Denis, of June 12, 1857, Walewski replied within the day.

I am sorry not to be able to meet your desire. If you wish to request an audience of the Emperor your best plan is to apply direct to His Majesty. A thousand compliments. Walewski.

Three days later — an unwonted delay — Leon delivered personally to the Palace of the Tuileries a letter requesting an audience. The Tuileries remained closed.

On June 11, 1857, Leon had once again submitted his candidature for a seat in the Assembly; and this move proved to be a more effective catalyst than his personally-delivered letter to the Court, for on June 27 Leon received from Manceaux, the Secretary-General of the Council of State, a note to call at his office between nine and ten o'clock on the following morning, Sunday.

If Leon expected some new suggestion — even a novel rebuff — he was to be disappointed, for Manceau merely passed on the regards of his master Billaut, the Minister of the Interior, and advised Leon to write direct to Napoleon III who was spending a late spring holiday at Plombières-les-bains in the Vosges, where the hot and cold sulphur springs had been renowned from Roman times as a specific for gastric troubles, and where the Emperor had been preceded by such renowned *curistes* as Montaigne, Beaumarchais and Voltaire.

Whatever benefit Napoleon III received from the waters was not shared by Leon, for he again received no reply from his cousin.

When Leon received a setback he did not retire in disorder but merely attacked on another front. This time his target was Rouher, the Minister of Public Works and the subject was Leon's claim on the Ministry and on Baron James de Rothschild for sums he had advanced for the Northern Railway.

Paris had a sufficiency of ministries, and before awaiting the reaction of the Ministry of Public Works to his ten year old claim Leon turned to the Treasury, where during a visit M. Magne the Minister of Finance promised a serious consideration of his claims. Had Leon not been a born optimist the phrasing of the Minister's response would have sounded ominous enough.

The day after he visited the Treasury, Leon sent to Alexandre Walewski at the Ministry of Foreign Affairs yet a third copy of the letter which he had sent to the Tuileries and to Plombières. The new ploy was for Walewski to carry a copy of Leon's request for an audience to the Court at Biarritz, a French village across the border from the Spanish town of San Sebastian. The Empress Eugénie's ambition was to do for Biarritz what the Duchess de Berry had done for Dieppe and in a few short years the fishing hamlet of a few simple huts was transformed into a busy resort following the building of the Villa Eugénie in 1854.

Meanwhile, the promised consideration of his *bout de papier* by the Minister of Finance not having evidenced itself, Leon again wrote to Magne. While reiterating the objects of his previous approach to the Treasury, the economically-minded Leon incorporated into his latest letter details of his candidature for the Assembly and his three letters to Walewski for Napoleon III; and concluded with a request to Magne himself to open to him the gates of the Tuileries.

Leon must have mused wryly on the summer which had started so promisingly with the distribution of the Emperor's will of St. Helena, and turned so soon to gall, for shortly after he had moved into 163 Rue St. Antoine there occurred a bizarre repetition of

Mme. Buelle's disastrous encounter with Leon and the bailiffs at 39 Rue Neuve St. Augustin. 'While I was claiming from the Minister of Finance the sums owed to me by the State,' said Leon, 'or at least a little on account to satisfy some of the creditors who were hounding me, one of them — Desprelles, a businessman and an assignee of an amount of 3,000 francs from M. Barillon, my former advocate, had the audacity to effect the seizure of some furniture which did not belong to me at the home of Mme. Jonet whom I have to marry . . . '

Françoise-Fanny was obliged to go to court to recover her bits and pieces. The court held on to the furniture, however, and Leon asked Mocquard to intercede with the Emperor to pay the 3,000 francs for which Desprelles was still pressing.

Mocquard's response was not encouraging and presaged a bleak autumn, 'I regret to inform you,' wrote Napoleon III's *chef de cabinet* on September 1st, 1857, 'that the Emperor, before whom I hastened once again to lay your request in accordance with your wish, is not prepared to entertain the matter.'

In desperation and in the knowledge that — as Leon himself expressed it — Mocquard had destroyed all his hope, he went to see Dr. Conneau, the Emperor's chief physician, who two years previously had lent him 1,000 francs. The debt had been repaid by Leon's receiver, the lawyer Boudin, and Leon had hopes of re-borrowing the money. Unfortunately Boudin had remitted the debt by way of Perron the head of section at the Ministry of State, and the 1,000 francs seems never to have reached Conneau. After several unsuccessful attempts to obtain a refund from Perron, Leon complained to his chief, M. Fould, Minister of State and Comptroller of the Imperial household. Writing on November 8, 1857, with a multiplication of detail dear to the bureaucratic mind, Leon added that M. Soubeyran, the Minister's private secretary, had been informed of the matter by Monsieur Dar, who would furnish M. Fould with all the necessary details.

Leon had for the past eighteen months been in receipt of his pension of some 10,000 francs annually. His cousin the Emperor had granted to Leon, for himself, Françoise-Fanny and their two boys, a yearly sum which represented about one tenth of the Empress Eugénie's dress allowance.

As Fould was obviously disinclined to bring pressure to bear on his subordinate Perron to reimbourse Dr. Conneau, Leon now turned to Prince Napoleon Bonaparte, the son of Jerome and a broken reed if ever there was one. He had returned from the

Crimea after losing some 16,000 men and was only just re-
surfacing.

Leon wrote to 'Plon-Plon' on November 17:

I have the honour to address to His Imperial Highness, two
printed mémoires relating to my claims against the State for
two sums of money which are quite legitimately due to me.
The first of these mémoires deals with the sum of 935,407
francs 55 centimes, capital and interest granted to me by the
Emperor Napoleon Ier on the Mosel forests. The second
concerns the indemnity and the reimboursement of my
advances on the Chemin de Fer du Nord amounting to the
sum of 500,000 francs.

His Majesty has already graciously allotted to me under the
will of St. Helena the sum of 255,319 francs, of which I
enjoy the income and of which the capital has been given to
M. Count Walewski; the 35,000 francs remaining being placed
at the disposal of my lawyer, M. Boudin, to satisfy my
creditors. But as these 35,000 francs do not suffice, my
creditors have all with one voice arisen, and are today stirring
up difficulties more distressing than ever before.[3]

I shall need, Prince, 10,000 francs to draw them off
awhile, and I believe I may have every confidence in address-
ing myself to Your Imperial Highness. I should be very
grateful, Prince, if you would advance me this sum of
money ... [wrote Leon to his affluent cousin, and sadly
concludes:]

I respect the Emperor's wishes and those of the entire family
in refusing to receive me; but I believe that His Majesty and
the Imperial family might at least interest themselves in my
welfare, and help me out of the perilous state in which I find
myself.

To this plea from the unsalubrious Rue St. Antoine in the ghetto
of Paris's East End 'Plon-Plon' remained unmoved. From the Palais
Royal which now housed a host of Napoleon III's grace and favour
hangers-on, Leon received a curt note from the prince's private
secretary.

'Instructed to reply to your letter of the 17th,' wrote Hubaine,
'in which you request of His Imperial Highness the Prince
Napoleon the granting of an audience and the loan of 10,000
francs I regret to have to inform you that the Prince is unable to
grant your request ...'

Ten days later Leon approached Alexandre Walewski with a

Françoise-Fanny, wife of Count Leon

Count Leon and
Françoise-Fanny
in old age

similar plea and received the standard letter of refusal from Chatelain, the count's private secretary.

On December 10, 1857, Leon approached the Count de Morny, the illegitimate half-brother of Napoleon III. Morny at least replied personally and in human terms.

Monsieur le Comte, I have received your letter in which you ask me to lend you the sum of 10,000 francs, which you find indispensable for liquidating certain temporary embarrassments. I have myself unfortunately many obligations to meet which make it impossible for me to make any kind of advance whatsoever. I would have been happy, you may have no doubt, to render to you the service you ask, and I doubly regret not to be able to do it. I shall not fail to call to the attention of the Minister of Finance when I see him again your claim, and ask him to do all in his power to hurry on a solution which will end the difficulties from which you have had to suffer . . . [4]

Reflecting on his various rebuffs of the past year Leon considers 'all there is of sadness and pain in these successive refusals on the part of such highly placed personnages who should have opened their hearts, were it only in memory of my august father, His Majesty the Emperor Napoleon, to oblige me by offering a friendly hand.'

Indeed the Imperial family could not bring themselves to receive in public or private a relative who was unique among royal bastards in having no official cover which would permit the family a loophole — fictitious or not — to satisfy the pompous court etiquette of the Second Empire. It is Napoleon himself who is credited with the observation — 'Etiquette is the prison of kings.'

Leon's advocate, Boudin, now advised him to have another go at Perron, who, he averred, still wished him well, in spite of Leon's letter of complaint to his chief at the Ministry of State. Boudin could not have been more wrong in crediting the under-secretary with benevolent thoughts!

Ever optimistic, Leon hurried round to the Ministry on November 26, 1857, a Thursday, at four o'clock in the afternoon, only to be advised that Dr. Conneau had authorised Perron by letter to devote the proceeds of the repaid loan to pious works. Leon thereupon asked Perron to show him Conneau's letter and warned the civil servant that the money was owing to Dr. Conneau and that he, Leon would not approve the accounts of his liquidator Me Boudin until the letter was produced.

'I have nothing to say to you; you are a scoundrel for making such a complaint against me!' shouted Perron. 'I'll wring your blinking neck, you miserable wretch!'

Leon (according to his own report) replied urbanely, 'Since this is the way you have reacted in this matter and since I only came to you on the advice of my lawyer, Mr. Boudin, I shall not approve his accounts; and tomorrow I shall inform your superior of this trap. I shall also send copies of this new complaint to all the members of the Commission for the Will of the Emperor Napoleon.'

It was Perron who, as Secretary of the Will Commission, had informed Leon that he was to receive only three per cent annually from Napoleon's immense bequest, and that the capital would devolve on Alexandre Walewski. The withholding of Conneau's 1,000 francs must therefore have come to Leon as the last straw that broke the camel's back. The day after his stormy interview Leon wrote to Fould, the Minister of State.

After describing the scene at the Ministry Leon goes on, 'What is M. Perron trying to make of this matter? Was he trying to provoke me into losing my temper and take reprisals? In that event he would have rung the bell for members of his staff and I should certainly have been taken in charge; and in the absence of an independent witness of this scene, M. Perron would have had no hesitation in saying that I had come to do him an injury. How can it come to pass that under the Imperial Government of Napoleon III I am insulted in such an unworthy manner by an underling!'

Smarting under these insults, and above all at the loss of Dr. Conneau's 1,000 francs, Leon the next day laid his case before Count d'Ornano, Governor of the Invalides and President of the Commission for the Will of St. Helena. As always Leon incorporated particulars of the Emperor's bequest of 255,319 francs; and as always added a little something extra. Complaining of Perron's behaviour Leon comments, 'He exhibited a singular lack of the obligations imposed on him by his official duties, and above all of a man decorated with the order of the Legion of Honour.'

Baron Ducasse, General d'Ornano's aide-de-camp, replied on December 1, 1857, with the surprising news that the Governor would receive Leon at the Invalides at midday on the third. However, Count d'Ornano could only regret that Perron still insisted that the sum of 1,000 francs had been paid over to Dr. Conneau.

This storm over a bagatelle must by now certainly have reached the Tuileries; and one might have expected that Napoleon III would allay the scandal by instructing someone — anyone — to pay Leon the paltry sum at issue.[5]

At this stage Leon sent a short note to Dr. Conneau at the Palais Royal appraising him that he had still not been able to lay hands on the 1,000 francs.

Leon now decided to write on December 12 to another civil servant, Perron's superior at the Ministry of State, M. Blance, the secretary-general no less, recalling the visit he had made to M. Blance a week before when the permanent under-secretary had promised to lay before his Minister Leon's complaints. To Perron's defalcation was now added the affair of the sinister trap.

He inserted into his letter a note of menace; and inevitably added an original topical note to his argument.

I have since read in my newspaper, *la Patrie*, a remarkable article entitled *Equality before the Law*, which treats of the severity which the Emperor has visited on certain senior public servants guilty of a lapse of duty in the town of Saint-Etienne. I have taken great solace from this, and also the hope that this power might be used no less justly in my own behalf concerning the legitimate claims I am making on the State, and particularly against M. Perron, in insisting that he restore promptly to Dr. Conneau the 1,000 francs he has been withholding for such a long time, against the express will of the doctor . . .

A hurried postscript notified the permanent under-secretary that Leon was enclosing the two mémoires that were prescribed reading for his correspondents — the claim on the proceeds of timber from the Mosel forests and the claim on the Northern Railways.

Leon's letter produced some action; for Perron made a sudden call on Dr. Conneau promising to repay him his 1,000 francs 'very soon'. Perron seems to have been in some financial straits himself: Conneau never received his money.

Leon now resolved to send the two famous mémoires to Baron James de Rothschild. 'The second', he wrote on December 17, 1857, 'consists of the indemnity which was promised to me at the time of the adjudication of the Northern Railway, in respect of my trouble, care and labour, and for the advance of 20,000 francs, which I made for the preliminary studies on this railway for which I had been promised the concession by M. Thiers's administration.'

After rehearsing the story of Napoleon's bequest Leon continues,

I wish to regularise and assure the position of my children — two fine boys — and I am just on the point of contracting marriage with the woman who has presented them to me. Last week I informed Count d'Ornano of my marriage and the general assured me that Count Walewski had always entertained the good intention of transferring the capital of the 10,000 francs investment to my children as soon as I married. Being obliged in some sort to satisfy the creditors who are pursuing me, and in order to meet the costs of my marriage, I need the sum of 25,000 francs and I believe I may be permitted to ask you for this loan; because no one can appreciate better than yourself the validity of my rights — above all my claim on the Northern Railways . . .

Leon concluded:

Knowing the generosity of your character and the goodness of your heart, I ask you to do all you can in the circumstances to help me out of the embarrassing position in which I find myself.

On this occasion Rothschild's generosity of character was not in evidence. Leon put off his wedding.[6]

There seems to be some substance in Leon's claim on the Northern Railways, however. In 1831 an engineer named Cartier had formed a company to build a railway line to Belgium by way of Beauvais, Amiens, Arras and Lille. Cartier had been promised the concession by the Minister of Public Works, Thiers, and Leon had been lured into furnishing capital for the preliminary studies. Cartier died in 1838 and seven years later James Rothschild took over his concession. Accordingly Leon accused the Minister of Public Works of stealing his plans and sued him for 500,000 francs damages. The claim failed.

Leon had been persuaded to invest in the enterprise — which was fully backed by Louis Philippe's Government — by General Bertrand and a deed to this effect was accordingly legalised by Doste Noël, a notary. Leon was invited to a meeting of financiers which included General Rumigny and Baron Athalin, but he seems to have been completely out of his depths. They told him that Thiers had promised their syndicate the concession. The trusting Leon handed over his 20,000 francs and, while a certain Becu was present, Cartier gave him in return a memorandum on the project together with an imposing set of fourteen maps. Leon never seems to have taken the elementary precaution of being accompanied by his own witness!

Unfortunately Cartier's plan was not the only study under consideration. M. A. M. Vallée was also in the market for the concession. But preference was admitted for M. Cartier's plan on the grounds of its opportunities for employment, for the economy, and for the *salubrité des voyageurs*.

The engineer Cartier died in 1838 and the scheme lost its figurehead. Application after application was submitted to the Ministry; but more powerful influences were at work who had seen the financial gains which had followed the development of the railways in England during the previous decade.

The concession for the Northern Railways was awarded to Rothschild.

'Confident in my capacity and rights resulting from an authentic deed legalised before Maître Doste Noël, notary, on 30 September, 1835,' wrote Leon to the new Minister of Public Works, Monsieur Jayr:

I deposited with you on 16 April, 1841, an application for a concession supported by a provisional scheme illustrated by fourteen drawings. Four years after receiving these documents you gave the concession to a private company — whose plan is nothing more than a copy of our study. Over and above the capital expended on this project, the intellectual labour itself constitutes a proprietary right, especially when the time and energy involved in drawing up plans, together with the capital, are considered.

Leon went on to mention that among the names of the men who had succeeded Thiers at the Ministry of Public Works was that of M. Teste —

who figured among the members of my family council, had told me that as soon as he assumed office I would never lose the fruits of my participation in M. Cartier's plans which I supported with my capital. It is quite certain that morally and legally I must not be the victim, Monsieur le ministre, I would even dare to say the dupe, of my good faith,

concludes Leon — summing up in his own words his own weakness.

The year after this letter was written saw the fall of Louis Philippe and Leon's claim was effectively quashed.

Six months after the birth of his son Gaston, Leon asked Napoleon III for a loan and he decided to send his letter to the

Emperor by hand of his newest *amicus curiae*, Dr. Conneau.

'Several of my creditors have unleashed themselves on me and I am worse off than before,' wrote Leon on December 22, 1857, 'due to their hounding me to the point where I am threatened with imprisonment.'

He mentions again the million francs due to him by Napoleon's grant of the proceeds of the sale of timber from the Mosel woods. But Napoleon III who so sedulously planted his feet in the traces of his uncle the Emperor was not prepared to re-assign the lucrative sales of timber which had been confiscated by the restored Bourbons. The second Emperor, however, had no compunction in sequestrating the Orleans lands — an action which precipitated the resignation from the Government of his half-brother, Count de Morny.

In vain Leon piled on the mellifluous phrases which his father had known so well how to employ.

Your paternal cares will lead Your Majesty to appreciate the solicitude which preoccupies me with regard to my own children, of whom I must — by marriage — assure the future existence. I shall teach them, Sire, to love and respect your dynasty, being myself full of sincere affection for the person of Your Majesty and full of admiration for all the glorious acts of your reign.

Christmas is but three days away, and Leon writes:

I humbly pray you to accept my most sincere wishes for Her Majesty the Empress and for Monseigneur the Prince Imperial. Three years ago I received my new year gifts from your private secretary, M. Mocquard. Since then I have been forgotten. It would give me great pleasure to receive them this year, because they would be a certain proof that Your Majesty wishes me well and reserves for me a place in your heart . . .

Leon's little cousin, unmoved by the spirit of the festive season, refused.

Leon's letter to Napoleon III seems to have succeeded in raising some action in the Tuileries, however, for Mocquard asked Leon to send him particulars of his debts. This request drew from Leon an uncharacteristically short note.

'As you asked me this morning,'

he wrote on January 8, 1858,

I am sending you a copy of my letter to His Majesty, as well as the demands of the various creditors who are pursuing me and of whom I shall be happy to be rid. Be well persuaded that the day I am able to see His Majesty will be the most beautiful day of my life.

CHAPTER 14

A Correggio painted on Agate

Paris had been widely informed that on January 14, 1858, Napoleon III and the Empress Eugénie would attend a gala performance, and at 8.30 in the evening an impressive cavalcade crossed the Place de l'Opéra to the old theatre. Preceding the royal pair was a carriage filled with officers of the Imperial household, followed by a troop of Lancers of the Guard.

The first party had already driven past the facade of the Opéra, and the royal carriage was slowing to a halt at the royal entrance when three bombs loaded with shot, and thrown with deadly accuracy, landed between the wheels of the Emperor's coach, killing the horses and destroying the carriage. High velocity pellets tore through the Emperor's hat, and flying glass cut Eugénie on the eye and cheek. Her white evening gown was spattered with blood from the horses, and the cloak of General Roguet — who had been sitting opposite the Imperial couple — was peppered with holes.

Thus had Orsini and his *carboneros* once more reminded Louis Napoleon of his long-unfulfilled promise to free the Italian people. Although eight persons died and the Place de l'Opéra was strewn with a hundred and fifteen wounded from among the mounted escort and the waiting crowd, Napoleon III and the Empress were able to continue on foot into the performance, The Emperor appeared badly shaken; but Eugénie — who had immediately placed herself in front of her husband to protect him — appeared perfectly calm.

The following day Leon wrote to Dr. Conneau:
Please tell the Emperor and the Empress of the joy I feel at their renewed escape from a dastardly attempt on their lives. I thank Divine Providence for this further blessing and trust she will prevent the repetition of another such deed, the like of which must fill the whole of France with revulsion and anger. May the perpetrators be eternally damned!
The lack of response to all his approaches, and the cold days of late winter seem to have resulted in an unwonted lack of activity;

but during March Leon was visited by a party of *medaillés de Sainte-Hélène*, who shared with him the amenities of the Faubourg St. Antoine — then the eighth arrondissement. 'Moved by the plight in which he had been left by the Imperial Government,' they asked him to represent them in Parliament.

This prompted Leon to make a second approach to Count de Morny, the President of the Assembly: 'Several of the electors of the sixth ward,' he wrote on April 5, 1858, 'in which I have been living for two years — all bearers of the St. Helena medal — who take the most lively interest in me, wish me to stand for the Chamber of Deputies in place of M. Goudchaux.[1]

These gentleman and myself [went on Leon] must hold a private meeting in the very near future to decide on the terms of my profession of faith. My unique affection for His Majesty the Emperor and the profound respect and admiration for the nobility of his character and the magnitude of his politics that I regard as sublime, monsieur le Président, place on me a duty to address myself to Your Excellency — of whose distinguished qualities I am aware — to ask you to vouchsafe to me a moment's audience to discuss all these questions with you. I should also like to bring to your notice a letter that my honourable friend Dr. Conneau has put into the hands of His Majesty, and on which action is already being taken. I should be grateful for the earliest possible reply — since in the event of His Majesty approving my candidature I shall barely have time to make adequate preparations.

Leon received cold comfort from Morny:

I received your letter informing me of your intention to stand as a deputy to replace M. Goudchaux. I have no doubt that you will understand the reticence imposed on me by my position. It is my practice always to abstain from personal involvement in questions of this kind, since the Minister of the Interior must be allowed an entirely free hand. This reply is in no wise dictated by my personal sentiments towards you; it is the consequence of a rule of conduct from which my position allows of no departure.

The not so subtle allusion of de Morny to the Minister of the Interior was as good as a nod to Leon, and the following day he presented himself at the Ministry, where Monti, the private secretary, immediately passed him over to the Prefect of the Seine who had personal charge of the elections. Leon was received at the prefecture by another civil servant de Janvry, an assistant under-secretary, with whom he left a copy of his election address.

Adapting his style to the changed circumstances in which he found himself as a pensioner of his cousin, Leon presented himself to the people of St. Antoine as the *éminence grise* of the Second Empire:

If I cast a glance at the situation in which France has found herself during the last few years, and with which we compare the situation today, the line of conduct we must adopt is clearly indicated. The disorders of the past presage immense dangers for the future. The Emperor Napoleon III re-established the institutions which have already prevented the downfall of the country and built-up its power. Immediately the prospect changed; the energy of His Majesty, the nobility of his character, the loftiness of his thoughts, restored France to that rank which belongs to her in the councils of Europe. My aim — should you honour me with your confidence *Messieurs les Electeurs* — is to second with all my energies the Emperor's admirable policies, and to co-operate devotedly in the maintenance and development of those Imperial in-stitutions which are the power and the glory of France. Comte Léon Rue St. Antoine, 7 April, 1858.

Napoleon III was appalled by this unsolicited promise of support from a tenement in the Paris slums. Appropriately enough he entrusted the quashing of Leon's political aspirations to the man who was busily ridding the capital of its congeries; a man so single-minded in his enthusiasm to redevelop Paris that he had without hesitation pulled down his own birthplace. The forty-nine year old Prefect of the Seine who declined to give the *estampille officielle* to the candidature of the son of Napoleon was George Eugène Haussmann. The prefect had just signed on behalf of the Government an agreement with the Paris municipality for the implementation of the second stage of his plan. Paris would bear two-thirds of the cost, estimated at 180 million francs.

It was Haussmann's departmental head who broke the news to Leon.

Two days afterwards, I saw M. de Janvry, who said that he had discussed my candidature with the Minister of the Interior and advised me — in view of the undertakings given to M. Perret, the former Mayor of the eighth arrondissement — to drop my candidature for the sixth ward and to write to the Minister of the Interior.

Yet again Leon was being sent on his circular tour from bureaucrat to bureaucrat. But like his father the Emperor he would never admit defeat. Leon accordingly visited the Minister of the Interior to request authorisation for his candidature. Here he was seen by the Minister's private secretary, Monti, who told him to take the matter up with the Prefect of the Seine. At the Prefecture Leon was advised to raise his application with the Ministry of the Interior!

Janvry, the secretary of the prefecture, had indulged in a good deal of smalltalk during which he purported to pass on to Leon the views of his master, Haussmann.

I was told that the time was not ripe for my nomination, at least for an intra-mural constituency; that the Government would accept my nomination for the next elections at St. Denis — and that I must first consolidate my position by marriage . . .

Leon reported all this in a letter of April 19 to the Minister of the Interior, General Espinasse; and he inevitably brought up to date his account of his various démarches to which he now added Conneau's name while enclosing the indispensable memoires on his two claims against the State.

'I am a father,' he wrote.

I have two sons whom I wish to legitimise and to bring up in a manner in keeping with my rank and birth; if I am unable to fulfil this duty by means of official appointments, this is yet one more reason why I should energetically defend my inheritance . . .

The general remained unmoved; but his *chef de cabinet* Monti answered briefly, 'His Excellency deeply regrets that his manifold duties do not permit him to receive you at the moment, and he instructs me to tell you to see the secretary-general who will pass on to him details of any documents you may have.'

Ruefully Leon observed that since he had no more documents to produce to a Minister whose many preoccupations prevented a personal interview, there was no point in pursuing the matter further with the Ministry of the Interior.

Having exhausted all other means of raising money, Leon bethought himself of the souvenirs he had thus far jealously guarded, and from which he could not, even in his most need, bear to be parted. On May 1, 1858, he wrote to his uncle Jerome:

Having today a pressing need of money to satisfy several creditors who are hounding me without pity, and to meet the

expenses of my marriage — which must be solemnised as soon
as possible to legitimise my two boys — I would like to sell
this picture, even though to me its value is without price
because of the giver, and because it would cause me much
regret. I am therefore going to offer it to you, Prince, and to
facilitate your acquisition of it, I have fixed the price at
25,000 francs. Were Your Imperial Highness to buy the
picture I should be filled with delight, knowing that this
precious object would remain in the hands of the family.

Leon possessed Napoleon's love of detail and he added the tit-bit,
Your Imperial Highness will no doubt recall that at that same
period Her Majesty Queen Hortense made me a gift of three
small shirt buttons in your presence, and you asked to see
them. I have preserved these small objects most preciously,
because in other circumstances of my life when I wore them I
believe they brought me luck.

(Leon was referring to his duel with Captain Hesse at Vincennes.)

The picture referred to in the letter to Jerome was a Correggio
painted on agate. Framed in gilded copper and enclosed in a green
morocco leather case, it represented an angel offering the cup to
Jesus Christ in the Garden of Gethsemane.[2]

The 'giver' who had bestowed such inestimable value on the
painting was the eccentric testator of 1840 — Leon's great-uncle,
Cardinal Fesch. One day in 1834 while they were both leaving
mass in the private chapel of the cardinal's palace in Rome, he
took the twenty seven year old Leon by the hand and led him into
the picture gallery where he presented him with the painting.
Fesch had for years lived in terror of having the picture taken
from him by Napoleon to hang in the Louvre.

D'Hérisson describes a visit which the son of Joseph Jerome
Simeon made to Cardinal Fesch in his archbishopric of Lyons at
the end of 1812. A valuable Correggio of small dimension stood
on a little table in a corner of the bedroom. Simeon admired the
painting and the cardinal remarked: 'It never leaves me, I have it
always under my eyes. Otherwise I should be afraid that *he* would
take it form me.'

The little picture had some narrow escapes. In 1838 Leon tried
to sell it to Queen Amélie, the wife of Louis Philippe, for 40,000
francs, but after keeping the picture a short while the king sent it
back to Leon. In 1840 he used it as a pledge to obtain 600 francs
from a moneylender. Fifteen years later, Boudin — while disen-
tangling Leon's finances during the liquidation of Napoleon's will

— recovered the painting by repaying the original 600 francs; and it may well have been the little Correggio which was the subject of Leon's early resort to the courts when in the summer of 1837 he gave a picture valued at 6,000 francs to the rascally Dubois to sell — and ended up in Clichy prison.

Two days after offering the Correggio to Jerome Bonaparte, Leon received a curt note from Drut, his uncle's secretary, informing him that the prince had no intention of buying the picture.

'Imagine my astonishment at the reception of this letter,' wrote Leon to Cardinal Morlot.

Was it not entirely natural that in the difficulties in which I find myself — and urged to legitimise my children by marriage — I should with confidence approach Prince Jerome who is the brother of the Emperor Napoleon? Was it right that I should expect such a dry and indifferent response?

Writing on May 25, 1858, to Morlot, Leon cries:

What then is the mystery which keeps me away from the Emperor and the Imperial family? And how does it come about that under the reign of Napoleon III I am thus spurned, without consideration and without pity. Monseigneur, I have confessed to you the whole of my life since I made the acquaintance of M. Coëssin, as I am meet to do before a Prince of the Church, invested with the confidence of the Emperor. Furthermore, the Holy Apostolic See has placed upon us the obligation of realising the Work of the Children of God under the direction of the bishops. It is imperative and entirely natural that we should have recourse to the bishops in all our difficulties. I cannot remain idle until I know the reasons — existing to this day — which oblige Prince Jerome Bonaparte not to receive me, and until I penetrate the mystery which has denied to me the presence of the Emperor ever since my life was poisoned by an odious slander. After all the fruitless attempts I have made, I see only Your Eminence, Monseigneur, who might be able to bring about the reconciliation I desire. This is why I have addressed myself to Your Eminence with all confidence and I do pray you to obtain from His Majesty the audience that I have for such a long time asked in vain.

In an apologia for his disastrous trip to London, he says:

The purpose of my journey Monseigneur, was to accomplish the mission with which I was charged by Archbishop Quelen

— to reclaim from the Count de Survilliers, ex-King Joseph
Bonaparte, the 500,000 francs that my great-uncle Cardinal
Fesch had left to me; and to conclude with Mr. Parker, an
important London businessman, an ambitious commercial
operation for the lamps described as having a revolving base
which M. Coëssin had invented and of which he exploited the
patent in the plan of the Work of the Children of God
gathered together in spiritual families.

At that period M. Coëssin owned magnificent workshops
for the manufacture of these lamps at 290 Rue St. Honoré,
near the church of St. Roch opposite the Rue des
Pyramides, in the former Montmorency mansion where he
employed a hundred workmen. By the strength of his
intellect and with the help of a small number of Children of
God who had rallied to his generous plan, he had created
more than a hundred thousand valuable pieces of equipment;
and the spiritual families at that time possessed materials
worth more than 600,000 francs, which they had amassed by
their own efforts, not counting the landed properties worth
more than 500,000 francs from M. Coëssin's inheritance, and
from Sophie de Chefdebien who was the first to devote
herself to this great work.

In his all-embracing letter to Cardinal Morlot Leon finally revealed
the text of a brief letter of introduction given to him to facilitate
his business trip to London during his cousin's exile there. Louis
Napoleon's newspapers had largely based their allegations that
Leon had been sent to England as an Orleanist spy on this
innocuous piece of paper. Certainly the young Leon was much
under the influence of the considerably older philosopher at this
time, who saw advantageous possibilities in the use of a Bonaparte
as a commercial traveller. Leon explains:

M. Coëssin wisely believed that in view of the most lofty,
most noble, and most religious aim of this industrial and
commercial operation, the influence of the Bonaparte family
could perhaps be useful, using myself as an intermediary, to
realise in England this great operation on the success of
which he had founded the most handsome aspirations for the
development of the Work of the Children of God gathered
together in spiritual families. At the moment of farewell, M.
Coëssin accompanied me to the Ministry of Foreign Affairs
and arranged for Count Molé to give me the following letter
of recommendation for M. Guizot, the French Ambassador, a

personal friend of his:

Paris, 30 January, 1840

Monsieur,

This letter will be handed to you by Count Leon, who is travelling to England on private business.

I should be obliged if you would welcome him, as he merits to be welcomed, and to render him in so far as you are able an agreeable stay in London.

Leon had concealed the contents of this dangerous squib for almost twenty years hoping for a change of heart on the part of his cousin. The remotest acquaintance with Leon was enough to establish the absurdity of the 'police spy' canard. Nevertheless his publishing the note as a last desperate gambit in May, 1858 — when Paris was counting the cost of its good fortune under the second Emperor and his expensive Alsatian — cannot have endeared Leon to his little cousin.

'Should His Majesty Napoleon III persist in his error,' wrote Leon,

I could have no other hope but the Church; and following the word of His Eminence Cardinal de Bonald, I should have recourse direct to the Holy Apostolic See to reconcile me with His Majesty; because in the final analysis I am a member of the Imperial family as the son of His Majesty the Emperor Napoleon Ier.

One person was indeed uniquely responsible for Leon's eternal banishment to limbo. The man who had ordered his son to be christened Charles Macon after a dead general, who when Leon was an unrecognised two year old had ennobled the already titled son of Marie Walewska — was the Emperor Napoleon, of whom Leon spoke with such unwarranted affection. Even after the birth of Alexandre Walewski the baby Leon was held in reserve as heir-presumptive until the birth of the King of Rome. His future at the age of three was to be everything — or nothing.

Even Leon, at the risk of his meagre pension, had not the temerity to allege what many people believed, that Napoleon III himself was in fact the son of a Dutch admiral called Verhuel, or Van Huel. His father King Louis of Holland refused to admit paternity and was only prevented from divorcing the passionate Hortense by his brother Napoleon. 'Hortense always gets in a muddle over the fathers of her children,' was Napoleon's cynical comment.[3]

In the final paragraph of his letter to Cardinal Morlot, Leon was moved to doff the velvet glove:

> Since these slanders have exercised a destructive influence on
> my whole existence it is time that they should cease, and the
> Emperor and all his Imperial family take note that I remain
> ever worthy of my illustrious origin. I repeat, Monseigneur, I
> can now count only on the charitable intervention of Your
> Eminence with His Majesty to rehabilitate me in the bonds of
> affection of the Emperor, and I dare hope that my con-
> fidence in Your Eminence and the Church will not have been
> in vain.

Leon's confidence in the Archbishop of Paris and his church was
indeed in vain, for he received no reply; and printed copies of his
letter were confiscated by the Minister of the Interior — General
Espinasse.

Two months after his abortive approach to Morlot, Leon had a
conversation with an old friend, a wearer of the badge of the
Legion of Honour — a distinction which Napoleon had never
bestowed upon his own eldest son. Moved by Leon's precarious
situation and astonished at the difficulties he had met in attempting to see the Emperor, the Legionary insisted that his friend
should write to the Empress.

Leon followed his friend's advice; but he put his foot in it with
his very first sentence:

> Permit me as the son of His Majesty the Emperor Napoleon,
> the glorious founder of the French Empire, to approach and
> ask of Your Majesty a Grace — the grace of my reconciliation
> with His Majesty the Emperor Napoleon III, the restorer of
> the Empire.

Leon's letter of 28 July, 1858, to the Empress reveals that his
perambulations from ministry to ministry had served a purpose:
Napoleon III had finally responded to his plea for something for
the boys.

> . . . Nevertheless His Majesty has been good to me. In 1855
> he granted to me the investment of the 255,319 francs
> bequeathed to me by the Emperor on St. Helena; and last
> January His Majesty deigned to send to me by letters patent
> on vellum an annual pension of 6,000 francs from the Civil
> List.

Leon attempted to pluck Eugénie's heartstrings.

> You are a mother, Madame, and the religious and generous
> heart of Your Majesty cannot but tremble at the future
> prospects of my children, condemned by a species of

Count Leon's coat of arms

Portrait in wax of Count Leon, modelled by John Theodore Tussaud, great-grandson of
Madame Tussaud

ostracism, by a vain family grudge. In persisting in his refusal of a complete and sincere reconciliation, His Majesty the Emperor — your august spouse — would sever a link in the mighty chain grasped in heaven by the immortal founder of the French Empire, my illustrious father. This refusal would perpetuate family hatreds. Your Majesty could not without emotion contemplate such a future. And it is written in the Gospels, 'God will in no wise pardon he who has not from the depths of his heart forgiven his brother . . . '

I shall bring up my children to forget what is past; and to love the Prince Imperial and the Imperial dynasty, commending the rest to God who alone examines the depths of our hearts.

The religious and generous heart of Marie Eugénie de Guzman, Comtesse de Teba, Empress of the French was moved only by the sight of the latest creations of her dressmaker; and the doors of the palace remained fast.

In the autumn Leon received a savage blow when he read in the *Moniteur Universel* of October 28, 1858, that his half-brother Walewski had with unseemly publicity been granted country estates valued at 100,000 francs a year. Malicious tongues whispered that the Minister for Foreign Affairs had received the property for being the 'husband of the favourite': Marie-Anne Walewska came of an old Florentine family and claimed descent from Machiavelli.[4] Walewski had on more than one occasion importuned Napoleon III to pay off his debts; for in spite of a stipend of 100,000 francs a year as Privy Councillor and his senatorial fee of 30,000 francs, the count — who lived like a king and was a gambler and spendthrift — could never make ends meet.

Leon had despatched Françoise-Fanny to Belgium on business which can only dimly be divined from a letter he wrote to her on November 28, 1858:

Ma chère et bonne petite amie, ma chère et bonne femme,

We are all perfectly well here and little Charles asks every day after his *petite mère*. We told him you were in Brussels to get some nice cakes, rusks and buttered fingers. Every morning when he comes into my room he asks for his little mama and whether the cakes have arrived. Cecile takes him out in the square every day. He plays with his ball and sleeps every night without waking. Our little boy has had a bit of cold for two or three days but he is now much better. Your mother has given him her remedies, and today he is very well.

Leon describes how his two boys create a good deal of noise playing with their toy horses, animals and carriages in the apartment so that he cannot hear himself speak:

> We only get a bit of rest when Charles is in the Place Royale. [Place Vosges] Gaston does not go out: your mother is afraid to take him walking for fear he may suffer from inflammation of the chest. Here the temperature is very low — always damp and muddy. You know how I detest this weather, my *bonne petite*.

Leon gives Françoise-Fanny bulletins on the health of her mother and the servants — Cecile who has a stiff neck; and Anne who does what she wants 'but it is no great thing. The *pot-au-feu* is being prepared following the instructions you gave before you went away. She made a fine fat chicken for my little Charles, who says it comes from the foolish goings-on in Brussels.'

Francoise-Fanny was not likely to be cheered by the list of complaints in which Leon indulges:

> As for me, *chère amie*, I am not well. I cough a good deal and sleep badly. And to get warm I have made your bed in the salon which I have shut up: I only light a fire in my bedroom. Every day I dine out; breakfast each morning with your mother, and play with my children until three or four o'clock. Then I go out to dinner in the Palais Royal. Also I visit the Cirque Napoléon from which I come back home by omnibus to sleep. This then is my daily routine. How eagerly I have sought some distraction. Always I think of you; and when I return to my room I feel very low and my heart is inexpressibly heavy.

Leon is curious to know how Françoise-Fanny passes her time in the Belgian capital:

> I believe you are happy with Céline. She must look after you. You know that I wish her to be attentive to your smallest wish. You do not tell me how you fill your time. How do you spend your days; and what do you do in the evening? Do you go to the theatre, walk out in Brussels? Tell me all about it in your first letter. I want you to have a good time: business matters are important, but pleasure also is a necessity.

The trip also took Françoise-Fanny into the Belgian provinces:

> You will have to go to Namur to make good use of your journey. Above all, see Captain Huguet — and the notary. Better stay a few days longer to get to know all the family.

Leon enclosed a precious 100 franc note and on Françoise-Fanny's mysterious trip advises her to contact the local mayor and ask for his advice.

Françoise-Fanny also visited her grandmother at the Châteaux de Veaux, and her two sisters Jeannette and Francoise.

Leon shows his concern for her health once more:

I recommend you to eat only wholesome things, and strongly advise you to keep off coffee and liqueurs; and above all not to drink habitually of the Brussels beer. Buy good wine — don't choose to economise on that. And besides — I shall send you more money if you need it. I want you to take good care of yourself: live well, get out into the fresh air, go to the theatre; eat good dinners; be prudent and safeguard your health.

At last Leon's incurable optimism breaks through as he looks forward to their wedding:

I have seen Boudin and Aumont-Thiéville; also my mother. I will tell you all about it when you get back; it is too long to write. Everything is going well. My mother is becoming more agreeable: she will consent to everything — and she is coming to our wedding. She will be good for you. Bring your birth and baptismal certificates. And try to see Captain Huguet, to inform him of your marriage to me and to get his consent in writing.

Leon concludes his letter from the Faubourg St. Antoine with further reflections on his loneliness:

I have seen neither M. David nor Hélène. Nor Lugan. I see no one: I live for my children and in my beautiful thoughts for you. Take good care that nothing happens to you, my good little friend. And receive the assurance that my love for you will end only with my life. Receive this kiss from the very depths of my heart, and also one from Charles — who is sitting on my knee giving me kisses by the ladleful for his good little mother.

In spite of the electoral rebuff from his Imperial cousin delivered though the architect of the new Paris, Leon was not dissuaded from his pamphleteering and continued to proffer advice to Napoleon III.

The Emperor of seven years was still obsessed by *la gloire* and striving to put into action Napoleon's dictum 'government ought to be a continuous demonstration.' The third Napoleon expressed it more clearly: '*Il faut toujours étonner les francaises — ne jamais les laisser le dernier mot*'. And Louis Napoleon had always endeavoured to astonish — if it were only by dropping grapes on to the bald head of a man in Greenwich, or rowing Mr. and Mrs. Disraeli on to a mudbank in the Thames. But as Napoleon III he demonstrated his restlessness in the movements of entire armies.

Leon — his four months majority in the National Guard of St. Denis a quarter of a century behind him — continued to give armchair advice to his martial cousin.

> Since the restoration of the French Empire, [he wrote] by the accession of Prince Louis Napoleon Bonaparte, events have thrust political questions to the fore in a prodigious manner.
>
> We are faced with only one outstanding problem — like a cornerstone — and it would appear to defy the whole science of diplomacy at the same time as it arouses all the great hopes of the future.
>
> In the grave circumstances which at present hold all Europe in the grip of suspense and the attention of the entire world, two pamphlets — each equally remarkable — have been tossed into the arena and have excited lively public attention.

On March 20, 1859, Leon published a long pamphlet entitled *La Paix* which supported a tract — *The Emperor Napoleon III and Italy* — regarded as officially inspired.

Quoting Matthew's Gospel, chapter 28, verse 18 — *All power is given unto me both in heaven and upon earth* — he writes: 'We have noted with delight that the author puts the pope at the head of the Italian Confederation; but that he considers this confederation to be impossible. It is very natural even and very reasonable that he should renounce, at Rome, his temporal power, in favour of a well-intentioned prince, who would find it to his own advantage and would put all his prestige and all his ambition into being the executor of the wishes of the sovereign pontiff, in so far as they would be the exact expression of the radical and universal reform of which we have outlined the foundations.'

Leon goes on to quote from a pamphlet entitled *War* by a fellow-disciple of Coëssin — Emile de Girardin — and also a paper by his little cousin, 'the heir to the Imperial throne and to Napoleon's thoughts'; and he is confident that 'the imperishable discourse of His Majesty the Emperor Napoleon III of 7 February, 1859, leaves us in no doubt as to what we must do.'

What does it matter to the pope that he possesses a corner of the earth that the kings of France gave him and that he did not always possess? It is able to suffice him that all the true needs of the Corps Pontifical should be assured by rules to be laid down.

The 'rules' devised by Napoleon III were that Pius IX should retain only the Patrimony of St. Peter — which itself extended from the kingdom of Naples to Tuscany in the north — and give up the remaining papal lands in Umbria, the Romagna, and large stretches of the Adriatic littoral. The argument put forward was that the papal territories were in their rebelliousness a source only of trouble to the Holy See.

Pio Nono was less than enthusiastic: he preferred to take his chance with the moth, the dust and the thief, rather than with the benevolent troops of the Second Empire. Napoleon III's invasion of Vietnam and the occupation of Saigon 'to protect French missionaries' did nothing to persuade the pope to a contrary opinion.[5]

Napoleon III and Cavour, the Prime Minister of Sardinia-Piedmont, had decided the future of Italy in secret talks at Plombières in 1858. Austria was to be provoked into war by an unsubtlety of method which would have offended even the rising Bismarck. The pope would become President of an Italian Federation — excluding both Rome and Venetia — and France would receive Nice and Savoy. Part of the deal was that Prince Napoleon — 'Plon-Plon' — should marry King Victor Emmanuel's fifteen year old daughter, Princess Clotilde.

The carefully hatched plot mis-fired. Duly goaded into mobilisation, the Austrians were severely beaten. Nevertheless, alarmed by the military preparations of Prussia and sickened by his first real sight of mass-slaughter, Napoleon III concluded a hasty peace with Franz Josef in July. Austria was allowed to retain Venetia.

To Victor Emmanuel's Prime Minister, Louis Napoleon's withdrawal was a bitter betrayal of their agreement. Cavour had been laying his plans for three years. 'A lovely countess,' he wrote, 'is now enrolled in the Diplomatic Corps of Piedmont. I have asked her to flirt with — and if necessary to seduce — the Emperor.'

Virginie, Marchesa di Castiglione of the violet eyes, slept on black silk sheets and kept a night-light burning to show off the whiteness of her skin. She became the Emperor's mistress, and was so impressed by the experience that she asked to be buried in the batiste and lace nightdress of their night at Compiègne. Nevertheless it was several years after her first invitation to the château that La Castiglione — in common with Eugénie — was drawn into Napoleon III's life.

But in the international field the Emperor's tardiness failed to satisfy the impatient Florentine beauty. One evening outside her boudoir the Emperor narrowly escaped a stiletto waiting for him behind the arras; and it was not until six weeks after the bombs of Orsini that he dined with Cavour at Plombières.[6]

Viel Castel described La Castiglione's appearance at the famous *bal costumé* held at the French Ministry of Foreign Affairs on Tuesday, February 17, 1857: 'The proud Comtesse wears no stays. Her delightful bosom rises nobly like the bust of a Moorish damsel; and her two breasts seem to throw out a challenge to all women.'

Eugénie was outraged by the marchesa's *espoitrinément*; but the drooling Emperor gave to his twenty two year old 'Mina' an emerald valued at 100,000 francs and a pearl necklace worth over a quarter of a million.[7]

In 1860 the arrondissements of Paris were increased in number from sixteen to twenty and the land between the customs barriers and the ramparts incorporated into the city. This was a rude blow to the debtors of Paris, since their sanctuary of Batignolles disappeared in Haussmann's second stage of redevelopment. Leon was no longer in fear of the bailiffs at least; for the Tuileries ledger records that his debts were again paid from the Civil List to the paltry amount of 7,202 francs 50 centimes, almost the equal of the dividends he received on the capital — earmarked for Walewski — of a quarter of a million francs from Napoleon's legacy of conscience.

The arch-spendthrift Jerome Bonaparte — the only surviving brother of Napoleon — died on June 24, of a stroke while gambling with his aide at his country home, Villegenis in Seine-et-Oise; and 'Moustachu' and 'La Reine Crinoline' continued to devour capital as if there were no *lendemain*. It is difficult to accept that the Empress Eugénie's dress allowance of 100,000 francs was merely equal to that of Josephine, her predecessor of half a century; for the Spaniard wore a pair of shoes once only, after which — so tiny were her feet — they were sent away to needy schoolchildren. Her gowns were made in duplicate, so that she was able to disappear in the middle of a soirée and after a quick change of dress re-appear looking as fresh as at the start of the evening, while her guests drooped in the super-heated *Salle des Maréchaux*. The court dressmaker, Worth, had designed for her the celebrated 'Winterhalter gown' to show off her splendid shoulders.[8]

Napoleon III was more sparing in his dress; for it was not until his white waistcoat and breeches — woven of cashmere from his own goats — had survived three launderings that he discarded them.[9] But to greet his bedroom companions in the blue room at Compiègne, Louis Napoleon wore pyjamas of Imperial violet with a bee embroidered in gold.

In the late winter of 1861 Françoise-Fanny and the children were at the St. Denis estate, while Leon remained discreetly alone in Paris. On February 21 he sent her another touchingly optimistic letter.

> *Ma chère petite Fanny, ma bonne petite femme,*
> I received your letter, the reading of which gives me both pleasure and pain; because I notice that your health is not good, that you are ill. You were quite right in sending me Varenne's writ so promptly. But do not torment yourself over the matter: there is nothing to fear from that quarter.

Leon placed an unwarranted confidence in Prince Napoleon — 'Plon-Plon' — for he goes on:

> I wrote my letter to the Prince and gave it to M. Hubaine, his secretary. I am happy at the way things are shaping. I took the opportunity of mentioning our children and also my marriage to you, my dear; and I have good reason to believe that he will act shortly and that it will have the approval of the Emperor.

Françoise-Fanny was again pregnant, with Leon's third son Fernand:

> I am very happy with what you tell me concerning your condition. I shall be well content to have at my side again my fine Gascon who has my large head. So look after yourself and do not do anything imprudent. Do not make the handkerchiefs; I don't need them. You know that sewing too long causes you much distress. Your mother must redouble her care of you. Don't go out — the temperature is too low. I should like her to prepare some nice little meals for you. Get some good Bordeaux in St. Denis.
> I shall not come over as I promised last Saturday; and if the weather remains as bad and you are no better, do not come across on Sunday. I shall be at the station at one o'clock. If I do not see you I shall leave for St. Denis at half past two and it will make me very happy to spend the day

with you and our dear children.'

Leon's new attitude to the Establishment is reflected in his criticism of the actions of two anarchists, Mirès and Rougemont, who had blown up a prison. He roundly condemns them, and concludes:

> *Adieu, ma chère et bonne petite Fanny, ma chère et bonne petite femme.* Be prudent and take care of your health. I believe we shall be well content, especially if you and the children are well and so able to enjoy the new situation that Prince Napoleon wishes to provide for us — with the approval of the Emperor.
>
> *Adieu* once again — or rather *au revoir* until Sunday. I kiss you on your pretty blue eyes, *ma bonne petite femme*; and I remain for life your dear and most tender friend.
>
> Give a sweet kiss for me to my little Charles and my good little Gaston and give my best regards to your mother, Laporte, Eugène and Czar.

Leon — now far from the Tuileries in the Rue de l'Empereur at Montmartre — again looked down on the Promised Land. In a letter of July 10, 1861, to Delangle, Minister of Justice and Keeper of the Seals he wrote: 'Today, the 10 July, 1861, Monsieur le Ministre, I have still not been able to receive an audience of His Majesty.'

Leon's letter to Delangle rehearsed all his old arguments and incorporated copies of his many letters to prelates and ministers, secretaries and aides-de-camp; and because of the seizure by the Ministry of the Interior of his dossier to Cardinal Morlot, the forty page letter to Delangle had to be laboriously written by hand.

Louis Napoleon was a clement man, and it is difficult to understand why he could not allow himself to pardon the duel of twenty years before — a duel which he himself had by his rebuffs helped to precipitate — when both he and his cousin were in their early thirties. The reason for his refusal to receive Leon at Court lies deeper perhaps. Leon was a living reproach to the man who on such slender authority had taken upon himself the grey mantle of Austerlitz.

'He was the living image of the great captain,' said Louis Goldsmith. How could Louis Napoleon suffer daily contact with the eldest son of the Emperor, who 'bore his birth certificate on his face?' Napoleon III, except perhaps in stature, bore no resemblance to his uncle: 'Height one metre 66; thick body, eyes small grey, large strong nose; hair brown; medium mouth, thick lips, pointed chin, oval face, pale; large shoulders into which his head is ducked; rounded back,' as Thierra described him.

Leon received no further increase in his pension which in spite of inflation still remained at 13,000 or 16,000 francs a year; and complaints at the cost of *la gloire* steadily grew. The woodcutters and raftsman of the Morvand in the Massif central published a minutely documented budget which compared the Civil List of Napoleon III with that of Louis Philippe. The Emperor lived at the rate of 7,000 francs an hour; his servants cost him 1,300,000 francs annually. And whereas a meal for a peasant, his wife and child accounted for 45 francs worth of bread and potatoes, Napoleon III, Eugénie and the Prince Imperial relieved the country of 300 francs each time they sat down at table.

At Compiègne the autumn seasons continued unabated; and the November summons on vellum bearing the Imperial arms was a herald both of delight and terror. 'I have been bidden to Compiègne and have had to sell a mill,' observed one lady guest with a *frisson* of pleasure; and the Countess de la Pagerie also was heard to observe, 'One derives appalling pleasures from a stay at Compiègne.' Not surprisingly; for Anna Bicknell recorded that a wardrobe of fifteen dresses was a minimum requirement for a week at the château — no dress was to be worn twice.

Wearers of *le bouton* dressed in hunting uniform of green cloth trimmed with gold lace and crimson velvet.

In one afternoon of blood-letting the compassionate Emperor shot a deer, 51 hares, 213 rabbits, 73 pheasants, and 5 partridges; while Marshal Ney's son, the Prince de Moskowa, bagged a mere 225 of assorted game.

Eight guests normally accompanied the Emperor and his retinue. The latter comprised his aide-de-camp, and his *médecin de la vénerie*, and loader; plus foresters headed by an inspector and deputy inspector, with two gamekeepers, 12 foremen, 40 under-keepers, six labourers, and four constables. Nor was this sufficient for a simple day's hunting. In addition to the 60 men of the chase, Napoleon III was accompanied by a 182-strong detachment of soldiers made up of an officer, 20 NCOs, 160 troopers and a trumpeter. They all needed transport; and a further 20 men consisting of waggoners, whippers-in and gun loaders brought the total of the Emperor's attendance to 280 persons — roughly one man to each fowl destroyed.

While the *fête-impérial* waltzed its way to perdition Rome burned with indignation. Pope Pius IX had permitted himself a leisurely five years to prepare his reply to the advice he had been given by Leon and the regiment of pamphleteers; and his encyclical *Quanta cura*, published on December 8, 1864, was accompanied by a *Syllabus of Errors* which contained a comprehensive condemnation of all the enlightened ideas of the second half of the 19th century. Among the eighty propositions listed for damnation were liberalism, indifferentism, and freemasonry, together with all the benefits of modern civilisation.

The motto of the Second Empire was *enrichessez-vous*; and Leon was still importuning the authorities for Government contracts. He made a fresh bid for the railways and sought a concession for the boulevards Amandiers and Parmentières and for the construction of the highway from Tours to Montlucon — without success. The Tuileries, however, settled his debts to the tune of 60,000 francs.

Leon's wife, the patient and industrious Françoise-Fanny, now thought that they had for too long been kept outside of what de Morny's father called 'one great gambling casino'. She petitioned the authorities for some business for a Belgian mine in which she held shares. More successfully, she wrote to the Emperor saying that she was in urgent need of 5,000 to 6,000 francs; and Leon's two sons were thus allotted places at the Institute de Sainte-Barbe, reputedly the oldest school in France, at 4 Rue Cujas, off the Boulevard St. Michel in the heart of the Latin Quarter.[10]

Leon's lack of success in tapping the vast Imperial fortune may be explained by the fact that he was but one of many who importuned the Tuileries. An exchange of letters between Napoleon III and Lucien's son Pierre Bonaparte — a professional hunter who counted among his bag a journalist and a brace of papal guards — furnishes a weird echo to Leon's pleas of the previous decade. 'You granted me 2,500 francs a month as long as I stayed in Corsica,' complained Prince Bonaparte to the Emperor. 'This was but half the amount you had previously allotted me, and insufficient for the standard of living which I had assumed.'

The ingredients of Pierre Bonaparte's begging letters are uncannily akin to those of Leon — recognition of his children, marriage; the offer not of service to the Emperor but of property in Corsica. The unfortunate Archbishop of Paris was again roped in: 'This worthy prelate wishes to discuss it with Your Majesty. I beg you to listen to him and to accept the homage of my respectful devotion.'

To judge from Leon's evidence in the famous trial of the bed he had formed a close acquaintance with Pierre Bonaparte in Italy, calling his marksman cousin 'the head of the revolution'. It is quite possible that the two restless spirits had kept in touch and compared notes. At any rate they both received a similar response from their common cousin, Napoleon III.[11]

Walewski, Leon's preferred half-brother from Napoleon's Warsaw idyll, died during 1868; but his death did not benefit Leon who continued to enjoy only the three per cent of his father's legacy of a quarter of a million francs plus the increment on vellum of 1858. For a year Leon had mourned the co-author of his misfortunes. Once more, but sadly, he trod the *salle des pas perdus* — this time to sue the beneficiaries of his mother's will. True to form she had disinherited her son. Eleonore died on January 30, 1868, aged seventy-nine, at 20 Boulevard Malesherbes, and was buried near Volney's pyramid in Père-Lachaise, beside her father Dominique Denuelle de la Plaigne. Leon was now sixty-one. He and his mother had been reconciled ten years.

The family tomb of the Denuelles bore only the words *De Profundis* and the bourgeois legend: *Concession à perpetuité*.[12]

Six weeks after Eleonore's death, Leon addressed a petition to the Minister of Finance claiming the dowry capital of 22,000 francs which he had helped his mother to retain by paying her legal costs in 1828, and the reversion of which she had promised him in 1831.

On January 23, 1868, Friedrich Krupp, head of the firm's Paris bureau, had sent to Napoleon III two pamphlets describing firing tests of a new cannon. At the Paris Exposition the previous year Krupp's *Meisterstück* received a special prize; and in the resulting Franco-Prussian euphoria Alfred Krupp was created an Officer of the Legion of Honour. The pamphlets on the ballistic tests were passed to Maréchal de Boeuf who in a matter of weeks returned them with the General Staff's appraisal to Conti, the French Counsellor of State. The army's comments on the new Krupp artillery were sent to Essen; and in the bureau of the Ministry of Defence in Paris Krupp's pamphlets were endorsed: 'No action. File away.'

Less than three years later a lonely figure sitting painfully astride his charger remained all day in the face of the new Krupp cannon trying to get himself killed. Death ignored the Emperor but claimed thousands of his soldiers; and on that day of September 2, 1870, at Sedan, Napoleon III surrendered his Empire.

While Leon was trying without success to call upon the ex-Empress Eugénie and the Prince Imperial at Chislehurst in Kent, his wife remained in characteristic protection of the household goods at their apartment in the fashionable Rue Royale, a few yards from the now ever-to-be-forbidden Tuileries. Following the seizure of Paris by the Commune, Françoise-Fanny and her small daughter Charlotte, aged three, received a brutal visitation from the *fédérés* in search of loot. These 'officials' entered the apartment armed with a search warrant. They found nothing — not even Leon's two sons who had retreated with their father to London — and in their rage and frustration they sacked the house. After pillaging Leon's home, the *communards* turned it into a guard post and installed a sentry.[13]

Françoise-Fanny nevertheless succeeded in eluding the rebels and rejoined Leon and her sons in London.

Once again it was money that drew Leon to follow the ex-Emperor Napoleon III into exile. All Imperial payments had ceased with the proclamation of the Republic; but true to his character Louis Napoleon honoured his obligations and continued to pay Leon's pension from the ample funds which had been salted away.[14]

On January 9, 1873, at Chislehurst, Napoleon III succumbed to an operation for the removal of gall stones, the agony of which had clouded his last years.

Leon's benefactor was dead; but according to Max Billard there existed documents proving that he continued to enjoy an annual pension of 10,000 francs — paid through Baring Brothers, bankers — until 1877 'at least'.

Surprisingly, after all his wanderings he still possessed a small collection of Imperial objects including a striking terra-cotta bust of Napoleon's mother, modelled from a plaster cast taken in Rome after Madame Mère's death. Leon decided to sell his relics where they would perhaps revive memories of the Empire in a few romantic hearts.

CHAPTER 15

Leon and the Tussauds

Almost three quarters of a century after Napoleon had been modelled by Marie Tussaud, Count Leon sat for her grandson. The resulting likeness of Leon in wax bears an uncanny resemblance to Canova's marble bust of the Emperor — even to the style of the hair.

One morning in the early days of the Consulate, Marie Tussaud had been summoned to the palace of the Tuileries to take the likeness of the thirty year old Napoleon. The appointment was for 6 a.m., and when Mme. Tussaud arrived on the hour she found Josephine and the First Consul already waiting for her, accompanied by Madame Grand-Maison, the wife of a pro-Napoleon deputy.

Marie's early and furtive visit may have been due to the fact that she had taken casts of the guillotined heads of the royalists and revolutionaries; and the petulant Bonaparte was not anxious for Paris to know that his head was to join those of Madame Tussaud's dead clients.[1]

Josephine begged Marie to take particular care as her husband had consented to undergo the ordeal to please her — for whom the portrait was intended.

Marie was used better to handling lifeless heads, and when the cold plaster of Paris was about to be slapped on to the young general's gaunt features, she begged him not to be alarmed; adding the encouraging assurance that it would be quite painless.

This *faux-pas* provoked a characteristic response.

'Alarmed!' bellowed Bonaparte, feeling the need to assert himself before an exclusively petticoated audience, 'I should not be alarmed if you were to surround my head with loaded pistols!'

Seventy-five years later John Theodore Tussaud wrote in his diary:

I met Count Leon, the natural son of Napoleon the Great.
The Count was then nearing seventy years of age, and had taken refuge in this country after the great débâcle of 1870.
He lived in modest lodgings at Camden Town, and to pay his

way set about selling the last remaining relics of the Imperial
Family he had in his possession.
John Theodore Tussaud continues:

> In a diary I now have before me I find that my father
> [Joseph Randolph Tussaud] visited him on Friday the 31,
> January 1873, the Count having expressed a wish to show
> him the family heirlooms, with the view to their finding a
> permanent resting-place among the many Napoleonic
> memorials at Mme. Tussaud's.

The entry in Joseph Randolph Tussaud's diary reads:

> ... Extd. at 10 to meet M. Vignon. Went with him to Comte
> Leon at Camden Town. The Count is a son of Napoleon 1st
> and a most extraordinary likeness of the 1st Emperor in
> figure as well as face. The only things fit for us are a good
> miniature of Lucian, [sic] a bust of Madame Mère, a
> snuff-box left in the possession of the Countess Luxbourg,
> mother of the count, and containing the snuff the Emperor
> had partaken of, and a lock of Duke de Reichstadt's hair
> Nap^n the 2nd; and stayed an hour chatting with the Count.[2]

John Theodore Tussaud — Marie's great-grandson — adds to his
father's description of Leon:

> The Count bore a striking resemblance to the Emperor,
> except in two particulars: his figure was cast in a larger
> mould, and his eyes were hazel, whereas Napoleon's were
> blue-grey. Count Leon returned to France, leaving behind
> him in London his son Charles for whom I obtained a
> position in a City warehouse, where he remained for several
> years, being at no pains to disguise his identity.[3]

On his return to France Leon wandered far from Paris in alien
towns — Tours, Toulouse and Bordeaux — before returning to the
capital. In Paris his creditors were waiting.

The legal doctrine of the *legitimate portion* was introduced by
the ancient Romans to prevent the disinheritance of a child by his
parent's will. To postpone Leon's legal quarter of the estate to the
satisfaction of Eleonore's particular legacies instead of levying it
on the gross amount available seems a denial of the doctrine. But
this is how the court interpreted Leon's claim; and worse — he had
to take his place in a long queue of Eleonore's relatives, all
clamouring for the *droit légitime* — distant as they were.

The decision of the First Civil Tribunal of the Seine was
conveyed in a letter from the lawyer Eugène Dubois of March 13,
1873. There were four lots of claimants — mostly from St. Leu —

to share whatever might be left of Eleonore's money.

Judging rightly that there would be little left over for himself, and that little taken by his creditors, Leon stubbornly refused to acquiesce in the liquidation of Eleonore's dowry of 19,800 francs.

Maître Boudin, Leon's old receiver, had gone to his rest and it was his son, whose office was situated in the unfortunately-named Rue Bailiff *derrière le Banque*, who now begged Leon to give his assent to the winding up of the de Luxbourg will.

On the title page of his pamphlet *The Work of the Children of God*, printed in 1857, Leon had quoted from the Vulgate the words: *Ubicumque fuerit corpus illic congregabuntur et aquilae* — 'For wheresoever the carcase is, there will the eagles be gathered together.'[4]

At the first distant crinkle of franc notes Leon's creditors gathered around him like vultures.

'The widow Decreps has taken out an injunction to repossess the property at St. Denis,' wrote Boudin on March 14, 1873. 'If you are not going to pay your rent and hire appropriate furniture it would be better to let her take back the house, which is at present of no use to you.'

Still Leon refused to budge, and sent the unfortunate Françoise-Fanny to talk to his lawyer. She was all for settling for whatever there might remain.

'Let me know if you persist in your instructions,' pleaded Boudin a fortnight later.

One of Leon's creditors had come up with a debt of 1840; and even the conscientious Boudin could not stomach this:

What does appear to me to be exorbitant is the pretension of the assignée of Maître Doutre, who for an original debt of 15,000 francs is demanding that a sum of 45,000 francs should be set aside, on the grounds that the capital has been requested several times since March 24, 1840, the date of the inception of this mortgage obligation.

More and more do Boudin's letters read like extracts from Balzac. The lawyer finally gave up in a short note of April 19, 1873,

... the instructions you have given me do not permit me to act in any way whatsoever in the liquidation, since their effect is to hold it up for as long as possible.

There was one more claim outstanding. And — irony of ironies — the debt represented the finery of a vanished Empire. On April 23, 1874, Françoise-Fanny and Leon were sued by Madame Tourillon, a dressmaker, for clothes supplied during the five years from 1866 to 1870. Leon had never given up hopes of breaching the Tuileries; for Mme. Tourillon's debt concerned a court wrap of red velvet lined with white satin and embroidered in gold.

True to form the sixty-seven year old Leon counterclaimed. His advocate, Maître Ferdeuil, submitted that Leon had long ago paid Mme. Tourillon her dues, and that in any case her action was barred by a limitation clause — article 2273 of the Civil Code — which cancelled debts between traders and private clients after the elapse of one year. Further, Countess Leon had deposited with the couturière certain materials which had not been returned, including sixteen metres of blue *pou de soie*.

Leon demanded a judgment of no-claim and the restitution of Françoise-Fanny's fabrics. It must be assumed that after a delay of five or six years the grained blue taffeta would be somewhat moth-eaten.

Judge Bernier of the Third Republic was more impressed by the arguments of Mme. Tourillon's advocate — Maître Racle, and in the fifth chamber of the Tribunal of the Seine he condemned Count and Countess Leon to pay 6,373 francs *with interest* and ordered Mme. Tourillon to return the materials to her old client.

Wearily Leon turned from the city that once had gathered him as a hen gathers her chicks, and settled briefly in alien towns of South-West France.

Writers — both English and French — have dealt severely with Leon. The former largely through ignorance and an uncritical acceptance of opinions sanctified by the passing of the years; the latter for less pardonable reasons, for Leon's failings were possessed by the other Bonapartes to a lesser or greater degree. Almost alone, Ginisty speaks of Leon with compassion:

It is certain that he foolishly dissipated his fortune; that he had a chequered life, that he was obsessed by chimerical enterprises and ambitions; that his incontestable gallantry made of him only a duellist, fighting for inordinately trivial causes; and that Napoleon III — who while paying him a generous pension had him watched — did not underrate him . . .

But when we think about it — never did circumstances more perfectly combine to make of a man a black sheep. Napoleon, who begot this son by a chance liaison, had tenderly cherished him — in the beginning — to the point where at one moment, careless of the Code he had established, considered making him his heir. There is proof enough that this idea sometimes obsessed him. Illegitimate as he was, the child born of his amours with Eleonore de la Plaigne had been treated like a prince, entrusted to Caroline Murat, recognised — at the very least — morally. Up to the fall of the Empire he had been cosseted — even after the birth of the King of Rome — raised for great destinies; nourished in the Napoleonic cult by Madame Letizia (Madame Mère).

Then, suddenly, there came the collapse of all his dreams, and that moiety of the name which he bore became yet more burdensome. He was born active, and he grew to maturity in the worst possible period for the utilisation of his energies — in the middle of the suspicious atmosphere of the Restoration. While still young, he yet belonged to the past. If he had never previously been acknowledged by Napoleon — and with some paternal pride even — he could have gone his way in obscurity. But his origin, so patently manifest, was becoming a crushing burden. He lived among the faithfuls of the Emperor who would not be reconciled. Naturally his ideas were distorted. Nowhere did he have his place, neither in the Imperial family, which, little by little, now that it was no longer dependent on a master, set itself at a distance; nor in bourgeois society, which as the son of such a father he found too shabby. Had he been able to enter the army he would perhaps, nay surely, have become a fine soldier. Who knows that for his own part he did not possess a need to lose himself, a precocious loathing for the whole of existence, which stemmed from the knowledge that he would forever remain short of his desires, when he threw himself into dissipation; into the tortured life which led to all his eccentricities?

Philibert Audebrand describes Leon's massive physical presence: For thirty-five years Count Leon was one of the curiosities of Paris. Very tall — at least six foot — of noble bearing and carrying himself bolt upright, he was like a living photograph of Napoleon exaggerated by enlargement. It could be said of him — and it was said everywhere — that he bore his birth certificate on his face.

Take the sublime general of the army in Italy striding through the thunder and lightning, small, pale and thin; the crowned victor of Austerlitz, still pale, but heavier; the prisoner of St. Helena in a straw hat, who in five years had aged a quarter of a century and had lost the eagle's glance.

Cast them into the crucible whence flowed Cellini's Perseus
and there will emerge the head of Leon. He was big: the
spitting image of Napoleon; a Napoleon with a giant's stride.

Sir John Falstaff was made to say by Shakespeare, 'I am not only
witty in myself but the cause that wit is in other men;'[5] and it was
this characteristic that endeared Count Leon to the *boulevardiers*
— who while they believed that Paris was the best of all cities in
the worst of all possible worlds, eagerly sought relief from politics
and military adventure. Indeed — as Philibert Audebrand states —
Paris had always claimed to the *'capitale de la Blague'*.[6]

Speculation on what would have happened had Napoleon
survived, or if he had recognised Leon in an open and forthright
manner, is not a very fruitful pastime. But if Leon *had* been
acknowledged by Napoleon and ennobled, what then? He was
neither the best nor the worst of the Bonapartes. Whichever career
he undertook would have unfolded under the great shadow of the
Emperor. And the fate of the Duke of Reichstadt was not a
consummation to be wished.

Nevertheless, the letters and pamphlets of Leon are evidence of
a keen intellect and a capacity for marshalling facts. They are not
ill-considered documents; and certainly in administering a
kingdom Leon could not have done worse than Napoleon's
brothers. Significantly Leon seems to have been much attached to
the compassionate Lucien Bonaparte, who founded a dynasty of
scholars.

Romancing on what might have been is idle. In Leon the world
sees only a William Claude Fields-like character whose knock at
the door of a *chef-de-cabinet* was calculated to empty the whole
building within minutes. Such men are necessary.

Leon's precious few existing letters to Françoise-Fanny reveal
an un-Bonaparte-like tenderness: he sacrificed even the faintest hope
of a career by marrying the mother of his children, and outside the
spurious Bonaparte nobility. A vicious irony: for how could he
marry within the nobility? He was *sui generis* with a vengeance.

After living variously in Toulouse, Bordeaux and Tours, Leon
returned to his ancestral regions. His penultimate home bore the
imposing title of the Villa Davenport and it stood in a leafy garden
near the banks of the Oise. But to Leon it might have been a
lonely rock in the Atlantic Ocean.

CHAPTER 16

The St Helena of Seine-et-Oise

The French have a saying — 'to return from Pontoise'. It is used of a person who wears an air of bewilderment or confusion. The phrase dates from the middle of the 18th century when it was the custom of Louis XV to banish to Pontoise troublesome courtiers, and even whole governments, who took the wrong decision.

Leon never returned from Pontoise. His exile was ended only by his death.

Capital of the Vexin and only twenty miles north-west of Paris, Pontoise is a charming little town whose narrow climbing streets and riverside meadows have been made familiar in the paintings of Camille Pissarro.

During the period following 1870 when Leon was living in Camden Town, Pissarro — also a refugee from the post-war chaos of France — was trying without success to gain acceptance at the Royal Academy for his paintings of the Crystal Palace and Penge railway station. Of London he complained, 'Here there is no such thing as art; everything is treated as a matter of business' — an echo of Marshal Lefebvre's oft-misattributed observation — 'The English are a nation of shopkeepers.'

Pissarro remained in Pontoise until 1882 and knew every field, building and person in the little town. He boasted that he was familiar with each copse and hillock; and the townspeople furnished an inexhaustible collection of types for his brush.

There is little doubt therefore that the artist encountered Leon more than once in the streets of Pontoise. And he can hardly have failed to be struck by his resemblance to the Emperor; a likeness that grew more uncanny with the passing years.

In the winter of 1879, Leon, in deep poverty, set up house at No.4 Rue Beaujour. The single-storey dwelling was in an old farmyard at the base of a steep cliff, atop which stood the ancient ramparts of Pontoise.[1]

On the wretched walls of the old farm cottage there still hung proudly four portraits of Napoleon, and a picture of a beautiful twenty-one year old girl dressed in the fashion of the early Empire, with a rich shawl thrown negligently across her white shoulders.

A screen, delicately embroidered in tapestry, now become old and fragile, held pride of place in the bedroom. It was a souvenir of Eleonore's idle hours as Countess de Luxbourg. Pictures and bits of furniture had gone one by one to pay for food; while Victorine, the faithful servant, tried to perform miracles on a miniscule budget.

Ashamed to be seen in his threadbare old clothes, Leon ventured rarely into the streets of Pontoise. But the forty-three year old Françoise-Fanny was too busy fighting poverty to be proud; and with the help of kindly neighbours the thirteen year old Charlotte did not go short.

Leon spent whole days sitting in an armchair before the empty grate; or wrote long letters which he immediately tore up. No one now wished to help the Imperial bastard: Napoleon had been dead for sixty years past.

Only a few precious objects remained from the house in the Rue Royale whence the family had been driven by the Paris mob. Whatever articles had not been lost or stolen over the years had been sold or pledged.

Leon received frequent visits from his landlord, Monsieur J. Fleury, who came as a friend, having long since given up any hope of receiving his rent. He testified to the lively memory and fine appearance of his seventy-five year old tenant, who left him with a profound impression of a human being deeply unhappy and ashamed of his condition.

But Leon had on occasion to flee the tongue of the devoted maid Victorine. And his appearance has been described by a neighbour — Monsieur Penaud — to whom Leon confided some documents including those dealing with the celebrated cases involving his mother. It was upon this friend that Leon called on his last visit to the outside world. They talked about gardening and other trivial matters.

Leon was wearing a shabby overcoat which barely concealed a patch of frayed shirt. Suddenly becoming aware of his wretched appearance, he instinctively held up his two hands to hide his neck.

'Please excuse me,' said Leon. 'I am here on a neighbourly call.'

His latter days recall in their poignancy Gustave Flaubert's harrowing account of the extinction of Charles Bovary. Leon could not even find a coin for halfpennyworth of tobacco.

Catching a glimpse of the servant of his neighbour, the carpenter Harvard, he resolved on a desperate strategem. Rummaging through his pockets he brought out a penknife.

'Here,' he said to the woman, 'would you like to make a deal?'

'What kind of a deal?' she asked.

'I'll give you this knife for a sou's worth of tobacco.'

The woman took the knife, but returned with *two* sous' worth of tobacco in a paper twist.

Paul Ginisty's description of Leon's last days as recounted by his neighbours has been disputed by his daughter Charlotte:

At that time we had several servants one of whom, Victorine, raised me. I possess an indignant letter from her refuting the libels that the press printed about him. 'How dare you, Charlotte, allow such lies to be written.' The story of the penknife, a souvenir of Napoleon Ier that my father is supposed to have traded for a couple of sous' worth of tobacco, is absolutely untrue. I still have this little knife in my possession.[2]

Françoise-Jonet resembled the Empress Eugénie to such a degree that at the Théâtre des Italiens she loved to occupy the opposite box. She dressed like the Empress and it amused her to receive the homage destined for Eugénie. I still have quite distinct recollections of the life in society led by my parents. My mother — always most elegant — went often to the theatre and to society receptions: I can still see her silk robes with their fluttering lace. This proves that my father was not wretched as legend has pleased to portray him. Fortunately the abbé Driou, Curé of Pontoise, the son of an officer killed at Wagram and whose future had been assured by Napoleon, out of gratitude did for my mother what my grandfather had done for him: he paid for her boarding school. Thanks to him I have been able to take up teaching. It was our salvation: all our remaining souvenirs were sold or dispersed . .

In the face of conflicting accounts; one by a writer who had indeed interviewed Charlotte Leon; the other from the daughter herself it is only possible to echo the Prefect of Judea's cry: 'What is truth?'

Writing on the amours of Napoleon and Eleonore Denuelle, Frédéric Masson observed: 'What romance could rival this true story of which we can only glean fragments from law reports, public registers, circulars and electoral addresses . . . '

Leon succumbed to the disease of the Bonapartes — gastric cancer. He was conscious up to the end, and suffered abominably.

Only one of his sons was by his bedside at the last.

According to his friend and landlord, M. Fleury, Leon's striking resemblance to the Emperor was still more pronounced on his deathbed. His shaven face exactly recalled the famous mask of Napoleon; it wanted only the legendary lock of hair.

Like the registration of his birth, Leon's death certificate contained inaccuracies. He was described as 'Sieur Le Comte (Leon)', an error that was corrected in the margin. The entry recorded that he died 'on the morning of April 14, 1881, at ten o'clock at No. 4 Rue Beajour, Pontoise, the husband of Françoise-Fanny Jonet, of independent means, aged forty-five, married in Paris.'

The witnesses were given as M. Gaston Leon le Comte, aged twenty-three years, a clerk living in the Rue Quatre Septembre, Paris; and M. Joseph Fleury, aged forty-eight, landlord of Vallangoujard, Seine-et-Oise.

Such was Leon's wretched condition at the end, that on his death the neighbours were obliged to give shelter to Françoise-Fanny and the little Charlotte, and provide a cheap coffin; for the son of the man who today lies in a marble sarcophagus beneath the golden dome of the Invalides.

Leon's body did not long remain at peace; for after a short interval the common grave in which he had been laid was turned over and his bones scattered.

NOTES

NOTES TO PRELUDE

J'ai un fils!

1. Some confusion has arisen between Napoleon's alleged sterility and his rumoured impotence. The two are, of course, quite different conditions. Impotence is an inability to perform the sex act while sterility is the state of being infertile. In his *Napoleon: Bisexual Emperor* — a physician's view of the Emperor in which Frank Richardson gives an admirable exposition of Dr. Corvisart's opinions — he says (in Chapter II — *Napoleon and the Doctors*): 'Doctors have differed about Napoleon's medical history ever since those who were present at the post-mortem examination of his body quarrelled about whether his liver was enlarged or not . . .'

2. There are several versions of the manner in which Napoleon received the news of Leon's birth. The account used here is contained in the sketch of his father by the present Count Gaston Leon, of Le Raincy, and appeared in the *Intermédiaire des Chercheurs et Curieux* for 1904. Even within the family version of the anecdote there are variations: in a wartime broadcast from Paris, Leon's daughter — Madame Charlotte Mesnard-Léon — said, '. . . *son enfant, qui devait naître le 13 Décembre, 1806. Ce jour-la assurait la fortune d'Eléonore et la disgrâce de Joséphine. Caroline exultait! Toute heureuse elle dépêcha aussitôt un courrier spécial à l'Empereur qui combattaient victorieusement en Pologne. C'est le Maréchal Lefebvre qui lui annonca la bonne nouvelle, le lendemain de la bataille de Pulstuck, la veille du Jour de l'An:*
— *Non Général, soyez heureux . . . vous avez un fils!*
— *Un fils? Enfin, je suis comblé de joie! Que l'on donne a Eléonore ce quelle voudra, mais qu'on lui retire l'enfant, et que ma soeur en prenne soin!*
— *Mon Général on a déjà donné à votre fils la moitié de votre nom: il s'appelle Léon.'*

3. In his will, Napoleon — enjoining on his executors the utmost secrecy — had bequeathed to Leon 300,000 francs, specifying 'that this sum shall be employed in buying land in the same year as my death.' And General Bertrand, writing to Leon on May 30, 1833, confirmed:

Napoleon forbade his testamentary executors to communicate to anyone whatsoever the secret codicil of 24 April, 1821, which contains among other dispositions the Emperor's legacy, and the circumstances which had frustrated its fulfilment in a deed executed before the notary Fermin Virgile Tabourier: 'The Emperor has, by a secret will,

of which the communication must not be made except to
interested parties and only so far as concerns them, in favour
of M. Leon, a legacy of money to be charged on his codicils
Nos. 4 and 5 of 25 April, 1821, by the gratitude and honour
— these are the exact words of the codicil — of the Empress
Marie Louise and of Prince Eugène. General Montholon
further declares, that the testamentary executors have made
all possible démarches to the Empress and to Prince Eugene
and his legatees. They have gone so far as to obtain from the
Tribunal of the Seine a judgment for the blocking of the
funds of sale of the Navarre lands; but Prince Eugene's
beneficiaries having opposed the law on the settlement, the
judgment could only be applied to the liquid funds, and at
this moment they have disappeared. As for the Empress
Marie Louise, the testamentary executors have without
success employed all legal means and even diplomatic
channels.

Napoleon's old valet, Marchand, also wrote in these terms:

M. le Comte arrived at my house. I consulted the instructions
dated Longwood, 25 April, 1821, as I had the honour of
telling you this morning, a desire expressed in the following
sense: 'Article 37: I should not be annoyed if the little Leon
entered the magistrature if that were to his liking'.

Notes to Chapter 1

Marie Antoinette's Chamber-Maid

1. It seems to have been considered not quite lady-like to handle
books, for Jeanne-Genet Campan had commenced her auspicious
career by acting as reader to the children of Louis XVI.

2. The advent of the young Eleonore came to the Murats like the
answer to prayer. Jealous at the advancement of Josephine's
children (Eugène de Beauharnais was made Viceroy of Italy, and
Louis Bonaparte, the husband of Hortense de Beauharnais, was
made King of Holland) Caroline Murat and her husband, whom
she had wed against the wishes of Napoleon, felt slighted.

3. In her memoirs Mlle. George noted Leon's birth: 'Napoleon's

first child was born a mere week after St. Marc's play was taken off . . .' And as to Eleonore's effect on the Emperor the supplanted Georgina tartly commented, 'She had neither interested him nor yet given him pleasure.'

4. De Bausset, the Court Chamberlain, described with what difficulty and fear of stumbling he carried the fainting Josephine down the winding stairway after Napoleon had announced his intention of divorcing her. As the Emperor and de Bausset were carrying her down to her own apartments, Josephine whispered to the Court Chamberlain, 'Careful! You are holding me too tightly!'

Notes to Chapter 2

An Absent Father

1. Revel was arrested for forging commercial documents. To pay for his wedding banquet and other expenses he had given a promissory note to Sorel, an innkeeper at St. Germain-en-Laye, backed by a fellow-officer — La Feuille, quartermaster of the 10th Regiment of Light Artillery. Sorel promised not to float the bill; but he put it into circulation and La Feuille declared his endorsement to be a forgery. Revel was condemned to two years imprisonment and jailed at Versailles; but he was granted a transfer to Dourdan.

2. Act II SC. iv.

3. Napoleon was in Paris or the surrounding district during the following periods:

26 January, 1806	to	25 September, 1806
27 July, 1806	to	16 November, 1807
23 January, 1809	to	13 April, 1809
26 October, 1809	to	4 April, 1810
1 June, 1810	to	28 August, 1811
11 November, 1811	to	30 April, 1812
18 December, 1812	to	14 April, 1813
9 November, 1813	to	24 March, 1814
20 March, 1815	to	11 June, 1815
21 June, 1815	to	28 June, 1815

Notes to Chapter 3

The Angel of Malmaison

1. Revel left Dourdan jail in March, 1807.
2. The 'Madelonettes' at 14 Rue des Fontaines in the 6th Arrondissement, was the former convent of the *Filles de la Madeleine,* and subsequently became a prison for women arrested on criminal charges.
3. *'Sur les vieillard qui font l'amour'.*

> *Téméraire vieillard: quoi! ton âme insensé*
> *Ose encore se nourrir d'un amoureux plaisir*
> *Pareil gibier fait mal: étouffe un vain désir;*
> *Car l'heure du déjeuner pour toi s'est écoulée*

4. Although William IV had left the Navy forty years before he came to the throne, the *Gentleman's Magazine* of April 1831, printed a new loyal song, *Long Live Our Sailor King:*

> *The vessel of the State*
>   *Has a seaman at the helm*
> *And how'er our foes may hate*
>   *They old England can't o'erwhelm —*
> *For while we rule the waves*
>   *We may firm and fearless sing,*
> *'Britain never will be slaves*
>   *While they have a Sailor King!'*

Notes to Chapter 4

Wellington's A.D.C.

1. Napoleon shared Cardinal Richelieu's abhorrence of the duel. It was the Emperor's belief that duellers made bad soldiers; and he once turned down a challenge from King Gustavus Adolphus — offering to despatch a master swordsman to the Swedish court. Although a professional artilleryman, Napoleon despised fighting with pistols as ignoble. 'The sword is the weapon of the brave,' he declared. 'For the brave man a gun is only the handle of a bayonet.'
2. It seems that Leon assumed the title of count sometime during

the early years of the reign of Louis Philippe. Writing in *l'Illu-stration* of August 15, 1931, Albéric Cahuet, author of *Pontcarral*, stated: *'On le nommait le comte Léon . . . titre figure dans l'armorial du Premier Empire, du vicomte Révérend. Le rédacteur de la notice ajoute, il est vrai: 'Le titre de comte qu'il a porté ne parait avoir été l'objet d'aucun decret, bien qu'il ait été mentionné avec ce titre dans des actes publics.' N'importe. Sur ses voitures le comte Léon faisait peindre ses armoiries, suffisament parlantes:*

> *Coupé 1°   d'azur à l'aigle au vol abaisé d'or empiétant*
> *en foudre du même (qui est de Napoléon et de*
> *l'Empire francais);*
> *2°   de geules à deux barres coticées d'or, accompagnées*
> *de deux étoiles du même, l'une en chef et l'autre*
> *en pointé (ce qui est de Bonaparte de Corse ancien.).*
> *Couronne de comte.*

3. For over eighteen years the legitimate Bonapartes had been denied entry to France. The official announcement — which had appeared in the *Moniteur* of January 14, 1816 — read:

> The forefathers and descendants of Napoleon Bonaparte, his uncles and his aunts, his nephews and nieces, his brothers, their wives and their descendants, his sisters and their husbands are banished from the Kingdom forever and are bound to leave it within the period of one month under the penalty incurred by the Article 91 of the penal code.

The spirited Hortense, however, had defied the ban several times.

Notes to Chapter 5

Unquiet Days in Clichy

1. Delpech can only have used the name of Eleonore's first husband derisively. Leon was never known by the name of Revel.
2. As one of the definitions of the word 'magnetism' *Littré* gives the practice of diagnosing bodily ailments by the inspection of a drop of blood from the patient's body, and the subsequent remedial treatment applied *to the blood sample itself.*

Notes to Chapter 6

Igniferous Balls and Incendiary Bullets

1. Francis Fenton had taken over the building at 63 St. James's Street — formerly Pero's medicinal baths — in 1800 as a coffee house, and turned it later into an hotel. The building now occupying the site serves as offices to the whisky firm of Johnnie Walker.

2. Colonel Bouffet de Montaubon, who was forty-six years old at this time, had been aide-de-camp to Josephine's son, Prince Eugène de Beauharnais. Serving under Murat and Napoleon, he fought in the advance to Moscow and at Waterloo. After the fall of the Emperor, Montaubon crossed the Atlantic for a spell in the army of Colombia, and at one time managed a soap boilery in Richmond, Surrey.

3. Maximilian-Joseph-Auguste-Eugène-Napoléon, Duke of Leuchtenberg, Prince Romanovsky, was the youngest son of Eugène de Beauharnais. He married the Grand Duchess of Russia, the daughter of Czar Nicholas. Queen Victoria described the Duke's three sons — Josephine's great-grandchildren — as 'nice intelligent boys,' and their sister Maroussy as 'ravishing.'

4. Barry Edward O'Meara, born in 1786, was an English naval surgeon of Irish origin who — thanks to his knowledge of Italian! — was accepted by Napoleon as his doctor on the island of St. Helena, and was later dismissed the Navy. Although the Bonaparte family took O'Meara to themselves, it seems he had been devious in his dealings with the Emperor and with Sir Hudson Lowe — Napoleon's custodian — taking money from both. In 1822 he was threatened with massive damages for libel by Lord Londonderry. O'Meara who became celebrated for his memoirs of St. Helena died in 1836. A tooth which the doctor had extracted from the exiled Emperor was exhibited at Mme. Tussaud's.

5. Hertford House, much enlarged and even more bare than in Guizot's day, now shelters the Wallace collection. Ironically enough, much of the magnificent armour in the museum was purchased by Sir Richard Wallace from Count de Nieuwerkerke, the lover of Princess Mathilde — Leon's cousin and Jerome Bonaparte's daughter . . .

6. The building is of considerable historic interest; Lord Northcliffe died at No. 1 Carlton Gardens on August 14th, 1922, and it is now the official residence of the Foreign Secretary.

7. Almost exactly thirty years later Napoleon III's ambassador would be turned away from a door at a small town in the Rhineland. The affront to Louis Napoleon's representative at Ems led directly to Sedan and the loss of his empire; the snub to Leon — Bonaparte's son — resulted in a duel manqué on Wimbledon Common.
8. Robson's *Commercial Directory* (1840) has an entry which reads: 'Buckley and Sanders, solicitors, 14 Grays Inn Square'.
9. For good measure Monsieur Guizot had received an audience of Queen Victoria earlier that day — and all this only two days after his arrival in London!
10. Louis Napoleon was then thirty-three and Leon thirty-four years old.

Notes to Chapter 7

The Duel on Wimbledon Common

1. In his *Réponse au gérant du journal le Capitole,* Leon insisted that Count d'Orsay, Prince Louis' second, had agreed upon the use of pistols.
2. Appointed to Bow Street Court in 1839, David Jardine, who was born at Pickwick, near Bath, in 1794, was a noted writer on historical and legal topics. Among his works were, *A Reading on the use of Torture in the Criminal Law of England previously to the Commonwealth,* which Macaulay described as 'very learned and ingenious'; and a translation of F. C. F. Mueffling's *Treatise of Equivocation.* Jardine — a member of the Middle Temple — died in 1860.
3. Baring's Bank played an important part in the lives of the exiled Bonapartes. Like the Rothschilds, the Barings were of German origin. Henry-Francis Baring was a Lutheran pastor of Bremen who towards the end of the eighteenth century settled in England. His son John became a textile manufacturer in Exeter, and later with his brother Francis came to London to found a successful dye works. It was John — the eldest brother — who left industry and became a banker. He earned the title 'the merchant prince' and stood in good favour with William Pitt, who in 1793 created him a baron. Alexander Baring, the son of Francis the dver, inherited considerable wealth which was added to by his

American wife. During the Restoration Alexander lent money to France on a grand scale; so that the Duke de Richelieu could exclaim: 'At this moment there are in Europe six great powers: England, France, Russia, Austria — and the House of Baring Brothers.' Known as 'Alexander the Great', he was created Lord Ashburton in 1835 and died thirteen years later. Napoleon III's transactions with Baring's occupy a whole page of Poulet-Malassis.

4. M. Vouillon, *negociant,* from whom Leon borrowed the 30 louis for his fare back to Paris was probably the 'F. F. Vouillon, silk mercer, at 12 Princes Street, Hanover Square,' listed in Robson's Commercial Directory of 1840.

5. Leon's chroniclers do not mention these other alleged *rencontres.*

6. Lady Morgan, the Irish writer, had lived for many years at 11, William Street, near Belgrave Square. Among the Bonapartes she had entertained was Jerome, whom she described in her diary as, 'the youngest Bonaparte; idle, extravagant, inconsiderate; dueller.'

Charles d'Este, Duke of Brunswick, owner of a Paris newspaper and immensely rich, was one of the few German princes to have lost his domains in the disturbances of 1830. Prince Louis Napoleon and the Duke later drew up an extraordinary pact in which each promised to aid the other to gain power. As part of the agreement Louis Napoleon also received a loan at five per cent. By the time the terms were agreed, Prince Louis was a prisoner at Ham and the pact was smuggled into the fortress for his signature disguised as a satin handkerchief.

7. It was Lucien 'the most intelligent of the Bonapartes' who on November 10, 1799, (the '19 Brumaire') clutched a shattered Napoleon from the edge of oblivion — and spent the rest of his life regretting it.

8. François-Claude-Auguste de Crouy-Chanel was born at Duisburg, near Düsseldorf, on December 31, 1793. Given a colonelcy by the Bourbons in 1814, he amassed and lost a fortune in financial speculation and was sent to prison for political activities. Leon and Crouy became friendly when they were both detained in the jail at Clichy; and Crouy seems — inevitably! — to have helped Leon financially. According to some reports Crouy-Chanel acted as a secret agent for Louis Napoleon and helped him to power. At any rate, on becoming Napoleon III, the prince granted Crouy a pension of 3,000 francs *'sur sa cassette privée, en récompense d'ancien services.'*

9. In his *Réponse*, Leon insisted that Parquin was not a colonel.

This was true. At the time of the Strasbourg attempt — on October 30, 1836 — Parquin was a captain in the Municipal Guard of Paris. Louis Napoleon had procured for him the uniform of a general of brigade. Parquin agreed to wear it — but only until the coup had succeeded. In fact the attempt failed — not least because Louis Napoleon entered a vital barracks by the wrong door.

10. The approximate equivalent of £1,000 in present day purchasing power.

Notes to Chapter 8

The Return of the Ashes

1. The equivalent of the French measurement of 5 feet 2 inches, plus 4 'lines'.

2. Sometime after Napoleon's death his custodian Sir Hudson Lowe observed in a letter to Lord Bathurst that it had been Montholon's wish to take the heart to Marie-Louise, whose family custom it was to preserve the hearts of the Habsburgs in a Vienna church. But Hudson Lowe disagreed: 'Uninformed as I naturally must be in what light, after so long a cessation of any relations together, whether of a public or domestic nature, such request might be viewed, I, however, refused it.'

3. It was the belief of one English writer that the escape was connived at in Paris. Sir William Fraser records a conversation between Louis Napoleon after he had reached England and was attending the wedding of his ex-fiancée — an adopted daughter of Mrs. Fitzherbert. The prince 'communicated to his companion that King Louis Philippe had given him ten days to escape from his prison at Ham; that he was liberated by sanction of the King. This was told to me by the recipient of the statement many years ago. After a long interval I put to him the question as regards this fact; and received precisely the same particulars.' He goes on, 'I have carefully read the account of *The Prisoner of Ham*, a book evidently published by authority: I can find nothing inconsistent with this statement. I believe that the friend mentioned as providing a passport was Lord Malmesbury.' It is significant that Lord Malmesbury visited Louis Napoleon at Ham in April, 1845; and it is extraordinary that the prince was able to walk through several open gates — given the large strength of the garrison. There

were 400 guards: 60 soldiers in attendance daily; three jailers, of whom two were always on duty, a picket at the gate, a sergeant, turnkey, sentry, and a post of 30 men.

Notes to Chapter 9

An Affiliation Order against a Mother

1. Delpech was one of Leon's most troublesome creditors, and much capital was later made out of this fact to Leon's detriment. Did he then get into the clutches of Delpech — who finally had him committed to Clichy — in order to raise the 25,000 francs for his mother's lawsuit against the Henrys? A further significant fact is that Delpech himself mentions that Leon was a prisoner in St. Pélagie — the debtors' section of which was closed down in *1834* and the bad payers transferred to Clichy. Fleischmann quotes only Delpech on the St. Pélagie episode. Leon did not enter Clichy until 1837. It follows therefore that his mysterious stay in St. Pélagie must have occurred sometime before 1834 — if Delpech is to be believed.

2. While these cases were proceeding a further illegitimate child had been born to Louis Napoleon during his imprisonment in the fortress of Ham. The mother of his two sons was a humble artisan's daughter. Her name — *Eléonore*.

Notes to Chapter 10

An Open Letter to the Prince President

1. Nevertheless, Jerome Bonaparte had been living for a year in the Rue d'Alger in Paris; and at the time of the abdication he was about to receive from Louis Philippe a peerage and a pension.

2. Leon refers to the letter which he received from Coëssin in March 1840 and which is quoted in *La Réponse*.

3. Napoleon was crowned King of Italy in Milan cathedral on May 26, 1804. He appointed as his viceroy Josephine's son Eugène de Beauharnais. The Emperor began his address to the Italian priests with the words: 'It was my wish to see you all gathered together here solely to have the pleasure of letting you know in person my

sentiments on the Catholic religion, Apostolic and Roman ... In the conviction that it alone is able to assure the happiness of any well ordered society, and consolidate the foundations of every good government, I assure you that always and by every means I shall remain its protector and its defence. I regard you who are the ministers of that religion — which is also my own — as my dearest friends; I declare to you that I shall know how to mete out exemplary punishment with the most rigorous penalties, even — should it prove necessary — the penalty of death, to all those who, as disrupters of public calm, would offer the slightest insult to your religion and mine, and who would dare, in any manner whatsoever, to scorn your sacred persons.' Leon might also have quoted the Emperor's more characteristic views on religion. 'Priests,' declared Napoleon, 'are the worst of things — or the best ... The Christian religion will always be the most solid support of every government clever enough to use it.' And on St. Helena he dismayed the strait-laced Gourgaud with his perceptive observations on Christianity and the Deity.

Notes to Chapter 11

Leon and the Second Emperor

1. Leon spoke truly; for the Rue St.-Thomas-du-Louvre, although situated between the two palaces of the Louvre and the Tuileries, lay in one of the most unsalubrious spots in Paris. Before it was swept away in Hausmann's plans the neighbourhood was a favourite haunt of bohemians, including Gautier, Gerard de Nerval, and Arsène Houssaye.
2. Application for possession of Napoleon's will was not in fact made to the British Government until February 17, 1853, when the request for its removal was immediately granted by the Earl of Aberdeen's administration.
3. General,

   You have acquired great renown as a man of war; but as a citizen you have been immortalised by the praiseworthy blast of indignation with which you covered with your scorn — on their judgment seats the assassins of Marshal Ney. This noble defence of an old warrior struck into silence, and froze into terror, those peers who under every regime have played the rôle allotted to

them by their master: members of the Convention, senators, peers
of 1814, peers of 1815, peers of 1830, France has seen them
condemn the views of the defeated ones only to vaunt the same
people on the morrow of their triumphant return. But you,
General, repudiated to the very face of that brilliant Chamber the
unanimity of its acts. Your glorious tirade was greeted with shouts
of acclaim and the galleries echoed to its cheers. The judges'
silence revealed not their remorse but their cowardice; not one
among them dared to stand up and declare: *I judged according to
my conscience*! In fact, where political judgments by political
assemblies are concerned conscience counts for nothing; the
interest of the moment is their sole motive. Your words were not
adopted by the peers of the July revolution; and so it is to be
conceived that the men who govern us, who choose the peers, are
the turncoats of Ghent. They are the ones who in the *Moniteur
universel* — published on foreign soil by M. Guizot who is today a
Minister — insulted our national glories in honouring them with
epithets like *wretches, scoundrels, bandits* and *traitors*, while they
eulogised the *valiant* Wellington, the *foreign nobles*, the *allied
generals* with fulsome praise. Oh! I have no doubt that the men in
Ghent who outraged your gallant comrades-in-arms, who urged the
enemy to war against our country, who were overjoyed at every
bulletin steeped in French blood that they printed in their
infamous paper, would again today condemn in judgment the
bravest of the brave. Here, General, is the manner in which M.
Guizot's newspaper reported the disaster of Waterloo:

Not being able as yet, in the absence of official bulletins, to give
an exact report of the successives skirmishes and manoeuvres
which took place during these operations, we must confine
ourselves to a very incomplete account of the immense results of
which we have been informed. On the 17th the English army was
in position at Waterloo, a village situated on the edge of the forest
of Soignies. They were drawn up in line with the Prussians, who in
the meantime had been rejoined by General Bulow's division, and
it is the *memorable day* of the 18th which brought to a conclusion
in the HAPPIEST manner for the Allies, the stubborn and bloody
struggle which had waged since the 15th. The *audacity* of the
usurper, his plan of aggression, which he had been long contem-
plating, executed with that obsessive activity which characterises
him and which redoubles the fear of outright defeat, THE
FEROCIOUS RAGE OF HIS ACCOMPLICES, the FANATICISM
of his soldiers — their bravery worthy of a better cause — all

succumbed to the GENIUS OF THE DUKE OF WELLINGTON, to that *superiority* of TRUE GLORY over a DETESTABLE REPUTATION. The army of Bonaparte, *that army which is French in name only* since it became the *terror* and the *scourge* of our country, was beaten and almost entirely destroyed; an immense amount of artillery initially estimated at 150 cannon fell into the hands of the ALLIES. The number of prisoners is not yet known, but it is considerable. At any moment we expect to have details of this GREAT VICTORY which is decisive to the outcome of that social war of which it must bring nearer the *happy conclusion.*

What then were France's crimes, that she merits to be governed by a man who has sullied himself with the publication of so gross a libel? Does not the presence of this man on the Government benches, who speaks of national dignity in the name of the king, oppress the heart — even to the drawing of tears — of you, the distinguished relict of the old army? We forget everything in France: a Minister who after having extinguished liberty has depleted the public finances, can nevertheless expect to receive the indulgence of honest folk; but the Frenchman who against his country solicited foreign arms, who rejoiced in the *complete destruction* of the French army and in Wellington's victory, this man bears on his forehead the ineffaceable imprint of infamy. His fellow men only utter his name in disgust, and if he occupies an eminent position in the State then the nation is delirious or kneels to the foreign yoke. General, M. Guizot is a Minister, Wellington is a Minister, Ney's judges are peers of France; a war, a new Ghent; another Waterloo, and another political murder — perhaps your own . . .

Count Leon,
Paris,
18 December, 1834.'

4. Archbishop Sibour was murdered on the altar steps of the church of St. Etienne-du-Mont on July 3, 1857, by a suspended priest called Verger. A supporter of the July revolution and a contributor to Lammenais' *Avenir*, Sibour nevertheless supported the régime of Louis Napoleon and celebrated a Te Deum after the *coup d'état.* It was for this change of views that he may have been assassinated.

5. Born in 1801, Armand Leroy de Saint-Arnaud organised the *coup d'état* of December 2, 1851. He died of an illness three years later during the campaign in the Crimea.

Notes to Chapter 12

The Children of God and the Ink Factory

1. A few weeks before he became Emperor, Louis Napoleon declared to the new deputies at the Tuileries: *'Depuis trop longtemps la société resemblait à une pyramide qu'on aurait retournée et voulu faire reposer sur son sommet; je l'ai replacée sur sa base.'*
2. The *Marseillaise* was banned by both Napoleons; and only in 1814 and the late 1860s — when the going began to get rough for the First and Second Emperors — was the Hymn of the Republic allowed once more to be heard.
3. Equal to about one million pounds in present day purchasing power.

Notes to Chapter 13

The Intendant's Daughter of St. Denis

1. Napoleon III's only legitimate child was born on Palm Sunday, March 16, 1856. The Prince Imperial grew up possessing all the good characteristics of his father and none of his defects. After the prince's birth, Eugénie was warned that the bearing of further children would endanger her health and she retired with no regrets from sex-life; while the Emperor continued to give rides to the pretty ladies of the court on his roundabout at Compiègne. On the occasion of the Prince Imperial's christening on June 14, 1856, the Empress received from the pope the Golden Rose — an honour she shared with King Henry VIII.
2. Praxedés Mateo Sagasta was born in Torreçilla de Carreros, Logroño, on July 24, 1827. By profession an engineer, Sagasta was elected to the Cortes in 1854. In 1856 after taking part in an abortive revolution he fled to France. He again took refuge in France in 1866, but thereafter rose to high office in the Spanish Government.
3. Napoleon's will was published on August 5, 1854, when a decree dated at the royal villa in Biarritz disposed of all outstanding funds. Nevertheless it was three years before Leon benefited from the 'codicil of conscience' made by his father the Emperor

Napoleon on St. Helena twenty-three years previously. In publishing Leon's legacy the *Moniteur Universel* of May 6, 1855, described him as 'the ward of the father-in-law of Meneval.'

4. *The Times* had described de Morny: 'To every man acquainted with Parisian society in the five years from 1843 to 1848 it was well known that M. de Morny was more deeply engaged on the turf, at the Jockey Club and the gambling table, and in the foyer of the Opéra than in parliamentary business. His coolness, courage and quick faculties no one doubted. He was an excellent judge of horse flesh, understood écarté well, and could criticise an opera or a ballet with accurate science — but no one believed him to know anything about, or to care anything for, parliamentary government.' August de Morny was the illegitimate son of Napoleon III's mother, ex-Queen Hortense, and Count Charles de Flahaut de la Billarderie, himself the bastard son of the legendary Prince Talleyrand, and another of Napoleon's innumerable aides-de-camp at Waterloo. On his elevation to a dukedom Morny incorporated into his arms the hortensia, or hydrangea, as a symbol of his birth. This infuriated his half-brother Napoleon III who in a lively altercation accused de Morny of insulting his mother. It is arguable that had de Morny lived the disastrous Franco-Prussian war of 1870 would not have occurred.

5. Napoleon III's annual grants to his Imperial relatives totalled 1,310,975 francs. During the eighteen years existence of the Second Empire they received in all some 70,187,796 francs. Official figures admitted to an outlay of 58 million francs. Papers seized after the sacking of the Tuileries revealed an expenditure of 4,362,562 francs on Prince Joachim Murat alone, of which 180,000 francs was spent on his wedding. The christening of the Prince Imperial cost the state 898,000 francs.

6. James Rothschild was himself not entirely passed over by Nemesis; for after the fall of Paris his best champagne was looted by Bismark. Whether Fürst Bismarck also appropriated the baron's silver *pot-de-chambre* is not recorded.

Notes to Chapter 14

A Correggio painted on Agate

1. Goudchaux, a Jewish financier and non-juror, stood as a moderate. On July 6, 1858, he and Carnot were the only two

candidates to be elected in the first of two ballots.

2. The critic Mengs records: 'There remain in France only old copies — principally of small pictures, including *Christ's Prayer in the Garden of Olives* which is in the Escorial.'

3. Louis Bonaparte — who disconcerted Napoleon by becoming a popular and conscientious King of Holland — also provided the future Napoleon III with a half-brother. His illegitimate son was named François Louis Gaspard de Castelvecchio after the family's Italian estates, and in 1856 he was given a job in the Ministry of Foreign Affairs. He was discreetly transferred to the French provinces and became a senior offical in the Alpes-Maritimes, dying in 1869.

4. One French writer quipped, 'She has certainly descended.'

5. A contemporary remarked: 'We fought in Cochin China side by side with the Spaniards to avenge the murder of an Andalusian monk. The Chinese war was waged to avenge the death of a missionary. The Syrian expedition was undertaken to avenge the deaths of several Christians of Lebanon massacred by the fanatical Druses.'

6. Louis Napoleon was aware that forty-five *carboneros* were ready to take his life in default of a united Italy; and while it is disputed that even in his tearabout Roman days he was himself a youthful *carbonero*, he was certainly regarded as such by the freemasons of the *Loge des Vengeurs*.

7. After Castiglione's death the necklace was sold for 422,000 francs.

8. Charles Frederick Worth was born at Bourne in Lincolnshire. Apprenticed to Swan and Edgar he became intensely interested in French dress materials and models. At the end of his apprenticeship in 1846 he entered the service of Gagalin and at the Paris exhibition of 1855 a lady's train designed by Worth was on show. Leaving the silk mercer, Gagalin, he entered into partnership with a Swede named Bobergh. His ladies' tailoring establishment quickly became patronised by Princess Metternich, the wife of the Austrian Ambassador. It was, however, the Comtesse de Pourtales who introduced him to the Empress Eugénie who henceforth had first call on his novelties from the Rue de la Paix. Worth is credited with being the first couturier to use human models — instead of the customary dolls — and with making the first ready-to-wear coats and suits. He also designed clothes for the stage, notably Hortense Schneider's elaborate hussar pelisse for her leading rôle in Offenbach's opera *La Grande Duchesse de Gerol-*

stein at the time of the Paris Exhibition of 1867. To facilitate the Empress's ascent to her apartments in her wide flouncing skirts, Worth superintended the installation of an outsize lift in the palace of the Tuileries. Ironically enough, he bought and erected in his garden at Suresnes a portion of the masonry from the palace after its destruction by the fire of 1871.

9. The first Napoleon had also worn white kerseymere breeches!

10. The Institution of Sainte-Barbe was founded in 1430 by Jean Hubert, a doctor of canon law. A new building was started on August 8, 1840, and inaugurated on St. Barbara's day — December 4, 1853.

11. Prince Pierre Bonaparte was married to Lady Dudley Stuart, whose brother refused to receive him. He had been tapping Louis Napoleon as early as 1837 when Pierre arrived from New Orleans and put up at Jaunay's Hotel in Leicester Square. His precipitate departure from America was due to a bizarre incident in which he had stabbed a dog and subsequently appeared before a magistrate. Prince Bonaparte's murder of a Paris journalist, Victor Noir, was said to have hastened the end of the Second Empire, after the fall of which Pierre Bonaparte retired with his wife to London and opened a milliner's shop in Bond Street.

12. So far as it is known Leon never referred to his half-sister Amélie who was born on November 3, 1825 — while Leon was with his mother in Germany — and who died on August 3, 1856, leaving two daughters and a son.

13. As the ex-Empress fled from the palace of the Tuileries with the help of her American dentist, Dr. Thomas W. Evans, France was being taken over by a new Government which included Crémieux — Leon's brilliant advocate of the mid-1840s in his celebrated affiliation suit against his mother.

14. Papers seized in the Tuileries showed that in 1854 Napoleon III had 4 million francs at Baring's; 1855 — 6 millions in the Bank of Victoria; 1856 — 3 millions at Kindlet's in Vienna; 1860 — 14 millions in Mexico; 1863 — 10 millions on mortgage at Brown Brothers of New York; and in 1867, 6 millions in St. Petersburg. After the ex-Emperor's death Eugénie received an income of £80,000 a year, increased by further legacies and savings. In addition there remained two buildings in the Rue d'Albe worth £36,000; three houses in the Rue de l'Elysée worth £80,000, and the Jouchère estate, £20,000; the Solferino estate in the Landes, £60,000; Biarritz, £40,000, another estate in the Basses-Pyrénées worth £48,000, and the unfinished Imperial Palace at Marseilles,

£64,000. The sale of the Marseilles palace and a chalet in Vichy paid off the debts of the Civil List. Yet Eugénie kept the unfortunate Prince Imperial so short of pocket money that he was obliged to borrow from his guests!

Notes to Chapter 15

Leon and the Tussauds

1. Napoleon was evidently pleased with Marie Tussaud's finished likeness, for some time after her visit to the Tuileries he brought to her studio Massena and one of his aides-de-camp.
2. According to W. Wheeler's note in Tussaud's catalogue of 1901, Joseph Randolph Tussaud was introduced to Leon by the Count de Lally Tollendal.
3. Tiring of his stint with the London merchant, Charles Leon joined the French army, serving as a corporal of horse in the 16th Light Cavalry Regiment stationed at Vendôme. He married a Baroness d'Elgert at St. Germain-en-Laye; and — having inherited his father's restlessness of spirit — emigrated to Venezuela, obtaining a railway concession in Caracas. The inhabitants of that capital erected a monument to Napoleon's grandson. Leon's second son, Gaston, having left Paris to become a commercial traveller for Larousse in the Atlantic port of La Rochelle, returned to canvass the voters of the capital. In *Le Figaro* of November 6, 1893, in a first leader entitled *Les Femmes de Bonaparte*, Maurices Barrès wrote ' . . . May I be permitted to add that his son, Count Leon, grandson of the Emperor was a candidate *investi* at the elections for the *Conseil municipal* in 1890. On our part, we recall canvassing General Boulanger on behalf of a candidate in whose favour, among other virtues, was the fabulous beauty of his origins.' In the *Intermédiaire des Chercheurs et Curieux* of 1904 appeared a letter to the editor, Georges Montorgeuil: 'I am sending to you a rough sketch written by my son. Please excuse the fact that his delicate state of health does not permit him either to round it off or indeed to finish it. Comtesse Leon.' Montorgeuil published the fragment of Leon's son Gaston under the heading *The Story of the Son of Napoleon I by his Grandson, lycée scholar*:

In 1881 Count Leon — my grandfather — left a widow, a daughter and three sons. What are they doing now? Where are they? Countess Leon — my grandmother — died in 1899 at Vitz-Villeroy in the Department of the Somme. My uncle, Count Charles Leon, died in 1894 in Venezuela, after having obtained a concession for railways. My father Count Leon is at this moment working and struggling to raise us and make us worthy of the name we bear. He is a man of whom the sincerity and integrity in no way belie his origins. The firmness of his gestures, his eloquent speech — which could if need be make the crowds to tremble — amply demonstrate the blood which flows in his veins and the spring at which he has drunk. My mother — the present Countess Leon — is a person of simple tastes who never in the least seeks either sensation or grandeur. What she desires and it is after all nought but commonsense, is her family's happiness. Who would ever have believed that the Count Leon her husband is a commercial traveller? None at all! In the evenings when I think about all this; when my eldest sister sings a sweet melody, and retires to seek her daily rest, I myself ponder and meditate the famous lines of the poet: *Can one at the same time be so great and yet so small?*

Gaston Leon,
Pupil of the Lycée St. Louis.

Fernand, the youngest of Leon's sons, also heard the call of the Americas and joined the travelling *Wild West Show* of Buffalo Bill — Colonel Cody — in which he is said to have appeared as a star performer when the rodeo visited the French capital. Fernand Leon was killed in 1917 on the Western Front.

Leon's only daughter, Charlotte, became a schoolteacher in an obscure village in Algeria before returning to France and continuing to support her mother — Françoise-Fanny — at Vitz-Villeroy, Somme, where they settled. Here in 1899 Leon's widow died and was buried. Somewhat tardily the Bonaparte family interested itself in Leon's descendants. Charlotte returned to Paris where her children were educated at the expense of Prince Roland, Lucien's grandson.

4. Matthew xxiv, 28.
5. Henry IV Part II, Act I, sc.1.
6. According to Charlotte his daughter, Leon was a friend of Lord Henry Seymour ('Milord Arsouille'); and Charlotte described how on one occasion they bought up the whole supply of oysters at Les Halles.

Notes to Chapter 16

The St. Helena of Seine-et-Oise

1. The whitewashed house at 4 Rue Beaujour — not *Beaujon* as given in Fleischmann and Ginisty — has been lovingly restored by its present owner; who acquired the building in a ruinous condition. The road has been re-named Rue Jean-Paul Soutumier after a Resistance hero. A short distance away, in the Rue de l'Hermitage, at No. 58, stands the Villa Davenport, also well-maintained, but now used as a company office.
2. The tiny folding pocket-knife is now in the collection of Mme. Colette Tillie and her father, M. Repiquet, together with other objects including an ivory rouge-container which once belonged to Eleonore — Mme. Tillie's great-great-grandmother.

SOURCES

Writing in 1905, Georges Montorgeuil, the editor of the *Inter-médiaire des Chercheurs et Curieux*, appealed to his readers for information about the story 'at one and the same time famous and obscure' of Eleonore Denuelle de la Plaigne. He observed with evident astonishment that the task had never been attempted by any writer, *'pas même par M. Frédéric Masson qui déclare ne pas vouloir dire tout ce qu'il sait.'*

Masson (1847-1923) was entrusted by Prince Napoleon with the task of cataloguing the family papers and the result was several volumes of biography. In 1919 Frédéric Masson completed his work, *'Napoléon et sa famille'* which filled thirteen volumes. Yet in *'Napoléon et les femmes'* (1894) the same writer had allotted a mere eight pages to Eleonore and Leon.

But even Masson with the enormous bulk of the Bonaparte family papers at his disposal felt bound to explain, 'What romance could rival that true history, of which we can glean only fragments from law reports, civil registers, circulars, and electoral addresses?'

It is to Hector Fleischmann (1882-1914) that we owe the first — and only — full-length biography of Count Leon, selective, inaccurate, and biased (*'J'entreprends aujourd'hui de plaider pour Napoléon . . .'*) as he sometimes is.

Dr. Max Billard's slim 32mo volume, *'Un fils de Napoléon Ier, le comte Léon*, (1911) is well documented and more reliable; but as an expanded magazine article it is woefully brief.

For a great part of the story we are able to refer to the pamphlets and correspondence of Leon himself. Fortuitously he filled his letters with his past history and the dossier entitled *M. le comte Léon à Son Eminence Mgr le cardinal Morlot, archevèque de Paris, grand aumônier de l'Empereur* (1858) which occupies sixty-four printed pages contains the text of various letters, some of which reach back as far as 1839.

Owing to the peregrinations of Leon his family records suffered several mishaps. A trunk-load of papers left by his wife, Françoise-Fanny, as a lien with a Belgian innkeeper disappeared. And more recently the disastrous fire at Mme. Tussaud's, which destroyed many Napoleonic relics including his carriage from Waterloo, also claimed ledgers which may have revealed Leon's address in Camden Town during 1873. Wartime bombing of the British Museum's collection also destroyed books such as

W. Wheeler's Tussaud catalogue of 1901. Happily a copy was produced by Lady Chapman, the Archivist of Madame Tussaud's,
from her collection and by such means has the story of Count
Leon been pieced together.

The most important extant manuscript sources for an understanding of Leon are his *Voyage du 1823*, describing a trip down
the Rhine when he was sixteen years old, and the two letters he
wrote to Françoise-Fanny during the high years of the Second
Empire. These intimate notes add leaven to the stilted correspondence with Government Ministers and officials and throw new
light on the character of Count Leon.

BIBLIOGRAPHY

Abrantes, La Duchesse D,, *Mémoires de Madame la Duchesse d'Abrantes,*
   Paris 1893
Alhoy, P. M., *Les Prison de Paris,* Paris 1846
Alhoy, Philadelphie Maurice, *Physiologie du créancier et du débiteur,* Paris
   1842
Almeras, Henri D', *La Vie Parisienne sous le consulat et l'empire,* Paris 1909
Almeras, Henri D', *La Vie Parisienne sous la République de 1848,* Paris 1921
Almeras, Henri d', *La Vie Parisienne sous la Restauration,* Paris 1910
Almeras, Henri d', *La Vie Parisienne sous le Règne de Louis Philippe,* Paris
   1910
Alphand, J. C. A., *Les Promenades de Paris,* Paris 1867-73
Alton-Shee, E. D', Comte, *Mes Mémoires, 1826-1848,* Paris 1869
Antommarchi, C. F., *The Last Days of the Emperor,* London 1825
Aretz, G. tr E. & C. PAUL. *Napoleon and His Women Friends,* London 1927
Argenteau, M., *The Last Love of an Emperor,* London 1916
Ariste, P. d', *La Vie et Le Monde du boulevard, 1830-1870,Un dandy; Nestor
   Roqueplan,* Paris 1930
Arjuzon, Caroline d', *Hortense de Beauharnais,* Paris 1897
Arjuzon, Caroline d', *Madame Louis Bonaparte,* Paris 1901
Armorial, *général de la noblesse titré,* Paris 1929
Arnault, Antoine Vincent, *Souvenirs d'un sexagénaire,* Paris 1833
Arnault, A. V., *La Vie de Napoleon,* Paris 1825
Arnott, A. *An Account of the Last Illness, Decease, and Post-Mortem
   Appearance of Napoleon Bonaparte.* London 1822.
Aronson, T., *The Golden Bees: the story of the Bonapartes,* London 1965
Aubert, Francis, *Le Journal de Chislehurst (9-17 January, 1873),* Paris 1873
Aubry, O. tr H. L. STUART. *The Emperor Falls in Love,* London 1928
Audebrand, P., *Derniers jours de la bohême, souvenirs de la vie littéraire,* Paris
   1905
Audiffret-Pasquier, Duc D', *Histoire de mon temps; Memoires du chancelier
   Pasquier,* Paris 1893
Avrillon, Mademoiselle, *Mémoires sur la vie privée de Joséphine,* Paris 1833

Babany, C., Kotzebue, *sa vie et son temps, ses oeuvres dramatiques*, Paris 1893
Bac, F., *Napoléon III inconnu*, Paris 1932
Bac, F., *La Cour des Tuileries*, Paris 1930
Ball, Robert James, *Justices' Justice*, London 1845
Banville, Théodore, *Mes Souvenirs*, Paris 1882
Bausset, Louis F. J. De, *Mémoires anecdotiques sur l'intérieur du palais*,
    Brussels 1827-29
Bertaut, J., *Napoleon in his own words.*, London 1916
Bertrand, A., *Lettres sur l'expedition de Ste. Hélène en 1840*, Paris 1841
Bertrand, A., *Un amour de Dejazet, 1834-1844*, Paris 1907
Beugnot, A. Count., *Mémoires*, Paris 1871
Bicknell, Anna L., *Life in the Tuileries*, London 1895
Billard, M., *Un fils de Napoléon Ier, le comte Léon*, Paris 1911
Boigne, Comtesse De, *Memoirs*, London 1907
Bonaparte, Lucien, *Mémoires secrets*, Paris 1818
Bonaparte—Wyse, O. *The Spurious Brood*, London 1969
Bourguignan, J., *Corvisart premier médecin de Napoleon*, Paris 1937
Bourguignon, J., and H. Lachouque, *Mémoires de Marchand*, Paris 1952
Bourrienne, L. A. F. de, *Mémoires*, Paris 1829
Brazier, N., *Chronique des Petits Théâtres de Paris*, Paris 1883
Breton, G., *Napoleon and His Ladies*, London 1965
Briffault, F. F. , *The Prisoner of Ham*, London 1846
Broglie, A. C. L. V., Duc De, *Souvenirs*, Paris 1886
Brotonne, L. De. *Les Bonapartes et leurs alliances*, Paris 1893

Cabanes, Augustin., *Dans l'intimité de l'empereur*, Paris 1924
Castellane, E. V. E. B., Comte De, *Journal 1804-1862*, Paris 1895-1897
Castelot, André, *Paris the Turbulent City*, 1783-1871, London 1963
Cavaignac, Marie Julie *Les Mémoires d'un Inconnu (1780-1816)*, Paris 1894
Chaboulon, P. A. Fleury De., *Memoirs of the Private Life*, London 1820
Chamas, A. M., Comte de Lavalette, *Mémoires et souvenirs du Comte
    Lavallette*
Chandler, D. G., *Campaigns of Napoleon*, London 1967
Chapman, C. J. M. and B., *The Life and Times of Baron Haussmann* London
    1957
Chapman, M., *Imperial Brother, A life of the Duc de Morny*, New York 1932
Cheramy, P. A., *Mlle. George*, Paris, 1908
Cochelet, Mademoiselle, *Mémoires sur la reine Hortense et la Famille
    impériale par Mademoiselle Cochelet*, Paris 1907
Coessin, Francois-Guillaume, *Les Neuf Livres*, Paris 1809
Cole, H. *Josephine*, London 1962
Constant, *Mémoires de Constant, premier valet de chambre de l'Empereur,
    sur la vie privée de Napoléon, sa famille et sa cour*, Paris 1830
Corley, T. A. B., *Democratic Despot: a life of Napoleon III*, London 1961
Cottrell, Leonard, *Mme. Tussaud*, London 1965
Creston, Dormer, *In Search of Two Characters*, London 1945
Cronin, Vincent, *Napoleon*, London 1971

D., *La Cour de Compiègne*, Paris 1866
Didier, E. L., *The Life and Letters of Mme. Bonaparte*, London 1879

Diesbach, Ghislain De, *Secrets of the Gotha*, London 1967

Dixon, Piers, *Double Diploma*, London 1968

Dixon, Sir Pierson John, *Pauline, Napoleon's favourite sister*, London 1964

Dufey, P. J. S., *Confessions de Napoléon*, Paris 1816

Dufey, Pierre J. S., *Dictionnaire historique de Paris*, Paris 1828

Erdan, Alexandre (André Alexander Jacob), *La France Mystique*, Paris 1855

Fain, Baron, *Mémoires du baron Fain, premier sécrétaire du cabinet de l'Empereur; publié par ses arrére-petits-fils, avec une introduction et des notes par P. Fain*, Paris 1908

Fantin, des Odoards, Louis Florimond, *Journal du Général Fantin des Odoards*, Paris 1895

Fisher, H. A. L., *An History of Europe*, London 1935

Fleischmann, H., *Une maîtresse de Napoléon, (Mademoiselle George)*, Paris 1908

Fleischmann, Hector, *Une Maîtresse de Napoleon, Mlle. George*, Paris 1908

Fleischmann, H., *Batârd d'empereur*, Paris 1913

Fleischmann, H., *Dessous de Princesses et Maréchales d'Empire*, Paris 1909

Fleischmann, H., *Napoleon III et les Femmes*, Paris 1913

Fleischmann, H., *Roustam, Mameluck de Napoléon*, Paris 1910

Fleischmann, Hector, *Le Roi Joseph Bonaparte; Lettres d'exil inédites (Angleterre-Amérique-Italie); 1825-1844*, Paris 1912

Flenley, R., *Modern German History*, London 1959

Fleury, Gen. Cte., *Souvenirs, (1837-59)*, Paris 1897

Fleury De Chaboulon, Pierre A. E., *Memoires pour servir a l'histoire de la vie privée, du retour, et du régne de Napoléon, en 1815*, London 1819

Fraser, Sir Wm., *Napoleon III*, London 1890

Geer, Walter, *Napoleon and Josephine, The rise of the Empire*, New York 1924

Genlis, Stéphanie Félicité Brulart De, (Marchioness de Sillery), *Mémoires*, Paris 1825

George, Mlle., *Mémoires*, Paris 1908

Geyl, Prof. P. tr O. Renier, *Napoléon, For and Against*, London 1949

Ginisty, Paul, *Une petite-fille de Napoléon, in La Marquise de Sade*, Paris 1901

Goldsmith, L. *The Secret History of the Cabinet of Bonaparte*, London 1811

Gooch, G. P., *The Second Empire*, London 1960

Gourgaud, Général Gaspard, *Sainte-Hélène journal inédit de 1815 à 1818*, Paris 1899

Granges, Charles-March Des, *Geoffroy et la critique dramatique sous le Consulat et l'Empire (1800-1814)*, Paris 1897

Green, F. C., *A Comparative View of French and British Civilisation, 1850-70*, London 1965

Guedalla, P., *The Second Empire*, London 1923

Guerrini, Maurice, *Napoléon et Paris*, Paris 1967

Guest, Ivor, *Napoleon III in England*, London 1952

Guizot, F. P. G., *An Embassy*, London 1862

Halévy, Ludovic, *Notes et Souvenirs*, Paris 1889

Heppenstall, Rayner, *French crime in the Romantic age*, London 1970

Henrion, M. R.A., Baron, *Vie et travaux apostoliques de Monseigneur H. L. de Quelen, Archevêque de Paris*, Paris 1842

Hérisson, Comte D', *Souvenirs intimes et notes du baron Mounier, secrétaire de Napoleon Ier, pair de France, directeur général de la police;* Paris 1896

Hervé, Francis, *The Memoirs of Mme. Tussaud*, London 1838

Hortense, La Reine, *Mémoires de la reine Hortense publiéés par le Prince Napoléon*, Paris 1927 Houssaye, Henry,

Houssaye, Henry, *Correspondence de Joachim Murat*, Paris 1899

Howarth, T. E. B., *Citizen King, The Life of Louis-Philippe*, London 1961

Imbert, De Saint-Amand, A. L., *Les femmes des Tuileries* (Joséphine), Paris 1833

Irisson D'Hérisson, Maurice D', *Le cabinet noir*, Paris 1887

Jerrold, W. B., *The Life of Napoleon III*, London 1874-82

Jerrold, W. B., *On The Boulevards*, London 1853-66

Jerrold, W. B., *Imperial Paris*, London 1855

Johnston, R. M. *The Corsican*, London 1911

Jung, H. F. T. *Lucien Bonaparte et ses mémoires, 1775-1840*, Paris 1882

Junot, Laure, *Madame Duchesse d'Abrantes Mémoires*, Paris 1831

Kemble, J., *Napoleon Immortal*, London 1959

Knapton, Ernest John, *Empress Josephine*, Harvard 1963

Kurtz, Harold, *The Empress Eugénie, 1826-1920*, London 1964

Lachouque, H., *Napoleon's Battles*, London 1966

Langlé, J. A. F., *Funérailles de l'Empereur Napoléon*, Paris 1840

Larrey, Baron D. *Mémoires*, Paris 1862

Las Cases, Le Comte De, *Mémorial de Sainte-Héléne*, Paris 1823

Lavalette, Comte, *Mémoires*, Paris 1831

Lazare, Felix et Louis, *Dictionnaire administratif et historique des rues de Paris et de ses monuments*, Paris 1846

Lecomte, L. Henry, *Un Amour de Déjazet*, Paris 1847

Lecomte, L. H., *Virginie Dejazet après ses papiers*, Paris 1904

Lecomte, L. H., *Une comédienne au XIXe siecle*, Paris 1892

Lefebvre, Georges, *Napoleon*, London 1969

Lêvy, Arthur, *Napoléon intime*, Paris 1893

Lillywhite, Bryant, *London Coffee Houses*, London 1963

Loliée, F., *The Brother of an Emperor*, Paris 1910

Loliée, F., *Life of an Empress*, London 1908

Madden, R.-R., *The literary life and correspondence of the Countess of Blessington*, London 1855

Maigne, *Journal anecdotique de Mme. Campan*, Paris 1825

Malardier, P., *La Liste Civile de Napoleon III*, Paris 1862

Malmesbury, J. H. H., 3rd Earl, *Memoirs of an Ex-Minister*, London 1884

Manceron, C. *Which Way to Turn*, London 1961

Manceron, C., *Napoleon Recaptures Paris, March 20th, 1815*, London 1968

Marbot, Baron de. tr A. J. Butler, *Memoirs*, London 1892

Marceau, F., *Balzac and his World*, London 1967

Marchand, *Mémoires de, J. Bourguignon et H. Lachouque*, Paris 1932

Markham, Felix M. H., *Napoleon*, London 1963

Martial, A. P., *Ancien Paris*, Paris 1860

Martineau, Gilbert, *Napoleon Surrenders*, London 1971

Masson, F., *Napoléon et les femmes*, Paris 1894

Masson, F., *Marie Walewska*, Paris 1897

Masson, F., *Autour de Ste. Hélène*, Paris 1909

Masson, Frédéric, *Josephine, Impératrice et Reine*, Paris 1899

Masson, F., Rustam, *Souvenirs*, Paris 1911

Masson F. and Biagi G., *Napoléon inconnu, papiers inédits*, Paris 1895

Masson, K., *Histoire des chemins de fer*, Bar-le-Duc 1912

Masuyer, Joséphine J. V., *Mémoires, lettres et papiers de Valérie Masuyer*, Paris 1937

Maurice, Barthélemy, *Histoire politique et anecdotique des prisons de la Seine*, Paris 1840

Maurice, Charles, *Histoire anecdotique du théâtre, de la littérature et de diverses impressions contemporaines tirées du coffre d'un journaliste avec sa vie à tort et à travers*, Paris 1856

Maurois, A., *Histoire de l'Allemagne*, Paris 1965

Méneval, Le Baron Claude-Francois De, *Mémoires*, Paris 1894

Meyrac, A., *Les Amours Secrètes De Napoléon*, Paris 1925

Michaud, L. G., *Biographie Universelle*, Paris 1843

Miot, A. F., *Comte de Melito, Mémoires*, Paris 1880

Mollien, Francois Nicolas, *Mémoires d'un Ministre du Trésor Public 1780-1815*, Paris 1845

Montholon, C. J. F. T., *Mémoires*, Paris 1857

Mossiker, Frances, *Napoleon and Josephine*, London 1965

Murat, Princess Caroline Letitia, *My Memoirs*, New York 1910

Napoleon, Prince, *Mémoires de la Reine Hortense*, Paris 1927

Nauroy, Charles, *Les Secrets de Bonaparte*, Paris 1889

North-Peat, Anthony B., *Paris sous le Second Empire; les Femmes, la Mode, la Cour (1864-1869)*, Paris 1911

Oman, Carola, *Napoleon's Viceroy, Eugène de Beauharnais*, London 1966

O'Meara, Barry Edward, *Napoleon in Exile, or a Voice from St. Helena*, London 1822

Ornarno, A-P. R. D' Comte, *Marie Walewska*, Paris 1947

Oursel, N. N. *Nouvelle Biographie Normande*, Paris Rouen 1886-1917

Owenson, Sydney, (Lady Morgan), *Memoirs*, London 1862

Peat, Anthony B. North, *Gossip from Paris during the Second Empire*, London 1903

Pereire, Jacob Emile, *Compagnie du Chemin de fer du Nord*, Paris 1848

Pessard, Gustave, *Nouveau Dictionnaire Historique de Paris*, Paris 1904

Petit Homme Rouge, Le, *The Court of the Tuileries*, London 1907

Phyfe, W. H. P., *The Return from St. Helena*, London 1907

Poggioli, S., *Napoléon-Louis Bonaparte retenu en prison*, Paris 1846

Potocks, Comtesse A., *Mémoires, 1794-1820*, Paris 1897
Poulet-Malassis, P. E. A., *Papiers secrets et correspondance du Second Empire*, Paris 1873

Rabbe, Vieilh De Boisolin et Saint-Preuve, *Biographie universelle et portative des contemporaines*, Paris 1834
Rapport, Dr. A. S., *Napoleon III*, Paris 1915
Remusat, Mme De, *Mémoires de Mme de Rémusat, 1802-1808; publiés par son petit-fils Paul De Remusat*, Paris 1880
Roederer, P. L. Cte., *Autour de Bonaparte*, Paris 1909
Richardson, Frank, *Napoleon: Bisexual Emperor*, London 1972
Richardson, Joanna, *Princess Mathilde*, London 1969

Savant, J., *Napoleon in His Time*, London 1956
Savary, Anne Jean Marie Renée, Duke of Rovigo, *Mémoires du duc de Rovigo*, London 1828
Savatier, R., *Bonaparte et le Code Civil*, Paris 1927
Schuermans, Albert, *Itinéraire général de Napoleon Ier*, Paris 1908
Simpson, F. A., *The Rise of Louis Napoleon*, London 1968
Stirling, M., *A Pride of Lions: a portrait of Napoleon's Mother*, London 1961
Stoeckl, Baroness A. de, *Four Years an Empress*, London 1962
Strantz, Ferdinand Von, *Erinnerungen aus meinem Leben*, Hamburg 1901
Suddaby, Elizabeth and P. J. Yarrow, *Lady Morgan in France*, 1971

Tallis, John, *Tallis's London Street Views*, London 1839
Thibaudeau, A. C., *Le consulate et l'empire*, 1834-35
Thiébault, D. A. P. F. C. H., Baron, *The Memoirs*, London 1896
Thierra, H., *Napoléon III avant l'Empire*, Paris 1895
Timbeaudeau, A.-C., *Bonaparte and the Consulate*, 1908
Titmarsh, T., M.A., (W. M. Thackeray), *The Second Funeral of Napoleon*, London 1841
Treich, L., *Les Alcoves de Napoléon III*, Paris 1930
Trotter, John Bernard, *Memoirs of the Latter Years of the Right Honourable Charles James Fox*, London 1811
Turnbull, Patrick, *Napoleon's Second Empress*, London 1971
Turquan, J., *Souveraines et grandes dames, les soeurs de Napoléon*, Paris 1896 *Napoléon amoureux*, Paris 1897
Turquan, J., *Le roi Jérome*, Paris 1903
Turquan, J., *La reine Hortense*, Paris 1927
Tussaud, John Theodore, *The Romance of Mme. Tussaud's*, London 1920

Vieilh De Boisjolin, C. A., *Biographie universelle . . . des contemporains*, Paris 1834
Viel-Castel, Horace De, Comte, *Mémoires sur le règne de Napoléon III (1851-1864)*, Paris 1883

Wairy, Louis Constant, *Mémoires de Constant, premier valet de l'empereur*, Paris 1830-31
Walford, Edward, *Greater London*, London 1893-95

INDEX

INDEX